ordered 3-18-08

HEROIC FINLAND

Heroic Finland

by David Hinshaw

ILLUSTRATED

G. P. PUTNAM'S SONS

NEW YORK

Acknowledgments

I wish to express my sincere thanks to The Macmillan Company for its ready permission of my request to quote from Volume I of the Memoirs of Herbert Hoover.

I acknowledge my indebtedness and express my sincere thanks also to The Ronald Press, publishers of *Finland and World War II*, by John H. Wuorinen and to the Harvard University Press, publishers of *Space, Time and Architecture*, by Sigfried Giedion.

My warm thanks are extended to my lifelong close friend W. L. White for his having provided me with a copy and granting me permission to reprint his famous 1939 radio broadcast from Helsinki, "The Last Christmas Tree."

—DAVID HINSHAW

Dunmow Farm
West Chester, Pennsylvania
July—1952

Preface

While in the United States in 1947, I was calling on David Hinshaw in his New York office. His secretary suddenly came in and told him that United States Senator H. Alexander Smith was calling him from Washington.

The part of the conversation which I heard went something like this: "Oh goody! Goody! Yes, yes, sure, of course we will do it; will you make the changes in the bill, or shall I?"

"You will?" A pause, then, "That's grand, Alex, and so are you. The finest thing about it is that I now understand for the first time in thirty years why Helen married you!" Another pause and then, "Okay! Okay! Maybe I am one, but it's still the truth."

That one-sided conversation helped me to understand how a private citizen could reach out and enlist, as David Hinshaw had done, many congressmen and senators in the noble cause he had launched for my little country.

Later, after my return home, I followed the course of the legislation in my capacity as the Secretary of the Government Foreign Aid Board, through copies of letters Mr. Hinshaw received and wrote which he sent me. The source of his strength shone through them—it was personal and wide. American political leaders in both parties did for this cause what he asked of them because they had known him and his record for many years. This record was, as stated in the citation when he received the Theodore Roosevelt medal, one of "distinguished public service by a private citizen," and knowing him and his record so well they held his character and judgment in high esteem.

No one will ever be able to determine the measurable value to Finnish-American relations of what we in Finland refer to as "the David Hinshaw scholarships"—there is a movement in Finland to call them that officially, unless the State Department offers objections.

We have tried to show David Hinshaw our appreciation, but he has brushed it off with the remark, "I was only the feather that tipped the scales."

He told his audience at the University of Helsinki on November 14, 1951: "You owe me nothing for what I did. Rather it is I who owe you much for demonstrating by what you do that there are people like you in the world. Your record inspired the idea and made my self-appointed task extremely easy. I had only to explain the plan to Congressional leaders and government officials. No urging was necessary. The Congress of the United States unanimously made a glowing, warm human idea into law both to help a hard-pressed people and to give recognition to great and fine qualities. By doing so it furnished proof that virtue does not always have to be its own reward.

"My hope is that under the provisions of this law countless thousands of Finns and Americans will gain from their association with each other a deeper understanding of the brotherhood of man and glimpse in a new and fresh way that love is the greatest power for good in the world, and that out of this understanding there will come lasting friendships which may serve as bases for universal peace."

We believed him. What is more important, the American Congress believed him, and what is of greatest importance of all is the way this thoughtful, generous, neighborly act by the American people through their Congress has touched the heart and soul of Finland.

The people of Finland have long had close spiritual and cul-

tural ties with the people of America. The love of liberty, freedom, independence, the dignity and importance of the individual
human being, have never been separated from our hopes and
have never left our hearts. You made them reality in your Declaration of Independence. We longed to do so for centuries. When
we did finally gain them we felt that our achievement made
Finns and Americans blood brothers.

We like to believe also that our unrelenting effort through
the generations to do what the Americans had done has given
us a special place in your hearts for the reason one of your poets,
Joaquin Miller, gave when he wrote:

> Great is the man with sword undrawn,
> And good is the man who refrains from wine.
> But the one who fails and still fights on
> Lo! he is a twin brother of mine!

An American visitor in Finland will be able to see indications
all about him of the closeness of the Finnish-American relationship. A striking one will be the answer to the question, if he
puts it, to any Finnish audience: "How many of you have relatives in America?" All over the audience he will soon see a
forest of waving arms as they reach high above smiling faces.

Due to Finland's location in the world and the immediate
neighbors around us, we Finns have found it advisable to establish and maintain all of our international relations on a straight
business basis, and to make no sign of preference of one nation
over another.

The David Hinshaw scholarship fund created a warmth and
depth of special feeling for America and Americans such as we
have for no other people, except perhaps for our nearest neighbors and helpful friends the Swedes. Your creation of the educational fund now helps us to believe beyond doubt, and despite
all charges to the contrary, that America's international purpose
generally is high, fine and disinterested.

An illustration of how this has worked is furnished by the

fact that America's propagandist enemies—to our shame there
are a few such even in Finland—nowadays are unable to get
more than their own faithful to listen to their tirades. The general run of Finns do not believe them any more. They know
that bad people don't do such good things.

One other result which stems from the scholarship fund is
that it has helped to make English, next to Swedish, which we
regard as a domestic language, the major foreign-language subject in Finnish schools and institutions of higher learning. The
pupils are learning English if for no other reason than that they
cannot hope to be designated as a fellow under the fund without
the command of the English language—and almost every one of
Finland's students holds the earnest hope that he will be named
when the time comes. A few years from now any English-speak-
ing person who visits Finland will be able to find someone even
in the most remote places who speaks English. With their ability
to read and speak English goes something else significant, namely,
a better understanding of American life, ideals and problems.
This in turn serves to bring Finland and America even closer
together.

I have written so far about the effect of this unique, to Finland
at least, American action. A word seems in order concerning
its provisions and practical operating which started in the summer of 1950.

The Congressional Act provides that the Department of State
shall have direction of the fund's operations and the State Department's budget carries its administrative cost, thus the entire
amount of Finland's payments are used for scholarships and
other provisions of the fund. In addition to scholarships, these
include the acquisition for Finnish libraries of American books
and treatises on a variety of subjects which would not otherwise
be available in Finland; special scientific equipment for laboratories and other institutions; the assignment for service in Finland of such American educators and scientists as Finland may
request. Its provisions are also broad enough to permit the selec-

tion of Finnish newspaper reporters, shop foremen and stewards, social workers and the like for study in the United States.

The United States Legation in Finland has created a special department to work with a group of Finnish educational and other leaders in selecting the beneficiaries of the fund. The Finnish Committee on study and training in the United States announces the scholarships and traineeships open for application, recommends nominees and makes transportation arrangements for the successful candidates. Every year some forty or more graduates arrive for a year's graduate studies in American universities and technological institutes, and many others study for shorter periods in their special fields.

Another group of students will arrive in the summer of 1952, as they will continue to do annually until 1984, when Finland makes her final payment to America for the food you sent us when our entire population was starving in 1919.

All Finland is now doubly indebted to America.

—ARVO PUUKARI

Contents

	PAGE
Acknowledgments	V
Preface by Arvo Puukari	vii
Introduction	xv

PART ONE

CHAPTER

I. Finland's Location and Origin	3
II. The Country and Its People	13
III. Finland and America and Finnish Character	23
IV. Independence, and Creating a Government	35
V. Parallel Problems—External and Internal	44
VI. Growing Pains—1920-1939	52
VII. Finland's Exhaustless Green Gold Mine	65
VIII. Additional Finnish Industries	75
IX. Finland's Food Sources	85
X. How Finland Moves and Buys	94
XI. Labor and Management Organizations—and Woman's Place	104

xiii

CHAPTER   PAGE

   XII. Education   116

  XIII. Music, Literature and Press   131

  XIV. Art, Architecture and Sculpture   141

   XV. Social Welfare and Sports   148

  XVI. Finland's Hospitals   157

 XVII. War and Disaster   162

XVIII. Peace and Reparations   211

  XIX. Finland's Present Foreign Policy   229

Epilogue: "The Last Christmas Tree"   239

                        PART TWO

Biographical Sketches   245

A Declaration of Faith
   (THREE LECTURES DELIVERED BY THE AUTHOR IN
   FINLAND, 1951)

   The American Ideal   258

   A Brief Look Backward—and Forward   272

   What of the Future?   284

Bibliography   298

Index   301

           *Twenty-three illustrations will be found
           following pages 10 and 138 respectively.*

Introduction

Previous to 1913, Finland had been to me merely the name of a country and a colored patch on the map of Europe. In this I was not unlike other college graduates of that period whose impressions remained vague until events and circumstances had brought the Finns and Finland into sharper focus and thereby revealed that they and their country had distinctive, national characteristics.

That this was the case is not surprising since academic historians had treated Finland with only passing mention and, in doing so, had considered it either as having been part of Sweden, or as it then was, a part of the Russian Empire. Their telescopic treatment of Finland thereby failed to present the Finns clearly to most people.

This oversight of academic historians therefore failed to bring to public attention that the people of Finland had developed through long centuries of invasion or conquest a distinctive civilization, culture, character and institutions.

I mean by civilization that which the great majority of men of the western world mean when they speak of it: namely, cleanliness, honesty, kindness and the way womenfolk are treated. If western civilization uses these qualities as its yardstick, it becomes evident why Finland is generally admired. Civilization, it should be stated, is the means by which the culture of a people is nurtured and developed. If culture can be measured by education, then Finland ranks high among the nations of the world. And if one measures education by the proportion of public funds a government spends on this activity, Finland, which now expends approximately one seventh of its annual budget for education, ranks foremost among the nations of the world.

The academic historians could not have sharply presented these points to the average citizen forty or more years ago because at that time their existence in Finland was not readily apparent. The Finns' desire then to make them reality also was obscured by the overshadowing cloud of Imperial Russia's control.

This obscuring Russian cloud lifted in late 1917, when Finland declared her independence and became a free nation. Since then, Finland's remarkable record of social and economic achievement, as well as her principles of liberty, which have been seriously challenged and successfully defeated by the alternatives of both communism and fascism, has created a broad and general interest in this small country and its people.

It was a conversation with Theodore Roosevelt in 1913 that first brought Finland somewhat into focus for me. I was reporting to him on state by state political conditions of the country as they affected the Bull Moose party. When we reached the State of Minnesota, I mentioned the necessity of finding a new state chairman there.

"Have you found a suitable successor?" T.R. asked. My answer was that there were two available good men for the job, and after describing the qualities of my first choice, added: "There's a second good man by the name of Oscar J. Larson, a lawyer in Duluth."

T.R. replied instantly, "Larson's your man. He's a fighting Finn, the toughest-fibered fighting stock in the world. Finns can't be licked and they won't compromise. You can tie to them. Take Larson, cultivate the fertile territory; the Finns and the Scandinavians are our fertile territory in Minnesota."

Having given his judgment, T.R., fairly bursting with information, began to discuss the Finns and launched on an intensely interesting half-hour lecture of the history of Finland and the qualities and characteristics of the people.

Even with this inspiring introduction to Finland and the Finns, my interest in them was desultory until 1917 when they gained their freedom after nearly eight centuries of first Swedish and then Russian overlordship.

The devastation and human misery which followed World War I next brought Finland to my attention, since it was one of the many European countries which received aid from the American Relief Administration. The Finns, having just created their government, had no money. They insisted, however, upon aid on a loan basis. Finland's debt to the United States was contracted to pay for this aid and the Finns have scrupulously made payments on account.

Nurmi, the great Finnish runner, and the unmatched Sibelius also helped in a way to make me Finn-conscious.

A few years later through my friends the Wallenbergs, the Swedish banking family, I learned in considerable detail how the people of little Finland had been able to make such marked economic and social progress while much of the rest of Europe whined and lagged. The Finns did this by making a realistic appraisal of their assets and capacities. This done, they went to work to carry out their carefully planned program, a marked phase of which was that they left individual initiative untrammeled.

Then came the winter war of 1939–40 with Russia, when, until the mass weight of Russia crushed them, the Finns thrilled the courageous of the world with their magnificent fighting qualities and courage.

By this time the accumulating favorable evidence of the Finns should have brought them into clear focus for me. But it was not until 1945, however, when the American Friends Service Committee, of which I was a member, undertook a relief project in the Lapland Province of Finland that I began to see them through the right end of the telescope.

It may help the readers to an understanding of the situation by stating that the conditions in Finland which met Quaker specifications for a relief project were: (1) It was an area of great need which, for whatever reason, other relief agencies had neglected. (2) Adverse conditions which made operations difficult. (3) People who needed friendship as much as they needed food, medicine, clothing and shelter. (4) Strong ideological crosscurrents which challenged the Quakers in their efforts to project human service above creed, color, nationality or ideology.

Lapland, the northernmost province of Finland, was the area selected for the first Quaker relief effort. It had been laid waste by the German army in 1944 while the Finns were driving it from the country. Storm troopers had destroyed 87 per cent of Rovaniemi, the provincial capital. They had wholly destroyed Kittilä and other villages, bridges and highways and had scattered mines everywhere. They left the Finns only brave hearts to bring back to what had been their homes. Reports reaching the Service Committee offices in Philadelphia from staff members in Lapland were deeply moving. One said, "Conditions are terrible, but the people are wonderful." The impartial Quaker workers, who try to submerge their personal likes and dislikes and to make no sign of preference in their world-wide relief work, are nevertheless human and the Finns captured their hearts.

The Finns' homes were in ruins and much of their property had been destroyed or confiscated and their food supplies were inadequate. Although inured to Arctic cold, they were shivering through the winter with meager clothing. They suffered even more from spiritual loneliness. Once when some Quaker work campers attached a crude stretcher between two bicycles to carry to a doctor a farmer's child threatened with blood poisoning, the father said, "I had forgotten that there were kind people in the world."

Except for their Scandinavian neighbors, particularly the Swedes, all of their old friends seemed to have forgotten them. Their great and good friend and national ideal, the United States, against which they had neither declared war nor fired a shot, had not officially lifted a finger to help them. Being a proud and courageous people, they could not bring themselves to ask for help. When it came, it was doubly appreciated because, as they said, "You gave it without our asking for it."

The reports of Quaker staff workers on conditions and needs, of problems courageously faced and solved; the Committee discussions; association with Americans of Finnish extraction in an effort to secure funds for the work—all of these factors served to quicken and deepen my interest in this hardy, determined people.

This interest in Finland and the Finns was further quickened and deepened in the summer of 1946 when I included Finland in the itinerary of a trip to Europe. I went there to inspect the Quaker feeding and work projects and get copy that would help secure public funds.

I visited all parts of Finland and met with men and women of all classes; despite their phlegmatic obstinancy, introversion and wait-and-see tendency, I fell in love with the Finns. I liked their qualities of courage, industry, integrity; their ability to do much with little; and their unshakable belief that their country had a mission to fulfill for mankind.

According to Topelius,[1] the general traits of the character of the Finns are: "hardened, patient, passive strength; resignation; perseverance allied to a certain obstinancy; a slow contemplative way of thinking; an unwillingness to become angry, but a tendency when anger has been aroused to indulge in unmeasured wrath; coolness in deadly peril, but caution afterwards; taciturn

[1] Zacharias Topelius (1818–98) Swedish-Finnish poet and novelist, professor of history, University of Helsinki, 1847–78.

reticency, alternating with a great flow of words; an inclination for waiting, deferring, living for a day, interrupted sometimes by unseasonable haste; adherence to the old and well known, an aversion to anything new; attention to duty; law-abiding habit of mind; love of liberty; hospitality; honesty; a predilection for religious meditation, revealing in true piety. . . .

"The Finn is recognized by his close, distant, reserved attitude. It takes him some time to thaw and become intimate, but his friendship when won, is to be depended upon. Admiral von Stadinek said of him 'The Finn wants a petard in his back to make him move.' In outward appearance the Finn is generally of a middle height and strong build and his intellectual endowments want waking up. . . . Lastly, we must not forget . . . their love of songs, proverbs, riddles, exercises of thought and disposition for satire which mercilessly ridicules their own follies and those of others."

That which perhaps most stimulated my admiration for the Finns on this visit was their instinct, in the face of the impossible, to preserve and strengthen the eternal verities of justice, honesty and courage, those qualities on which western civilization rests.

I made my last visit to Finland in November, 1951, for the purpose of delivering three lectures which appear in the final section of this book under the title "A Declaration of Faith." Those who read them will find that my general theme was liberty. The Finns, on that bit of free soil which lies under the shadow of the Kremlin, accepted in their stride what I had to say on the subject.

Because it is symbolic of my relationship with Finland, I record that while driving by car from Lahti to Hämeenlinna over narrow, winding roads that were bordered by great forests of snow-burdened pine trees, something suddenly scurried hurriedly into the pine forest. I cannot be positive that it was, but it could have been Santa Claus. I feel sure that it was. The season and the setting were exactly right, and the unfailing faith and the good will of the Finns for all men convinced me that it was. May he live long in Finland!

Geography, which made Finland the home of Santa Claus, also placed her on the watershed between the eastern and western civilizations that today are engaged in a cataclysmic contest for supremacy.

Despite the eastern civilization's determined effort to force Finland into its orbit, her people continue to cling to and live by western civilization's free ways, culture, ideals and moral principles. Neither the military might, ruthlessness, false promises nor diplomatic intrigues of Communist Russia have been able to make the Finns give up their freedom or their independence.

Finland still is a free man's country. She holds democratic elections. Her press is uncensored. Her citizens are free to migrate abroad or travel freely at home. Foreign visitors may travel unhindered within her borders. She is troubled, as are other free nations, by Communist agitators, but no Communist holds a cabinet post in the Finnish government.

Finland is still a free and independent nation because her people so well understand Russian ways and know Russian habits. The Finns knew to a certainty that they would lose their freedom and their independence if they accepted Moscow's fair promises. They knew also that their refusal would call for heroic sacrifices. They refused. They made the supreme sacrifice—the result is that there still is a free Finland whereas today, Estonia, Latvia, Lithuania, Poland and Czechoslovakia, all of which yielded to Moscow's demands, are only tragic memories.

Had the nations of the free world possessed the wisdom, understanding spirit and determination that the Finns displayed in dealing with Communist Russia, their peoples would have avoided the heartaches which now trouble them and haunt their statesmen.

I have studied the Finns from afar and close up over a period of years and believe with Hudson Strode that: ". . . . they know things other races have forgotten . . . what is right and wrong . . . how to endure hardship and how to draw spiritual sustenance from natural forces about them." Their hardships appear to have sharpened their virtues and sustained their valiant spirits.

My hope is that this case history of free Finland's successful record of withstanding Communist brigandage may serve as a guide for the peoples of the free world.

—THE AUTHOR

PART ONE

Chapter one

Finland's Location and Origin

Finland, a small, compact republic with a literate citizenry that has been schooled in self-government, is the most northerly independent nation in the world. Russia lies to the east and Norway and Sweden to the west, thus it is the bridge and meeting ground of two civilizations. Its location makes it the crossroads and the buffer zone of conflicting ideas and ideologies between the east and west. It is natural, therefore, that since prehistoric times traces of both eastern and western influences have been discernible in Finland. But every important phase of Finnish life, however, whether in culture, religion, economics, politics, or undeviating adherence to belief in the dignity and importance of the individual, definitely places Finland with the west.

Draw a line across the top of the world's map and you will find Finland lying between the same degrees of latitude as most of Alaska, northern Canada, southern Greenland and the larger part of Siberia.

These latter countries are either sparsely settled or else uninhabited wildernesses, whereas Finland has a population density of approximately 29 per square mile, or about equal to that of the State of Minnesota. Finland contains more than one third of the people of Europe who live between the 60th and 70th parallels. Finland has about one seventh of the European land area that lies between those parallels. This comparative density of Finnish population is due to favorable climatic conditions which are caused by the Atlantic ocean's warm currents, as well as the wide gulfs of Bothnia and Finland, her sixty thousand or more lakes and her endless forests. The land is mostly low in character, rising gradually from the south to the small mountains in the far north whose highest peak is 4,340 feet.

Except for differences in language, anyone familiar with the State of Minnesota will find himself quite at home in Finland. Finland is the larger of the two places, but they are similar in shape, topography, forest areas and lakes. Finland has a total area of 130,159 square miles, 70 per cent of which is forest land, 9 per cent waterways and lakes, 9 per cent cultivated land and 12 per cent wasteland. Portions of both areas are covered with pine, spruce, white birch and aspen forests, but with this difference: Finland's forests, except those in the far north above the Arctic Circle, thrive throughout the entire country, whereas Minnesota's forests are largely confined to its northern two thirds. There also is this difference: Finland's more than 60,000 lakes and waterways are located in her southern two thirds, whereas Minnesota's ten thousand lakes are in the northern two thirds of the state.

Another difference between the two areas, and a marked one, is that Finland's summer days and her winter nights are far longer and her summer nights and winter days are much shorter than are Minnesota's.

Both Finland and Minnesota are places of striking beauty in summer, with their balance of the green of forests and fields and the blue of their lakes; with the trunks of white birches as lovely as that of children playing naked in the sun; the unbroken masses of forests. They are much alike in winter, too, with their crystalline seas of snow; and the stratospheric solitude which casts its spell and leaves its mark on the character of both populations.

Because of the similarities in climate, forests, lakes and crops, the traveler who is familiar with either place will find himself easily at home when visiting the other for the first time.

Scientists long ago rejected the once-held theory that Finns originally were Mongols of Asiatic origin. Finland is unique, except for the similarity of her language to that of the Magyars. Insofar as the Finns can be typed, they are Nordics and East Baltics, with light straw or ash-colored straight hair, gray, green or grayish blue eyes, prominent cheekbones, and oval or nearly rounded skulls. These are all similar characteristics that belong to the oldest European races which can be traced back for 2000 years without interruption. The Finns are homogenous socially, with only about 2500 Lapps—itinerant gypsies, all of whom enjoy civil rights. Anti-Semitism does not exist in Finland.

Fur hunters, presumably from Central Europe, pushed north across the Baltic in the first centuries A.D. and settled in what is now Finland. They created a new country, a new language, and a new type of people who over the centuries have earned the admiration of friends and the respect of enemies. They pushed the Lapps and their reindeer ever northward until now only about 2500 Lapps live on the cold northern fringes of Finland.

As a group the Finns came to be known by this name in the beginning of the eighth century. Even then their bravery and hardiness as a people were marked. Their gods included "Ukko," the God of Air, "Tapio," the God of Forests, and "Ahti," the God of Water.

Their repeated raids on the coast of Sweden forced the Swedish King, Eric IX, to set out to conquer the Finns in 1157. From that time until 1809 Finland became the cockpit of northern Europe in the almost continuous fighting between Sweden and Russia.

The first genuinely historical Finnish document is the bull which Pope Alexander III addressed on September 9, 1172, to the Archbishop of Upsala, Sweden. It is interesting to note in this first of all historical Finnish documents that the Holy Father in 1172 found the Finns difficult to contain, a quality which their enemies in this later distant, troubled day continue to find in them.

The Holy Father's lamentations in that bull concerned the inability of Eric IX, King of Sweden, to Christianize the Finns in 1155 by force of arms. During their more than one thousand years of residence in what is now known as Finland, the people of the country in 1172 offered, as they do today, a stubborn resistance to the new religion and to a form of foreign domination which they feared would lead to a new political and social system. Unlike the Irish, who are instinctively *agin* the established order, the Finns strive to maintain, improve and strengthen it. Then, as now, they were attached to the faith of their fathers, to their social order and to the principles of independence which they had wrought out of their hard existence.

There still stands the shell of a 700-year-old primitive cathedral on a hillside overlooking a lake in the Province of Häme. This well-preserved shell of granite and brick, under a good roof, offers mute but graphic testimony of the Finns of that distant day when the Swedes and the Roman Church were making such strenuous efforts to tame the Finns with Christianity. The walls of the interior of the cathedral, one great room with arched naves, still carry pictures in their original vegetable dye which tell a primitive story of the Bible. This pictorial biblical story was a necessary part of the people's worship, since few of them were able to read. In the entryway there still stand the racks where the worshipers stacked or hung their arms. In it, too, are the stocks in which the feet and hands of recalcitrant worshipers and community wrongdoers were locked. There also is an octagonal stone about two feet high on which the condemned laid their heads preparatory to losing them. A multitude of niches in the stone's top reveals that the blood of many Finns had flowed freely down its sides.

The Finns switched, without bloodshed, from the Roman Catholic to the Lutheran Church along with Sweden in 1527.

Since that time the Lutheran Church has been the established Church of Finland.[1]

There is a wealth of evidence available in the orally transmitted legends, in archeological, ethnological and philological investigations and a variety of comparative researches which convincingly establish the conclusion that by 1172 the Finns had turned from nomadic hunting to established farming. Social ties, with the sources in family life, gradually grew with territorial relationships.

Along with the customs to which the Finns have so tenaciously clung, to Pope Alexander III's annoyance, was their determination in 1172 to continue their way of religious worship: namely, veneration of their ancestors with the worship of various spirits, and some supporting magic and sorcery sidelines.

In the twelfth century the Finns at last yielded to the Roman Church's Pope and the King of Sweden, but did not do so until these two powerful leaders had worked them over through two wars which lasted nearly a century. Finally the Finns at the close of the thirteenth century said, paraphrasing St. Paul, "Enough, we want to be Christians."

Sweden and Finland eventually became unified. Armed intervention, however, played the minor rather than the major role in the unifying process. It is possible that the Finns still might be resisting Sweden, but, because of their piety, they would have accepted Christianity. Those other more powerful forces which were bringing about unification of the two countries were

[1] The Lutheran Evangelical Church, the established church of Finland since the Reformation, is closely allied with the government. The 1919 constitution grants full religious liberty to every citizen. 3,800,000 of the 4,000,000 Finns are Lutherans.

The next largest church group is that of the Greek Orthodox Catholics, with 70,000 members, most of whom originally lived in Karelia where they began to come under its influence about the twelfth century. All other denominations have a combined membership total of less than 12,000, of which twelve are Quakers. Percentagewise the Quakers are the fastest-growing religious group in Finland in that their membership has grown from three to twelve during the past seven years.

born of the need to unite in defense against the common enemy from the east, Russia. The women and menials, who formed the majority in Finland, also were receptive to a religion which preached love, humility and equality of men before God, and which also condemned the pagan worship of violence and material strength.

One other factor that limited Finnish opposition to Sweden's Christianization program was that the Swedish social and political order was as liberal as was that of Finland. The Swedes placed a comparatively light governmental yoke on the Finns, in that they only required the Finns to recognize the authority of a common king. The king was the unquestioned, all-powerful chieftain in war, but in peacetime his role was not so important. His job was to keep order, but in doing so he was not permitted to destroy the Finns' ancient rights. These considerations encouraged the Finns to swear allegiance to Sweden.

The Finns finally gave in and accepted Christianity and the working relationship with Sweden. Under unification with Sweden the Finnish provinces enjoyed political autonomy. They recognized only the authority of the common king. All citizens capable of bearing arms were required to help defend the country. During those six and a half centuries, 1157 to 1809, when Sweden and Finland were united, Sweden was the swaggering, fighting bully of Europe, and her defense was largely that of offense, and the fierce Finns became the fighting backbone of Sweden's armies. It is a common belief of Finns today that while Sweden had Finns fighting on her side she was sure to win. When she lost Finland to Russia, the warlike Swedes threw up their hands in despair and followed peaceful ways.

Despite occasional violations of the Finnish people's sovereignty during some of the periods of Sweden's foreign wars, Sweden formally maintained the principle that she could amend no Finnish customs which had the force of law, change her tax basis, or enact any new one without the consent of the representatives of the Finnish people.

In 1362, Sweden called upon Finland to participate in the election of the king and to take her seat in the Diet of the Four Estates. Even so, the scales were weighted against Finland during the six and one half centuries of Swedish rule in that the Diet expressed the will of the minority whose obligations, in time, were forgotten, but whose privileges were not. Neither workmen, town laborers nor women had any recognized rights. But this must be said in favor of the Swedish regime: it recognized and respected the inviolability of the individual and his property rights. Provincial laws adhered to this principle even before it was inscribed in the King's Act of the Law of the Country. All Swedish kings respected the individual freedom of the Finns.

In 1809, during the sunset period of her belligerent life, Sweden lost Finland to Russia. The history of nations is replete with ironic incidents in which old belligerents become allies and old friends become enemies. The irony of Sweden's loss of Finland to Russia at the end of the last of numerous wars between the two countries is that the first Czar of Russia was a Swede. The circumstance back of his selection was that the Swedes nearly 1500 years ago had struck off across Russia and established trading posts on their long treks to Byzantium and Kiev. According to the Russian Nestor Chronicle, the Kingdom of Russia was founded in the year 862 when some of the ancestors of present-day Russians said to the Swedes, "Our land is large and fertile, but there is no order in it. Come ye therefore and reign and rule over us." The citizens of Novgorod invited Rurik, a Swede, to rule them. From Rurik the Russian czars were descended.

The Swedes ruled Russia only a little more than a hundred years. When Vladimir I, Saint Vladimir, assumed the crown in 972, he found it advantageous to substitute the support of the Russian people for the support of Swedish swords, and Swedish influence consequently waned. All of this was changed when Russia finally defeated Sweden after intermittent wars which

were concluded with the peace treaty, in 1809, that transferred
Finland from Sweden to Russia.

Today, all that remains of the Viking giants' dreams of empire
of a thousand years ago are the blue-eyed and fair-haired men,
women, and children who live here and there among the Slavic
populations of Russia and the Baltic countries, throwbacks to the
one-time Swedish penetration of foreign lands.

From 1809 until Finland declared her freedom in 1917, she
was a grand duchy of the Russian Empire. True to her character,
Finland occupied a unique place in the Russian Empire in that
she was the only self-governing part of it—this habit of being
unique seems to be a characteristic of Finland. She is unique in
solving her problems with hard work; unique in having hope
when the light of hope seems to have gone out in many parts
of the world; unique in international good will and honest
dealing.

When Finland was incorporated with the Russian Empire in
1808–09, Czar Alexander I gave assurances to the Finns that
he would respect their laws and constitutional rights and that
Finland, he said, was henceforth raised to "a nation among
nations."

The honeymoon period with Russia began to fade in 1825,
and ended by 1855, when the spirit of Alexander's liberalism
was transformed into despotism by Nicholas I, in 1899. It was
then that political life in Finland came to a standstill. In July,
1901, Russia promulgated a new military law which to all practical purposes amalgamated the Finnish with the Russian military forces. Russian officials and the Russian language were
foisted on Finland in every possible way. In 1903, Russia in-
vested her Finnish Governor, General Bobrikoff, with dictatorial
powers which carried a spy system, domiciliary visits, illegal
arrests, and the banishment and suppression of newspapers.
The Diet was not convened, censorship was made oppressive,
and liberty of association was restricted by the Czar's government.

A reindeer train—West Lapland.

A typical group of workers' houses, situated close to the factories.

Sulphate and sulphite factories at Kaukas, East Central Finland.

Haystacks formed by pitching the hay onto long iron spikes.

The livingroom-kitchen-workroom of a peasant home. Note the flat round loaves of sour rye bread tucked between the rafters. This bread is unleavened and lasts for months.

Courtesy Finnish Nat'l Travel Bureau

Rovaniemi in winter.

A scene on Lake Saimaa, showing log booms.

Courtesy Finnish Nat'l Travel Bureau

Courtesy Finnish Nat'l Travel Bureau

The Great Square and Cathedral, Helsinki. Facing the Square on the left is the Main Building of Helsinki State University.

Market stalls at Helsinki's South Harbor, looking eastward.

Courtesy Finnish Nat'l Travel Bureau

A typical lake boat. (Vääsky Canal)

The Helsinki railway station, an early example of the architectural skill of Eliel Saarinen.

A modern apartment building, Helsinki.

Earlier in 1863, there had been a national re-awakening of faith in themselves by the Finns, proof again that hope for liberty in the human heart can never be stilled. Out of this re-awakening of faith in themselves came the enactment of new fundamental laws. They organized elementary education on a popular basis, greatly developed higher education and codified the laws pertaining to rural and urban communities. The Finns extended communal suffrage rights to women in rural districts and townships in 1872, and in the same year stimulated economic life by a law which proclaimed freedom of trade.

In the first decade of the twentieth century Nicholas II broke Russia's oath to Finland, which all previous czars had respected. After doing so he launched a campaign of oppression and Russification, during which he repeatedly violated the Finnish Constitution.

The Finns—as both the Swedes and the Russians have learned —have something of the qualities of the porcupine, an inoffensive animal until it is attacked. Being practical people, they knew that they would be crushed by Russia's might if they openly resisted, so they met the new oppression with passive resistance. This method quickly gained them the moral support of the western world, and Russia was forced to pull in her horns.

The Finns took advantage of Imperial Russia's shift from a hard policy to a softer one and in 1906, Finland was the first country in Europe to grant women the same political rights as men. That same year the Diet passed a law that provided for freedom of speech and the press as well as freedom of association and assembly.

Then came 1917, the Russian Revolution, and on December 6th, the declaration of independence of Finland's Diet.

The Finns did this on their own without the help of map-makers or the self-determination of the Peoples Committees at Versailles. Neither of these groups nor the Versailles Peace Conference were in existence when the Finns acted. Their action seemed right to them even though they stood alone in the world by doing it.

Due to their having so tenaciously preserved and protected these rights of free men throughout the centuries of Swedish and Russian overlordship, they had become experts in self-government and the art of political ways in governmental operation. They had learned to manage their public affairs with a thousand years and more of administrative experience in local government. They had learned, too, that political rights and individual responsibility go hand in hand if freedom is to be preserved.

They learned these hard but fundamental lessons of life through self-rule and thus were prepared and fit to guide a nation when finally, after God's good time of nearly eight centuries of foreign domination, they declared Finland to be a free and independent nation and a small but vital unit in the family of nations.

Chapter two

The Country and Its People

The law of compensation, because of nature's having withheld most mineral resources from Finland, seemingly has tried to make up for it by creating an incomparably soft beauty of countryside in which forests, fields, lakes, streams, moors, villages and industrial plants offer scenes that are moving and inspiring. This is particularly true in the summer when the green of the unending forests mingles with the blue water of Finland's countless lakes, with frequent breaks of farms and villages which help to lessen the fairyland, other-world effect.

Roads wind through endless green forests, with sudden glimpses of the blue waters of shimmering lakes in summer. In winter they run through a fairy world of stratospheric silence where the white of the snow blanket seems to make the pines and spruce forests even more green.

The summer sun which lingers over Finland nearly every hour of the day's twenty-four, as if to bless the country, reflects cloud, field and forest beauty on the still surfaces of its tens of thousands of lakes. Finland's gentle hills and endless green forests, broken with patches of lakes and desolate moors strewn with giant boulders, make it unlike any other country in the world.

Great patches of brilliant fireweed intermingled with Queen Anne's lace and white yarrow vie in their contrasts to give color and beauty to the countryside, along with bluebells, buttercups

13

and the ubiquitous dandelion. Lilies of the valley grow in great clusters in some of Finland's forests, and one occasionally sees an unusually beautiful pink and white wild rose, with delicate, silky petals. These constitute most of Finland's wild flowers. Perhaps because of their comparative scarcity the Finns love flowers more than most peoples. The southern windows of their homes are crowded with begonias, fuchsias, nasturtiums, geraniums and other potted flowering plants.

Harmony has its favorite home in Finland. Nature's beauty harmonizes with the clean, quaint towns, villages and great ultra-modern industrial plants with their colonies of workers' attractive homes—these all fit perfectly in their natural setting as if they too had grown there with the lakes and forests. There is harmony also in the way the Finns live and work.

The tourist too frequently visits countries where, though attracted by their past glories, he feels pity because later generations seem to have lost their way. The tourist in Finland never has this feeling of pity for the Finns; his enthusiasm for Finnish ways and accomplishments causes him to want to emulate the Finns.

There he finds the best of the old world and the best of the new existing alongside each other in perfect harmony.

Perhaps one of the greatest of all appeals that Finland has for the visitor, however, is that of her lakes and forests with their deep brooding silence. This is natural since deeply planted in the human mind and heart is the holdover love and awe of both of these from the time that his forefathers depended so largely on water and wood for his existence.

Finland's labyrinth of waterways, lakes and rivers constantly changes in an infinite variation of form and color, making her a paradise for campers and canoeists. Every lakeside or coast village and town has its yacht club or association where sailing is the main sport.

Finland also has a network of highways which reaches every section of the country, including the far north where the picturesque Lapps live. Finland's summer is short, bright, warm and sunny, and the summer nights throughout the country have a faint blue twilight, except in Lapland where the sun turns night into day for nearly three months. Every town of a few thousand inhabitants has one or more hotels ranging from comfortable to excellent. Many visitors hold a lingering memory of Finland's salmon, served raw in summer and salted the remainder of the year.

If the tourist is looking for gentle beauty, Finland is the place for him to go. There nature seems to strike a mystical chord, with constantly changing light and the continuous intermingling of water, land, forests, old and new civilizations.

Lake boat trips also offer fascination for visitors to Finland who are fond of the sheer spectacle of magical unreality. Some of the lake boat trips which are run on regular schedules are several hours long and a few last for several days.

One of nature's finest gifts to Finland's visitors who wish to give themselves up to nature's charms is the ability to get away from men and machines through the simple expedient of walking a few hundred yards from any town or village. If they do so, they will be completely lost from the buzzing noise and whirl of man's activities.

One of the greatest thrills any tourist in Finland can get is that of "shooting the rapids" in a large boat either in the upper part of Emäjoki, which has eleven rapids in about eleven miles, or in Lapland on the Swedish-Finnish border.

In the Lapland province of Finland, north of the Arctic Circle, one can catch glimpses of an inspiring beauty equal to that of the dawn of creation as one watches the setting sun's coloring on clouds slowly merge with the rising sun's coloring on the same clouds.

Three thousand years ago incomparable Homer in a beautiful phrase described dawn as "rosy-fingered." In Lapland the beauty Homer described in living words is doubled, because at the same instant one can see rosy-fingered sunset and rosy-fingered dawn.

It is an old, old act of nature's that has been performed countless millions of times yet never has lost its dewy freshness of beauty or become commonplace. Each performance is as wonderful as was the previous one, something that every individual should see, awesome beauty which will cultivate his appreciation of perfection.

Finland's winter-long, lasting snow blanket offers continuous skiing opportunities and the water of her lakes furnishes fine skating areas.

Since all Finns are nature lovers, they enjoy the forests and lakes even more than the visitors do who come from distant places.

Villages, whose houses have an ageless, old-world appearance, dot the countryside and bespeak an older culture. Here and there one passes through an industrial community which combines the old and the new world. Modern buildings of the western type are spotted amidst old-world and old-civilization buildings—a strange but not unpleasant marriage of eastern and western ways of living and working.

Careful observers, however, will note how little evidence exists in Finland of the eastern influence and, on the other hand, the great amount of evidence of western influence there is in the country. Even Finland's flora and fauna carry both eastern and western elements and the country and its people show permanent east-west ethnographic marks.

The Finns are an admixture of a little of the east and considerable of the west in culture, outlook and ways of living and working. Yet to an extent they are a race apart.

The Finns have overcome or at least brought under control some old-world characteristics but have not entirely rooted them out of their subconsciousness. This is fortunate for the Finns in that it helps them to have a better understanding of their close neighbors, the Russians, whose borders adjoin those of Finland on the south and east, and whose attempted domination of Finland never ends.

The Finns' knowledge of Russian ways of thinking and acting comes from proximity and long association rather than from similarity in ways of living, outlook or common origin. Evidence abounds in official statements and actions that Soviet Russia's leaders bitterly hate the Finns' stubborn, unyielding struggle for the right to live their own lives as they wish; that neither threats, wars, intimidations, economic pressure nor interference in internal affairs weakens the Finns' purpose to remain outside the U.S.S.R.

Evidence of a feeling of frustrated superiority exists in Finland toward the Russians. Its sources are Russia's long record of domineering treatment of the Finns plus the fact that they and the Russians are fundamentally different in temperament and tradition.

If pre-Soviet novels and short stories are accepted as accurate representations of Russian peasant life, it is easy to believe the Russian peasant to be dirty, incompetent, ignorant, easy-going and childishly naïve to a remarkable degree. His Finnish counterpart, on the other hand, is usually clean, competent, literate, hardworking, realistic and emotionally stable. The Russian peasant wears his charm on his sleeve where everyone can see it, whereas the Finnish peasant keeps his hidden.

These basic differences between the peoples of the two countries are understandable, since the Russians and Finns do not have a common origin.

The Russian peasant, schooled in a millennium and more of serfdom, has developed but little initiative, and because of this retarding influence he requires direction, control and authoritative leadership. The Finn, who has enjoyed a large degree of freedom during the same millennium, has become an almost purely direct-action individualist who abounds with initiative. One of the Finn's most striking characteristics is his way of getting things done without fuss and feathers.

Long, indoor, inactive winter nights which follow the calendar's active, long summer days have given Finns who live in rural areas ample time for reflection, and from this they have acquired a sense of timelessness in their consideration of the problems of life and living. It also helps them to see life whole and thereby avoid the jitteriness of people of other lands, whose hurried and complex times cause them to lose perspective of men, movements and events.

They never have, for example, relaxed in their efforts to develop and perfect their democratic processes. The author was privileged to attend an all-day conference in 1946 which Governor Hannula of the Province of Lapland held with his provincial Council. The meeting took place in a temporary building in Rovaniemi, a town which two years earlier had been almost totally destroyed by Nazi Storm Troopers. Except for those at the meeting, every able-bodied Finn was then working almost literally day and night helping his town, Phoenix-like, to rise from the ashes.

Each local Finn was given an opportunity to criticize or make suggestions. Each point so raised was replied to by the official in whose department it belonged. The postmaster, for example, stressed the need to push completion of the post office. He expressed the conviction that it was more important to care for the mails than it was to repair highways and railroads. The Minister of Communications from Helsinki explained that Finland's life and commerce directly rested upon her people's ability to transport food and goods, otherwise without open highways and operating railroads each community would be forced to live upon its own resources—which none could do.

As the meeting progressed, everyone had an opportunity to get his troubles off his chest and to offer suggestions. Everyone was able to understand the how and why of every official action, some of which had been modified by what had been said in the open meeting. It was democratic action which the Finns had worked out over the centuries, on the lowest as well as the highest level.

Centuries ago the Finns created popular assemblies to settle disputes in the villages between free peasants. These popular assemblies, in which the vote was confined to land owners and over which the nobility presided, made the laws. Primitive democracy though it was, this system in which the executive, legislative and judiciary powers were lodged in the people did express the will of the majority which was respected by the free consent of all members of the community. This seed bed of the elective system that the Finns planted carefully and nurtured with tender care was started a thousand years ago. Finns still cling to and protect it with fierceness. They have been difficult to conquer because their desire to govern themselves is so much an innermost part of every Finn born that it cannot be extinguished until the last living one has died.

The positive law, written or accepted as the common law, as it applied to local affairs, has been interpreted, administered and enforced in the communities by their residents since the earliest times. As early as 1340 A.D., Magnus Eriksson of Sweden guaranteed local self-government to all towns in both Sweden and Finland. Village communities and then larger areas conducted their public affairs at local councils and later to some extent at sessions of their district courts. In time some questions were decided at parish meetings and at meetings of land owners. Thus it was that local self-government, the creation and the administration of law and the enforcement of order grew out of the lives of the Finns and grew up with them.

A direct government by the people worked easily and naturally in those older Finnish provinces which had a comparatively primitive economic and social life. This was possible, in a measure, because the administered areas were small and the people could meet to make laws, settle disputes and agree upon policies in much the same way the residents of New England still do in their town meetings. It was a democratic and simple political system, but it had overtones in that it showed the Finns how to create and operate a national government with marked success many centuries later. The law to them was sacred. They them-

selves created it and retained it. They held it sacred because
they had found over the generations that it protected them
from their own misguided passions and the caprice of rulers.
In a word, the law assured them of justice, equal justice. Justice
next to liberty, which is the deepest and most inherent instinct
of the wildest animal ever born, was their prize of all prizes.

Professor Wuorinen, Professor of History at Columbia University, holds that:

Ever since the Finns became articulate about such things, they
have thought, written and talked about "law-bound" liberty. "Law-
bound" is a literal translation of a phrase every Finn knows; it is
probably more familiar to him than is "liberty under the law" to the
average American. It means that fixed rules, formulated by a demo-
cratically chosen legislature, determine what government can do
and cannot do. It can tax and coerce only within the rules. It has no
right to arbitrary action. What is right today is right tomorrow, and
what was within the law yesterday or is within the law today will
be within the law next week or until a new law properly enacted
provides otherwise.

The acceptance of and devotion to liberty under law was deeply
imbedded among the Finns. It is an interesting fact that the literature of freedom and liberty in the abstract does not loom large in
Finnish culture. This does not mean that the concepts or practices
of freedom have been ignored. What it means is that freedom, liberty and government under law have been taken for granted. National freedom and liberty of the Finnish citizen and Finnish cultural
independence—these have been accented more than the general ideal
of human liberty. Man's search for freedom has not been the important concern; the Finns' own desire to be free, to escape foreign
domination; to be masters in their own house, has been the inspiration. In a sense, this reflects provincialism and narrowness, no doubt,
but the provincialism it discloses violated nobody's interests and was
free from the notion that Finnish freedom could be or must be
achieved and maintained at the expense of someone else's enslave-
ment.[1]

[1] John H. Wuorinen, Ph.D., *Finland and World War II* (New York, The
Ronald Press, 1948), Foreword, p. 10.

One other important index to the character and quality of a people is the kind of homes in which it lives. Finland has no slums. Her people's homes usually are small, modest, well-kept places. The care the Finns give them bespeaks good taste and pride.

This is true also of Finland's farms, whether they are large or small. Each one is as nearly a self-supporting unit as its owner is able to make it. Many of them look like miniature villages, the home, barn, sheds and always the *sauna*, or Finnish bath-house, making a tiny unit. The *sauna* is as distinctive a part of Finnish life as are the honesty, industry, piety and tenacity of the people. Whether or not the Finns created and use it because they believe "cleanliness is next to godliness," or whether their instinctive desire to keep clean was the inspiration for its creation and use, is unimportant. Americans rely on more than 90,000,000 bath tubs as cleanliness aids, but when the Finns want to get clean, they hie to their *saunas*.

Nearly every rural and suburban home in Finland has its own *sauna*, and many of the lately built city apartment houses have one in the cellar. These are in addition to the public *saunas* in the cities, few of which, like the Uimahalli in Helsinki, are elaborate establishments. There the customers can get anything from a *sauna* to a swim, massage, hair-cut and manicure. The primitive *saunas*, from which the city and urban *saunas* have been perfected, usually consist of a small building which contains an entry-dressing room and a separate room for the *sauna* itself. A built-in corner is heated by a flat-top stove made of stones laid in mortar, on top of which a receptacle for water sometimes is placed. Terrific heat is produced by throwing a little hot water on the heated stones. The bathers sit on a series of step-benches attached to one wall. When they have thoroughly perspired they wash and then rinse themselves. An American has the feeling when he has completed a *sauna* that he is really clean inside and out. The effect of the *sauna*, due to the heat, leaves the bather invigorated rather than with the debilitating feeling which he receives from a Turkish bath, which has the steam room.

The *sauna* occupies an almost holy place in Finnish life. In rural areas mothers still retire to them for child birth. A Finn told the author that once as boy he had used a slang phrase in the *sauna*, whereupon his father, admonishing him, stated: "You are never again to say such a thing in the *sauna* or in church."

Chapter three

Finland and America
and Finnish Character

Those Americans who best know Finland and the Finns see constant evidences of a strikingly close relationship in outlook, ways and principles of the two peoples—Finns and Americans. The Finns' undaunted optimism is closely related to that of the American pioneers. The ability of both peoples to do much with little is identical. The capacity to fight against and overcome insuperable obstacles is their common heritage.

Both Americans and Finns like neatness and efficiency. They both have more than an average amount of initiative and hustle and both are direct-action people. Both Americans and Finns possess an open-minded readiness to try anything once, although the Finns proceed a bit more cautiously than the Americans. The peoples of both countries are alert in their efforts to improve governmental, social and economic organizations, and both readily adjust themselves to new ways of working and living. These are strange qualities to find in Finland, whose roots run deep into an old-world civilization, the most striking characteristic of which is a tenacity to cling to old methods and ancient beliefs.

One proof of the Finns' admiration for America may be found in the half million or more Finns and their children who have become American citizens. Another evidence of America's admiration for Finland exists in the large sums of money its government and banking institutions have loaned the government of Finland and its business leaders, largely on the character of the Finns. J. P. Morgan the elder once stated publicly that he would loan a man one million dollars with no security other than the borrower's character. So it has been with America's loans to Finland; they were character loans rather than commercial security loans.

There is a special reason why Finns hold a particularly warm place in their hearts for Americans. In the early days of their country's independence, when they had nearly reached the point of actual starvation as a result of destroyed crops, plundered and burned granaries, and stagnated imports and exports, they were eating bread made from the bark of trees. They were unable to establish foreign credits because other governments had not yet recognized their new government.

A delegation of Finnish officials called upon Herbert Hoover in Paris when he was head of the American Relief Administration and told him of Finland's desperate food situation. Mr. Hoover promised immediate help and to that end diverted some cargo ships of food then on the sea to Finnish ports. The Finns inquired how much the supplies would cost, and stated that they might not have sufficient funds to pay the bill.

I explained [Mr. Hoover has written] that I did not know what the cost would be, but if they could not pay, I would arrange to supply it on credit. They said, "We will pay. Our people will work and pay." . . .

I sent a mission of American Officers headed by Major Ferry Heath. The Finns are not only the most honest of peoples but they are able administrators. They had organized a capable Food Administration even before our mission arrived.

My urgent representations as to the necessity of the recognition of their independence to the Council of Foreign Ministers over months got nowhere. The French were the obstruction, as they believed Communist Russia would collapse and that the question should be kept open to settle with the expected new Russian Government. This action was such nonsense that I finally urged the President to raise it in the "Big Four" and let me do the talking. He asked for the usual memorandum to lay before his colleagues. This was sent on April 26th:

26 April, 1919

My dear Mr. President:

I am wondering if there is not some method by which the recognition of the full independence of Finland could be expedited. They have now had a general election, they have created a responsible ministry: this ministry is of liberal character. There are many reasons why this matter should be undertaken at once.

1. The United States has always had a great sentiment for the suffering of the Finnish people, and their struggle over a century to gain independence.

2. By lack of recognition, they are absolutely isolated from . . . the rest of the world. They are unable to market their products. . . . They have ships without flags; have no right to sail the seas. They are totally unable to establish credits, although they have a great deal of resource, as no bank can loan money to a country of unrecognized government. They are isolated by censorship. Their citizens are not allowed to move as their passports do not run.

I then described the relief operation and their financial situation, and continued:

If ever there was a case for helping a people who are making a sturdy fight to get on a basis of liberal democracy, and are asking no charity of the world whatever, this is the case. I am convinced from our reports that unless Finland is recognized within a very short time the present government cannot survive the difficulties with which it is faced. . . .

Nor do I see why any half measures need to be taken in this matter. They have gone through every cycle that the world could demand in political evolution, to the point of an independent people, and I feel that they would long since have been recognized had

*it not been for the terrible cloud of other questions that surrounds
the world. . . .*

> Faithfully yours,
>
> Herbert Hoover

The President asked me to see Clemenceau over the matter. As
always with me he was most co-operative. I did not need appear
before the "Big Four" with my short but prepared oration. They
sent my letter to the Council of Foreign Ministers with directions
to act at once. They met on May 3rd and agreed to recognition of
Finland's independence. But for some reason or other, it was agreed
that the decision should be kept secret from the Finns and the public
until a few days later, and then be announced simultaneously by all
Governments. A few hours after their decision was made, Holsti
came to see me full of emotion and gratitude. He informed me he
had seen my letter, but that recognition was not to be made public
yet. However, both the French and the British had communicated
to him confidentially what was done, and both had said that they
hoped he would appreciate their efforts. As it meant their blacklisted
ships could prepare to go to sea, Colonel Logan telegraphed to
Major Heath in Helsinki—confidentially over our wires—that recognition would be soon announced, and added:

*The recognition of Finland has been brought about entirely by
Mr. Hoover by his urgent and repeated representations to the various governments.*

Heath's immediate reply makes illuminating reading:

*You doubtless know that the news of England's recognition
arrived three days prior to the news that we had also recognized
Finland. Naturally, this resulted in a feeling of obligation towards
England which was only partially dispelled by the tardy arrival of
the news from the United States.*

*In addition to the general food supply for the population, our men
set up the usual organization of Finnish women to administer the
free child feeding. They gave a total of 35,000,000 free meals to the
youngsters. Our files are filled with thousands of letters from the Finnish organization for children. I give one example:*

"Three scourges, war, hunger and disease, have ravaged in Finland. They have sown sufferings and tears into many homes. But in addition to all this, the continued shortage of foodstuffs brought sufferings especially into the homes of the poor families. . . .

"And then arrived the gift of the American people for the children of Finland. When the poor mothers heard this their hearts brightened and their hopes revived. Now our small ones at least shall receive of God's real food.

"And then when the father or mother brought home the gift of the noble American people there was a holiday. The eyes of the children shone for joy and thankfulness toward their good benefactors. They were prepared into a meal which with glad hearts and thankful minds was eaten. Benedictions were asked for the great and noble American people living beyond the sea.

The Nurmes Committe" [1]

Every Finn knows it was America, through Herbert Hoover,[2] that assured and hastened recognition of their nation and fed them on trust when they were starving and unable to help themselves. And knowing this, their gratitude and affection for America and Americans is deep and genuine.

Alike though Finns and Americans are in many ways, they are quite unlike in several particulars. The Finns are less bumptious than Americans, more inclined to live and let live than are their great friends across the seas.

Having a longer and a homogenous history in contrast with the shorter polyglot history of Americans, the Finns possess clearer historical perspective. This is important in that it helps them to avoid the human tendency of confusing method with principle, something the Americans are not always able to do. Another of their differences is that *old* Finland has retained the

[1] *The Memoirs of Herbert Hoover.* (New York, The Macmillan Company, 1951) pp. 365–7.

[2] Mr. Hoover's name continues to be higly respected throughout Finland and has become a word in the Finnish language—"Hooveria"—which means gifts from America, be it food, clothing or other help. Mr. Hoover was made a Ph.D. with a sword by Helsinki University, founded 1640, in a special festival that was arranged in his honor when he visited Finland.

vision that *young* America seemingly has lost, the belief that the nation has a mission to fulfill for mankind.

Two of the more striking qualities which most Finns possess are strength and stamina. These are usually considered physical attributes. They are far more, however, in that strength is developed from right living, whereas stamina derives as much from human will and character as from the body.

The Finns' word for their stamina and strength is *sisu*. There is no English synonym for *sisu*. Its nearest is the ugly and inaccurate American word, *guts*. *Sisu* to the Finns means courage, tenacity, stubborn determination, energy and a will and an ability to get things done. A surprisingly large number of Finns possess these qualities to a marked extent. The factors in their life which have nurtured them include a poor soil, severe climate, adverse destiny, vast expanse of nature and the solitude which is a part of long winters and their long nights. This, at least, is a reasonable theory, since all animal life acquires something of the nature and climatic conditions in which it lives.

Toynbee [3] cites several historical examples in support of his belief that "ease is inimical to civilization." After asking the question: "Can we say that the stimulus toward civilization grows positively stronger in proportion as the environment grows more difficult?" he turns to China for his first example. Here he points out the different degrees of difficulties which the lower valleys of the Hwang-Ho and Yangtse rivers created for their respective peoples, and how they reacted. The Yangtse River, which seldom overflowed, was navigable in all seasons due to a relatively mild climate, whereas the Hwang-Ho River's frequent floods were devastating and, because of its shifting river bed and floating ice in the spring, it was not navigable. Even today, after three to four thousand years of human effort spent in draining swamps and building embankments, its occa-

[3] Arnold J. Toynbee, *A Study of History* abridgement of Vols. I-IV by D. C. Somervell (New York & London, Oxford University Press, 1947), pp. 88-89.

sional floods continue to be most destructive, yet Sinic civilization came to birth on it and not on the Yangtse.

Greece, in Plato's day, Toynbee states, had a light, stony soil that had been further impoverished by erosions which made human existence difficult. By changing from grain growing and cattle breeding to olive groves, whose trees can flourish on stony soil, the Greeks stabilized their economy and were able to undertake other business pursuits. Their improved economy enabled them to create and develop the political, artistic and intellectual culture which continues through the centuries to excite the admiration of men, whereas the peoples of the fertile areas to the north and west produced little that has not vanished and been forgotten.

To buttress his theory, Toynbee turned from Hellenic to Syriac history whose peoples, the Israelites, Phoenicians and Philistines, "distinguished themselves relatively thereafter in close proportion to the relative difficulty of the physical environment in the different districts in which they happened to have made their homes." Neither the Arameans on the rivers around Damascus nor in Antioch, nor the tribes of Israel who halted east of the Jordan to "fatten their bulls" on Gilead's fine pastures nor the Philistines who went to Syria as refugees from the Aegean, not as Barbarians but as heirs of the Minoan civilizations, earned the respectful attention of posterity.

It was earned instead by the groups who had to struggle against desert encroachments and thin and stony soil, who gave civilization its alphabet, discovered the Atlantic Ocean and, most important of all, arrived at a popular conception of God "which is common to Judaism, Zoroastrianism, Christianity and Islam, but alien alike from the Egyptic, Sumeric, Indian and Hellenic views of religious thought."

In the United States, Toynbee held, "taking all in all—climate, transport facilities and the rest—it is impossible to deny that the original colonial home of the New Englanders was the hardest country of all. Thus North American history tells us in favor of the proposition: 'the greater the difficulty, the greater the stimulus.' "

Finland's history supports Toynbee's theory.

Although difficulties and dangers cast constant shadows over their nation, the Finns appear never to have lost their sure faith that a better future awaits them, nor do they permit their love of their homeland to lessen or grow tepid. They have courageously and hopefully traveled their hard path through history which has been strewn with dangers, oppression, sacrifice and hard work.

The character of the Finns has been hammered out on the durable anvil of hard circumstance. They have worked hard for centuries to hold their own against nature, which seems to have developed a remarkable quality of niggardliness. Their struggles have not made the Finns perfect; they have made many mistakes. Their most serious and tragic troubles, however, seldom have been of their own making. Circumstances from the outside, over which they have no control, such as aggression and power politics, have made Finland a pawn. Field Marshal Baron Gustaf Mannerheim once expressed Finland's unyielding attitude about foreign invaders and her people's determination to live their lives as they wished when he said, "If we cannot have freedom to govern ourselves, we will fight to the last of our old men and the last of our children. We will destroy our towns and our industries—and what we will give the Russians will be cursed by nature."

In one national crisis created by invading hosts a Finnish statesman said, "Finland has been devastated before and her people have ascended again. The Finns can do it another time."

Foreign invaders have made a bloody battleground of her forests, fields and homes. The Finns, however, have never fought a war of aggression. Their greatest wish appears to be to live in peace and deal honestly and fairly with all men.

One reason why the Finns have caught the world's fancy is that their approach to life is the antithesis of cushion-chair thinking and push-button existence in that part of the earth where too many people believe the world owes them a living—a cock-eyed and unsupportable thesis.

Another possible source of the world's admiration of the Finns is that men still are thrilled by the spectacle of the winner against unequal odds. That is why the success story of little David and his slingshot in his contest with the mailed giant Goliath still grips the imagination of children and grownups. That is why Captain Carlsen's courageous fight in early 1952 to save his *Flying Enterprise* in its unequal battle with the might of a mad ocean and wild winds caught and for days held the attention and stirred the inspirations and aspirations of men all over the world.

It is a tendency of human beings to center their sympathies and interest on the party who has odds to overcome in a contest —provided only that that party never sinks below their highest ideals of courage, daring, determination and resourceful effort.

This tendency in men to claim as their own the heroic fighter whose chances are slender helps in a measure to explain why the people of little Finland have been able to create a distinguished place for their country in the family of nations. Finland fought for centuries to maintain the integrity of her principles of liberty and self-government.

There also is Finland's honesty, pure gold in a brassy world. Other nations, and among them the greatest in history, welshed on their debts to the United States and each other when the going got hard. True, they were hard pressed. So was Finland. But Finland made principal and interest payments promptly and uncomplainingly.

The human character is determined by so many influences and conditions that it is difficult to state definitely just which one has helped most effectively to mold this quivering mass into a stable and fixed form. This observation leads to the question: Why do Finns place kindness, justice, honesty, liberty and peace foremost in their lives?

Climatic and soil conditions certainly play a part in the process. So do the Finns' ways of living and earning a living, acquired through centuries of struggle by fifty or more generations to maintain an existence in an area which places a premium on initiative, industry and co-operation. These engendered qualities help in a measure to explain the hardy growth in Finns of the spark of kindness that God planted in the human heart.

The hardy conditions of life help also to an extent to explain their development of honesty. Nature is the most honest thing in the world. Observant men raised on the soil, and until a half century ago nearly 80 per cent of the Finns were so raised, quickly learn that nature demands absolute honesty from those who maintain their existence with her help. Nature cannot be tricked with short cuts. Soil must be well cared for, good seed must be planted in the right seasons, crops must be properly cultivated and the harvesting season met without evasions and delays. Indolence, delays and indifference carry heavy penalties in all of these particulars. Honest, hard work, a sense of duty and intelligence can win and hold nature's favor in nine seasons out of ten.

Whether or not the Finns have been conscious of this truth is unimportant. What is important is the fact that it has slowly but surely become a part of them, helped to mold their characters into a fixed, stable form. It has colored and influenced their national policies and international relationships.

By the same token the conditions of life which oppressed Finns over long centuries have had their part in developing other basic qualities of character which civilized men look on with high favor.

Nearly two thousand years ago Tacitus, the Roman historian, wrote that "The Finns are extremely wild." Long, hard winters, short growing summers, the Roman Church and the Swedes, followed by the Russians, combined to curb but could not entirely eliminate the wild streak in the Finns. It still shows up when they go to war, in internal differences, in insistence upon paying their just debts, and in their fierce love of liberty and justice. Few entirely tamed and balanced individuals who approach problems calmly and quietly, on *the-one-and-then-on-the-other-hand* basis, have retained these primitive, simple qualities which are a part of wildness. Life must be so simple that it can be readily resolved into clear-cut issues for an individual or a people to hold and live uncompromisingly the things in which they believe.

The simple, primitive way of life which still exists in Finland begets neighborly, helpful customs and practices. The fixed place of habitat, where generations of ancestors have lived, enables family roots to run deep into the soil until now Finns have almost become a part of it. All of these things serve as controlling agents on fractious spirits, creating in the hearts of the people an observance of those laws which exist in the vast domain of the unenforceable.

During the centuries between 1157—when the Swedes and the Roman Church brought the "wild Finns" to accept Christianity with swords—and 1809, Finland was the anvil on which Sweden and Russia hammered out their wars of conquest and which decimated her population. Finland's manhood fed their war machines in man's most futile and mad activity, and their invading armies destroyed the homes of her people and confiscated their property.

These tragic experiences planted the seed of peace deep in the hearts of Finns and caused them to seek by every honorable means to live in friendship, short of sacrificing honor, with all peoples of all nations.

These were the circumstances and customs, the tragedies and the hardships which have made the Finns what they are today, nurtured a pliant but unbreakable spirit, given them an understanding patience and a conviction that integrity, justice and determination to cling to principles will emerge triumphant in the end.

Proof that the Finns practice what they preach is furnished

by their concept of and adherence to the principles of integrity and justice. Corruption in public life is the exception in Finland. Callous sacrifice of public to individual ambitions seldom raises the ugly head there. Arbitrary government has gained no foothold with Finns.

Few men are qualified to say whether or not their circumstances, customs, tragedies and hardships are responsible for the Finns' failure in some respects to create and foster a culture and a civilization which equals in "depth and grandeur" that of many other lands. The fact is that they have not yet done so, but they do have a quality and character that is all wool and a yard wide, acquired by toil and perseverance; none of it by despoiling other peoples.

Chapter four

Independence, and Creating
a Government

The Russian Revolution broke out in March, 1917. The revolutionists deposed the Czar and created and established a provisional government in swift order in St. Petersburg under the liberal Prince Lvov.

The new Russian government acted on the Finnish question with unusual speed by quickly summoning the Finnish Diet to meet. It next removed the officials of the old regime and released political prisoners, with the apparent intention of restoring Finland to a contented and progressive state under Russian guidance.

The people of Finland had other ideas. They were uncertain about whether or not it would be wise to cut their working class adrift from all Russian connections. They were certain, however, that Finland must be permitted to decide about her own future.

The Finnish Diet expressed this conviction on July 18, 1917, by adopting with a majority of 136 to 55 what is known as the "Independence Bill." The Bill declared that the Diet could not be dissolved except by its own decree; that "the Diet of Finland alone decides, sanctions and decrees the execution of all laws of Finland, including those that concern State economy, taxation and customs" and that "the Diet decides concerning the Executive power in Finland."

This aggressive, decisive Diet action appropriated to itself all of the powers which Finland had gained and retained under the old constitution when it had been ruled by Czars in their capacity of Finland's Grand Dukes. The Diet conceded one point, namely, that Russia could continue to direct its foreign affairs and provide for its defense. There was a sharp difference of political opinion about this provision. Some leading Finns wanted to make a complete break with Russia, but in keeping with the Finnish wait-and-see characteristic of permitting events to clarify the situation, the Social Democratic majority voted to take one step at a time.

The Russian Provisional Government, which was dominated by Kerensky, insisted that the Diet's action took in too much administrative territory. Kerensky ordered the Finnish Diet to be dissolved and the election of a new Diet in the fall to decide the future of Finland.

Russia's action served to transform the normally phlegmatic Finns into the "wild men" Tacitus had called them so many centuries earlier. They were neither calm nor deliberate in expressing their feelings. The opposition to Kerensky's stand was expressed in violent acts throughout Finland that autumn.

The rank and file soldiers in the Russian garrisons in Finland even rose against their officers. In Helsinki "whichever way you cast your eye you saw only wild, armed bands with the expression of madness on their faces, carrying revolvers in their hands and the swords of murdered officers by their sides." [1]

Election day finally came. When the ballots were counted the results showed that the Social Democratic party had lost eleven seats, and a clear majority of the Diet's two-hundred membership, on a campaign program of "full internal autonomy."

One other factor which entered the involved situation, aside

[1] S. Soderhjelm, *The Red Insurrection in Finland*: A study based on documentary evidence (Harrison, 1919).

from the loss of eleven Social Democrat Diet seats, was that a new change had occurred in the Russian government in October. The Bolsheviks had now come into power. This last change in the Russian government carried a threat to the economic principles which were held dear by the middle-class majority in the Finnish Diet. Communist control of Russia served, however, to consolidate and coalesce the strength of the Finland-for-Finns movement. This more favorable situation encouraged the Finnish Diet to declare on November 15th, "The supreme power in Finland belongs to the Diet." After it made this momentous decision the Diet members and the people of Finland waited with fear and anxiety for the heavens to fall. When the skies continued to remain in their immemorial place and no threat of retribution came from St. Petersburg, the Diet took a momentous step on December 6, 1917, and drafted a declaration of independence which formally proclaimed Finland to be a sovereign state.

An earlier chapter has described how Herbert Hoover forced the Great Powers to recognize the new government in Finland.

The major question the Finns now faced was: What kind of independent nation will we have? Shall we create access to equality of opportunity for every citizen?

At home, hooliganism paralyzed existing organizations for preserving order and Finland again, as she has so often before, became the gnawed bone of contention with foreign powers.

The White Guard, composed largely of the "white army of peasants" and strengthened by Finnish officers who formerly had served in the Imperial Army, now numbered 37,000, but the Red Guard, which the Social Democratic Party had created, quickly grew into a powerful opposing force with thousands of recruits of Russian Communists, out-of-work Finnish laborers, and ne'er-do-wells. On Sunday, January 28, 1918, the Red Guard carried out a *coup d'état*. It seized and occupied government buildings in Helsinki, and later throughout the country, by the simple process of issuing orders to each local Red Guard unit to establish control in its own district. The following day the President of the Diet and the Chairman of the Senate, together with the Red Guard Chairman of the Trades Union, proclaimed Finland a Socialist Workers' Republic.

The *coup d'état* group created a civil war instead of a workers' republic. While the Red Guard was trying to organize an army in Helsinki, General Mannerheim, a Swedo-Finn who had seen service in the Russian Imperial Army, was active in creating a United White Guard Army at Vaasa in west central Finland.

Indecision reigned everywhere. The country was in the throes of revolution. The Reds held practically the whole of south Finland, its most thickly populated and wealthiest part. They lacked discipline, however, which created delays that soon put them on the defensive. The struggle's turning point came at Tampere, an industrial city of about 100,000 inhabitants, in southwest Finland. The Reds held the city. The White Guards began their final assault on April 3rd; on April 5th, Tampere fell and Mannerheim took 10,000 prisoners.

This White Guard victory, however, did not end the civil war in which the Reds still had 90,000 men under arms against the White Army's 60,000 to 70,000. How long it would have taken them to fight it out between themselves will remain unknown, because Germany sent 12,000 men to Finland on April 3rd with the immediate double objective of crushing the Reds in Finland and of preventing the Allied forces from effecting a junction with the Imperial Russian fleet, then ice-bound in the Gulf of Finland.

The White Guard and German forces' successful encounters with Red troops enabled them to move into Helsinki, the former Red headquarters, whereupon the Reds moved in full retreat to Viipuri, near the Russian border. Mannerheim's Finnish troops, aided by the German forces, captured 20,000 Red prisoners at Lahti, in south central Finland. This White Guard victory broke the backbone of the Red strength and was of decisive help in hurrying to an end the civil war which Finland now calls the War of Independence.

Following the successful end of their War of Independence, the democratic, liberty-loving Finns, who try to keep aloof from international politics, did the one glaringly inconsistent thing in their long history by inviting a German prince to come and rule over their country as king.

The German Kaiser refused the crown for one of his sons, but he did generously and graciously, as it were, permit Finland to name his brother-in-law Prince Friederich Karl of Hesse, King of Finland. This was done by a rump Finnish Diet, by a vote of 75 to 25, on October 9, 1918. The Armistice which ended World War I shortly thereafter saved Finland from a fate that could have been "worse than death."

The Finns' action is understandable if it is accurate to say that exceptions prove the rule. One possible reason for their taking this addlepated step is that the German Kaiser had exacted it in return for having sent Finland military aid in its fight against the Reds, but this point cannot be established until and unless German and Finnish files are all made available.

Another reason which had cleared the way to make it possible was that Finland's Regent, Svinhufvud, was pro-German. His personal sympathies could not, however, have determined Finland's course had it not been supported by a variety of strong Finnish-German ties.

These Finnish-German ties were first created in 1531 when the Finn, Michael Agricola, who made Finnish a written language, returned home from Wittenberg, where he had served as pastor under Luther. There was, in addition, the German-Finnish religious tie which grew out of the dominant position which the Evangelical Lutheran Church held in both countries. Another factor which had helped to bring Finland into a close relationship with Germany was that of her proximity to many excellent German universities at which several generations of

Finns had studied. This naturally led to the adoption by Finnish scientists of German methods of scientific research.

Still later, about a century ago at the time of Finland's Great Awakening when she began to establish new relationships in the west, the Finns conducted the greater share of their foreign financial business, imports and exports, with Bremen bankers, which in turn led naturally to increased commercial relationships. This became particularly noticeable following the expansion of German industry and its need for new foreign markets to absorb its exports.

The net result of all of these long-established German-Finnish religious, cultural and commercial relationships was that many Finns read German easily and spoke it fluently, understood German ways and thinking and had developed an appreciation of German music and literature.

Which one of these reasons or to what extent all of them helped to influence Finland's amazing action of seeking a German to rule over them, is unknown.

The fall of the German Empire carried with it the fall of the political fortunes of the Finnish Regent, Svinhufvud, whose moves Mannerheim had opposed. Mannerheim succeeded Svinhufvud as Regent. When Mannerheim came from abroad, in the files of the honor guard which received him, the former Regent Svinhufvud stood as a sergeant major of the White Guard.

Despite Soviet and German participation for their own ends, this bloody War of Independence really was a civil war of Finn against Finn. It was a contest of the old Finland's yeomen and pastors that was led in part by the Swedish-speaking educated classes against the new proletariat of the towns and the landless peasants. It was fought with the terrible brutality which always marks class conflicts.

The Reds killed in cold blood behind the lines an estimated number of 1,000 men, most of whom were land owners and university graduates. The White Guard, following victory, placed 80,000 Reds, men and women, in concentration camps of which an estimated 10,000 died of starvation.

The brutality displayed by both sides was an expression of the deep, inner, fierce quality of the Finns who, unless fired to white heat, are among the most humane and law-abiding peoples. When their passions had cooled, the Finns tried 70,000 prisoners in courts. By March, 1919, the government had carried out the death penalty on only 125. It had also reduced the sentences of those others who had been found guilty. National unity and independence had cost the lives of 24,000 Finns.

Although both World War I and the Finnish civil war had ended with the year of 1918, Finland's future looked black. The classes were farther apart than ever before. The country's export trade was throttled by foreign government regulations, and she had lost her best customer, Russia. The new government was unable to export enough goods to pay for necessary imports, including vital food supplies.

This combination of hard conditions created an alchemy that cleared the mists of unreality from Finnish eyes. With better vision they saw that they could not grow strong and become united either by bleeding themselves to death or by filling their hearts with rancorous hatred. They had become an independent nation because they were a meteor fragment of gigantic, clashing world forces. An inscrutable but generous fate had saved them from themselves when their Diet selected a German prince as King of Finland. Great powers, serving their own purposes, had helped hasten to an end their cruel, barbarous civil war. The sweep of great forces and events left them a tiny unit in a back eddy of the world. Their birth pains had been long and full of agony. Now, at last, they were on their own.

Fortunately, for the sake of a strong, united and purposeful Finland, her people seem always to be at their best when circumstances are most difficult. This is the trade-mark as well as the distinguishing characteristic of the thoroughbred. He never quits. The Finns did not quit! They went to work individually and nationally. Food and shelter came first, but hand in hand with providing food and shelter they revived business, began a search for new markets and started producing goods for export.

One of their early administration problems was that of creating and then of agreeing upon the exact form their government would take. The new Diet, which met in April, 1919, began to consider the new constitution, and after long and acrimonious debates the Diet ratified it on July 17, 1919.

The striking quality of this constitution, which is unmarked by dramatic surprises or half-baked proposals, carries evidence of the Finns' gift for compromise as well as their ability to establish sweeping reforms without ignoring the durable qualities of tradition. With minor changes, it continues to stand as the fundamental law of the country.

A swift examination of it shows that it contains a bill of rights that is in the tradition of the nineteenth-century democracies except in one important particular: it guarantees protection of the health as well as the property of the citizen, his labor and his personal liberty.

The new constitution declared that the power belongs to the people as it was expressed through the Diet; provides that Diet members be elected for a maximum of three years by the votes of all citizens, male and female over twenty-four years of age (later changed to twenty-one years) by proportional representation, in order that minorities might have their rightful representation.

The sole power of making laws was placed in the Diet, but the constitution provided that the President must sign all Diet bills before they can become law.

In addition to his veto powers the President's other powers are considerable—even greater than those of the President of the United States. He can issue administrative edicts, provided they do not contravene existing laws. He names his own cabinet but is not obliged to accept the advice of his ministers. He directs the foreign policy and the army. He may call for special sessions of the Diet or dismiss it when he wishes. He does not, however, have any authority over the budget. All of his decisions must be countersigned by the minister concerned. The Chancellor of Justice examines all presidential decisions and, if he finds them contrary to the constitution, may indict the President before the Diet, which by a three-fourths majority can bring the President before the Supreme Court on the charge of high treason.

The constitution provides that the President be named on February 15th, the anniversary of the day more than six hundred years ago when Finnish peasants first participated in electing a king. His term of office is six years. He is chosen indirectly through an electoral college of three hundred electors, the candidate receiving the majority of votes being declared the winner.

Under its constitution the Cabinet is required to balance its budget. It cannot borrow money except with the consent of the Diet. The Diet may not amend the constitution without the consent of the voters in a general election. Judges have life tenure and the Chancellor of Justice is made responsible for checking the legality of the acts of the Diet, Cabinet and President.

The new constitution drew heavily on Finland's 1772 constitution, but the Finns borrowed from other governments in writing it. They took proportional representation from Belgium; indirect presidential elections and other portions from the United States, and included many English and Dutch features.

Comprehensive and explicit as was Finland's new fundamental law, there were still the unanswered questions: Would it give free play and sufficient satisfaction to the varied interests and aspirations of the Finnish people? Did there exist in them a great enough spirit of good will to make the constitution workable?

To an appreciable extent, time has answered these questions in the affirmative.

Chapter five

Parallel Problems—External and Internal

The Finns in 1919 had decisively settled the problem of the form of government under which they wanted to live. It was to be a republic. They adopted the fundamental law and embodied it in a constitution which fixed legislative, administrative and judicial procedures and responsibilities. They now, by midsummer of 1919, on paper at least, were a free and independent nation with a responsible, functioning, representative government.

The immediate problem of how to keep body and soul together, was not insoluble, because each Finn was a producer who was able and willing to do much with little. They sought peace and strove for order because they believed that peace and order, permitting each of them to produce at his utmost capacity, would solve their problems in due course.

The new government's sailing course was not by any manner clear of danger both externally and internally. Externally, their problems included (a) the Åland Island question with Sweden and (b) the Karelian, or eastern boundary, question with Russia. Serious as were the two-dimensional external problems to Finland's future, they possessed none of the mercurial properties of internal problems which consisted of language use, rights of of the Swedo-Finn population, prohibition—Finland also tried that experiment—and the agrarian problem, the most complex and serious of all.

The Åland Islands question had become a serious external problem about one century earlier and it troubled the Finns because it affected their country's relations with Sweden on the west. The Karelian boundary problem, unless settled amicably, was sure to create bad relations with Russia on the east and south.

The sobering effect of responsibility which national independence gave the Finns helped to give them stability. Their industry hastened development, but their leaders realized, however, that successful settlement of the two external problems would depend upon their neighbors' agreeable acceptance rather than upon the amount of territory the Finns might gain, since without the lasting good will of both Sweden and Russia, Finland's continued independence could not be assured.

The new nation's foreign policy was simple and obvious. Its aim, that of peaceful relations with all nations, rested on scrupulous observance of commitments. It was a moral policy which was in complete harmony with established Finnish principles of justice and fair dealing to the extent that it sought to harm no one or threaten the security of any nations.

Napoleon once said, "Åland is the key to Stockholm." The Swedes, realizing this, undertook to "fish in troubled waters" during World War I. This group of nearly 300 islands, which lies between the Baltic Sea and the Gulf of Finland, stretches from the southwest coast of Finland nearly halfway to Stockholm. The islands were demilitarized by the Peace of Paris in 1856. Germany waived this clause in 1907; the Allies in 1914. During World War I, Russia built a strongly fortified base on the largest of the islands. The Swedes did not like this. In due course Sweden sent agents to the islands to collect petitions from the pro-Swedish population, nearly all of whom had Swedish antecedents. These petitions called for the surrender of the islands to Sweden. The feelings of the Swedish population were intensified when Finnish Red Guards in 1918 highhandedly took charge of everything on the islands.

The question was still in dispute when World War I ended. The islands sent a deputation to the Peace Conference and insisted upon the rights of self-determination. The League pigeonholed the question for the time being. In May, 1919, the Finnish Diet passed an act which granted a degree of local autonomy to the islands. This was not to the liking of the islanders, who sent representatives to Stockholm with a formal request to be annexed to Sweden. The Finnish government countered by sending a battalion of troops to the islands to arrest the island representatives who had gone to Stockholm. The Swedes retaliated by recalling their Minister to Finland. Talk of war between these old friends began to be rumored.

In 1920, the newly formed League of Nations Council invited Finland and Sweden to present their respective cases. The following year, 1921, the League sent a committee to the islands to make a careful study of the situation. It concluded that since the Ålander population consisted of only about ten per cent of Swedish-speaking people, the islands by right belonged to Finland. In June, 1921, the League Council recognized Finnish sovereignty of the islands. Some time later Sweden accepted the decision with good grace. In October, 1921, at an international conference, the League of Nations gained the signatures of all concerned governments to guarantee that Åland would not be used for military purposes. This action eased the gathering tension between Sweden and Finland.

The Karelian problem was a complex one due to the fact that the western part of the Karelian province (which is situated on the Russian border) always had been considered a part of Finland. This was the case both during the centuries when Finland was a grand duchy of Sweden as well as after it became a grand duchy of the Russian Empire in 1809. The inhabitants of both Karelias spoke Finnish and nearly all of them were Lutherans. The eastern part of the Karelian province, however, had been made a part of the Russian Empire proper in 1809, due to the fact that its people for centuries had been more under the Russian than the Swedish influence. Although eastern Karelians were Finns, they were adherents of the Greek Catholic Church. Its proximity to Russia and the influence of the Greek Catholic Church prompted its people in 1809 to want to become a part of Russia proper. It remained and was treated as an integral part of the Russian Empire. Late in World War I, after much buffeting around, an assembly of the eastern Karelian province unanimously expressed its desire "freely to manage its own affairs and to separate from the Russian Empire." Russia countered by approving the formation of a Karelian Soviet Commune.

When in October, 1920, Finland and Soviet Russia concluded peace negotiations and signed the Treaty of Dorpat, Finland recognized East Karelia as a part of Soviet Russia. Russia on her part ceded to Finland her claim on the two western frontier parishes. Russia also recognized the Finnish Republic and gave Petsamo, an ice-free port on the Arctic Ocean, and a corridor to it as well.

Finland through this settlement with Soviet Russia won her powerful neighbor's good will. It also brought about the resumption of commerce with Russia, and enabled Finnish Socialist refugees in Russia to return home.

The three major internal problems were mercurial in nature because their roots lay deep in centuries-old human customs, traditions and prejudices. They included the place the Swedish-speaking population of Finland would have in the new republic, prohibition, and land ownership.

The constitution had prescribed that "Finnish and Swedish shall be the languages of the Republic." It specified the right to use the common parlance of Finland: that is, the Finn-Finns and the Swede-Finns were permitted to use their mother tongue before the law courts and administrative authorities "so as to safeguard the rights of both language groups . . . (and) provide for the intellectual and economic groups in accordance with identical principles."

The phrase *identical principles* became the center of the controversy between the two groups. The extremist Swede-Finns insisted that it meant on a basis of equality, whereas the extremist Finn-Finns insisted that it meant "in proportion to numbers."

The ancient difference in social advantages caused by two languages, and the mutual distrust between the two groups, had simmered during their common struggle to gain independence. Once independence had been gained it began to boil over.

Finland's language problem has several unique qualities. Taking the negative phases of it first, one finds that it does not arise from religious differences, since above 97 per cent of Finns are adherents of the Evangelical Lutheran Church. It is not a regional controversy since outside of the Åland Islands there are few concentrated Swedish-speaking groups. It is not a racial problem since all but a negligible number of Swede-Finns have no more Swedish blood than do most Finn-Finns. The Swedish language speaking Finns in 1950 represented slightly more than 8 per cent of the total population of the country and they are scattered in the western, central and southern part of Finland.

Some Finns in the past had learned the Swedish language and adopted Swedish names largely because it was the surest road to advancement. The Swede-Finns represented the last group of die-hards of the old ruling class in Finland, an anachronism from the time when Sweden ruled Finland. In one way their stand was related to the old, old class struggle of the haves with the have-nots. Because class struggles tend to cloak their purpose, the Swedish-speaking Finns adopted Swedish culture as their slogan. Thus the conflict to an extent was one between the old ruling classes and the new group of nationalist Finns.

The constitutional guarantees of cultural and economic equality between the two language groups, the proven capacity of the Finn-Finns to grow in business and political leadership, the increasing stability of Finland economically and otherwise, the care and justice with which the government of Finland treated minority groups plus the inevitable and unvarying help that the passing years give to the solution of knotty problems, have all combined to make this conflict of diminishing importance.

It was not until after June 1, 1919, that prohibition enforcement became a problem in Finland. The problem of excessive use of alcoholic stimulants had long troubled the Finns, as it had the people of many other countries. The peoples of all ages and areas have taken some narcotic, either to lift their spirits or to dull the edge of the drab realities of life. In this respect the hardy Finns were not different from other peoples. But unlike many other peoples, they produced neither betel nut nor tobacco, coffee nor tea, grapes for wine nor sufficient grains for malt. They bridged this gap by distilling alcohol from wood and corn—a he-man drink.

Excessive drinking did not become publicly disturbing in Finland until the industrial revolution arrived at the turn of the century. In Finland, as elsewhere, it tended to increase tensions and lull restraints. The figures for 1906–10 reveal, for example, that Finland's per capita consumption of alcohol was *one sixth* that of Great Britain's, held to be Europe's most sober nation.

World War I years, with their concomitant breakdown of moral restraints and temperate customs, tended to increase the drinking habits of Finns as they did those of many other peoples.

The Prohibition movement in Finland, as in most other countries, was one phase of the religious revival that had gripped the country around the 1850's. It was led by the pastors. In time, as the Finns became more adept in governing themselves, they grew to believe in the magic of legislation as the cure for all social and economic ills. Mistakenly they believed, as have so many other peoples, that vice and injustice could be abolished by law. The more experienced, self-governing people of the United States also held this naïve belief. But human nature changes at a snail's pace and in a most laborious manner. Finland finally learned this lesson and repealed her Prohibition Law in 1932. But in Finland as in the United States an economic crisis helped to make repeal possible.

However, the land problem, which is as old as civilization, was the major internal one that the new nation faced. It first became a problem when man changed from a hunter to a grower, built his home on some land and produced his food from the soil. The yearning to own land and to put human roots down deep in it is an essential part of the human heritage. Self-respect and human dignity, security and independence, best grow and flourish there. Land hunger thus is as old as human aspirations and development upwards.

In Finland, where even today three out of every five people still live in the country, the struggle between those who own land and those who do not became acute when Finland declared her independence.

It early became evident that the new Republic's secure future would rest upon the courage, resourcefulness and energy with which its leaders undertook to satisfy the insistent land hunger of the people. The problem was twofold: first, that of enabling farmers and cottagers to secure full ownership of their holdings, and, secondly, how to provide new land for the landless.

In 1910, only 24 per cent of Finland's land-living families owned their farms; 33 per cent of the remainder were tenant farmers and the remaining 43 per cent were farm workers. Of the tenant farmer group, 66,500 families out of 160,000 held leases that the owners could revoke at will and only 84,000 of the 207,000 farm workers had cottages with vegetable plots.

The government took its first step to remedy this bad situation in October, 1918, when it provided state loans to enable tenant farmers to buy land at prices based on 1914 values, but it did not come to grips until 1922 with the problem of how to provide more land for would-be home owners. The greatest difficulty was that the land owners of Finland were Finns, not antinational aliens; therefore, their land could not be expropriated. The problem was so intricate that the government was unable to work out an acceptable compromise until October, 1927, when the *Lex Kallio* bill became law.

This measure provided for state aid to purchasers of two types of holdings of hitherto uncultivated land: small farms consisting of a maximum of 40 hectares (about 100 acres) of farm and woodland, and two-hectare plots for the purchaser of home and vegetable plot. The government agreed to pay the landlords for the holdings from which the new homes were taken in 7 per cent bonds per annum, 4 per cent of which was interest and 3 per cent for amortization, of the purchase price. The purchasers paid the government 9 per cent of the cost price of their properties.

Because expropriation became legal only as a last resort under *Lex Kallio*, the right-wing opposition to it softened. The Communists, who took their cue from the Third International and Soviet Russia, vociferously opposed it.

Despite strong opposition, the new agrarian reform worked smoothly and effectively. Within ten years 120,355 farm renters owned their own farms and 120,355 families had become owners of home and garden plots. The total area of land covered by the reform was about 3,500,000 acres. In less than a decade *Lex Kallio* brought over 2,000,000 acres of land under cultivation, increased the productivity of land per acre and enormously increased Finland's agricultural output. The country in 1914, for example, produced only 41 per cent of its consumed cereal foods, but in 1934 it produced 82 per cent. Finland increased her milk yield between 1920 and 1934 by more than 30 per cent.

Had Finland fumbled or evaded agrarian reforms, it is more than likely that she would today be a member of the family of so-called Soviet Republics, because the most stabilizing social or political influence is land and home ownership. It adds to human dignity and self-respect—which is God's most precious gift to man. In addition, it gives man courage to fight for his rights against odds and, because it makes him a paying partner in society and government, it prompts him to maintain law and order.

Finland's successful solution of these two major external and three internal problems within eight years of the adoption of her constitution augured well for the future of the country.

Chapter six

Growing Pains—1920–1939

Despite external difficulties, world economic collapse, internal dissension, including the rise of fascism, strained credit, inadequate industrial equipment and minor problems, the people of Finland maintained a stable government for the nineteen-year period (1920–1939), except for one period in the 1930's when they stood on the precipice of fascism.

The stability of Finland's government is revealed in part by the fact that four men served as president between 1919 and 1940. It is supported by the further evidence that her government was in danger only at one time during this trying period when deep moving forces were playing havoc with governments and peoples throughout the world.

During the same period, Hitler's Nazis transformed Germany from a republic to a barbarous dictatorship. Mussolini strutted through Italy and North Africa. The governments of Great Britain and the United States were rocked to their foundations and both underwent violent administrative and legislative changes. The government of France zig-zagged back and forth between communism and dictatorship. Japan's war party in the Far East started action which eventually changed ancient China more completely in a decade than had all other forces in twenty-five centuries.

Finland's government, however, remained stable and it made no important policy changes in those two momentous decades during which civilization underwent most profound changes.

The rise of one phase of fascism in Finland, which was her most disturbing problem in these two decades, had its roots in the causes which had brought it into being in some form in so many other countries. These causes included war's waste which had swept away or destroyed his spiritual inheritance, vitiated his moral standards and weakened his religious beliefs.

In addition to war destruction, life had been growing more complex. The individual was unable to fathom it, could not stand on his own feet and rely upon his own efforts as had his forefathers. He had lost his way both economically and spiritually. In error, he believed that his old gods had failed him. When he reached this belief he accepted the new god of strong central government under a despot, beneficent or otherwise, a mechanistic society which promised him food, clothing and shelter with the unfortunate result that he lost his soul for the time being.

This was not entirely true of the Finns. They had worked while many other Europeans whined. The majority of Finns kept to the hard way while the people of many nations sought the easy way. Hard circumstances had taught them to rely on themselves, made them responsive to Biblical truths, one of which is that a man earns his bread "by the sweat of his brow."

Their naïve belief indicates not so much that they are more gullible than other peoples, but that in some important ways they are like the experienced big bass which does not strike at every lure. As individualists, they went to work and as a determined people, they kept at it. As believers in law and orderly processes, they clung to both. As lovers of liberty, they shunned dictatorship. But in spite of all of these qualities, a form of the fascist movement did give Finland some anxious moments.

Finland's fascist movement was formed to check the spread of an ideological movement that was inimical to her free institutions, rather than to advance an ideology of its own. A large group in Finland, including members from all classes of society, decided that if their government would not or could not curb improper communist conduct and propaganda, they themselves would do so.

When the Finnish fascist movement got under way in 1930, it was heralded to the world in newspaper headlines—FASCISM IN FINLAND. The beginning of the trouble, like the source of great rivers, was a tiny affair. It was in the form of an announcement by the League of Communist Youth that it would hold a meeting at the end of November, 1929, in the village of Lapua. Their first mistake was in the selection of the place for holding the meeting. Lapua is in a conservative yeoman-farmer area, hard by the site of victories over the Russians in the old days. It also was the rallying place of the White Guard forces in the Civil War, and finally, its people were Pietists to whom Communist antireligious propaganda was most obnoxious.

The inevitable result was that when the partly armed contingent of 400 Communist Youths arrived at Lapua by train they were attacked by farmers who seized their arms and then put most of them back on the departing train. The farmers also gave the Communist Youth speakers an old-fashioned, vigorous whipping.

The incident might have ended there but it did not. Professor Lauri Ingam,[1] later successively prime minister and archbishop of Finland, has written that "a spark had fallen into the tinder at Lapua. And the tinder was everywhere in the country. The arrogant behavior of the Communists had raised feeling to such a pitch in all circles where religion and morals handed down by previous generations, love of country, and the independence and liberty of the Republic were still held in respect, that in a few days a mighty wave of anti-Communist feeling had spread like a conflagration throughout the country."

Anti-Communist leaders arose and called upon the people to help the authorities "smother the propaganda meetings and dis-

[1] L. Ingman, *The Lapua Anti-Communist Movement* (Helsinki, 1930).

graceful imitations of Bolshevik customs at birth . . . the will of the people must crush this illegal revolutionary party in all its phases."

Deputations from different towns called on the President and Prime Minister in Helsinki with a demand that the government act to suppress Communist propaganda activities. The law, as it stood, had slight power to do this. That was the case, because by changing its name, as it had in 1923, the Communist party had evaded the legal restrictions of the law. When the officials made this clear, the delegations then asked the Diet to adopt legislation which would suppress certain Communist societies. The Diet did so but refused to pass legislation which the deputations demanded for muzzling Communist propaganda, on the grounds that it would curtail the freedom of the press.

The direct-action farmer groups in March, 1930, after the manner of vigilante groups in our old West, took the law in their own hands. They formed an organization to challenge and stamp out Communist propaganda: in other words, they were going to fight the devil with fire. They called the new organization *Suomen Lukko* (Finland's Lock). Its first move was made on the night of March 27th, when its members destroyed, beyond repair, the printing press at Vaasa, which printed *Labor's Voice*. Reports soon began to reach Helsinki from all sections of Communist abductions, beatings, jailings or of Communists being escorted to the boundary and thrown over the wires into Russia.

Finland's central and local government-enforcement officers seemed either unable or unwilling to check the activities of the *Suomen Lukko* members. Its lawless activities created a storm of public opinion that blew the Prime Minister out of office, following which the President formed a coalition cabinet.

In response to the Lapua movement's demands the new Prime Minister, Svinhufvud, on July 9th, ordered the arrest of the twenty-three Communist members of the Diet. He secured approval of his action from the Diet and thereupon requested it to pass three emergency bills. The first to "forbid the entrance into Parliament of members of a party working for the overthrow of the State"; the second, to "restrict the possibilities of a misuse of the freedom of the press for subversive propaganda"; and the third, to give the government powers to deal with emergencies of this nature by ordinance.

Since the enactment of this legislation depended upon its being adopted as an amendment to the constitution, Svinhufvud dissolved the Diet on July 15th and called for an election in October.

Finland's political pot now began to boil over as one abduction of Socialists and Communists rapidly followed another. Civil war seemed imminent. Respect for law disappeared; belief in individual liberties was shaken; pastors preached intolerance as a Christian duty; disenfranchisement of a large part of the population was seriously urged; free speech and public meetings were threatened. A pall of madness hung over Finland and swept away the national characteristic of calm action in crises.

The factors which had combined to unbalance the Finns were largely alien and economic. Intolerance, hatreds, prejudices and a surging, rampant national selfishness fed the fires. These fires in turn were consuming trust, good will and the long view on which the foundations of social progress and commerce are built.

The impact of world economic chaos was felt in Finland in the late 1920's. The country's small landowners raised a poor crop in 1928. A severe drop in export trade struck industrial workers two years later. The conditions these circumstances created were so disturbing that they shattered the calm of the people. Also, more than any other country, Finland felt the potential menace of Communist Russia, because at that time Russia was dumping large quantities of lumber products on world markets at far below production costs. The Finns were seriously hurt, even angered, by this action because their country's existence depends largely on forest products. Added to these factors was the important position held by many Lutheran pastors in Finland who led the movement which sought to throttle Communist propaganda. The pastors' participation gave it a religious implication.

The October, 1930, elections returned a sufficient number of Diet members to insure passage of the bills outlawing Communists on November 11th, by 134 to 66 votes.

The Lapua movement should have ended with the passage of this legislation but it did not because terrorism, like the tail of a killed snake, does not stop suddenly. Kidnapings of Socialists and other so-called liberal supporters continued. Some capitalist interest, high army officers and private banks, which had been supporting the Lapua movement, seemed unwilling for Finland to return to Parliamentary democracy. In the presidential election in 1931, Svinhufvud was chosen by the narrowest of margins, 151 to 149. Public opinion was so favorable to the Lapua movement purposes that later in July, 1931, General Wallenius was acquitted of complicity in the early kidnaping of former President Ståhlberg. The Finnish Court acquitted him in the face of the General's full confession of his guilt when the charges were first preferred against him.

Finland's bad situation worsened on September 21, 1931, when Great Britain, Finland's best export customer, went off the gold standard and was followed a week later by the Scandinavian countries. These currency changes meant a loss of Finnish export trade and shortage of foreign currency, thereby making it impossible for Finland to pay for imports.

Finland went off the gold standard on October 19th, and thus saved her trade with Great Britain and Scandinavia, but this action put Finland at a disadvantage with those countries that had retained it. Chaotic international financial conditions hampered Finland's foreign trade activities while at the same time her producers of goods for the home market were placed at a disadvantage by her depreciated currency. Unemployment continued to increase and helped to make the bad situation worse.

To relieve the unemployment and financial situation, the government initiated a program of public works; ended the twelve-year-old prohibition experiment and gained new, badly needed revenue by making the liquor trade a State monopoly; adopted the principle that communes were responsible for relief but offered to pay half of the costs and up to half of the expenses of training courses for the under-twenty-year-old workers. These and other government measures furnished work or income for nearly 60,000 workers in the winter 1931–32.

The government also took steps to check the fall of agricultural prices by establishing higher tariffs on foreign cereals, pork, eggs, etc.

These palliative measures did not effect a cure but they did serve to ease the pressure in some areas. The feeling grew that nothing except improved world economic conditions could save Finland from insurrection. The situation became so bad that Lapua forces planned a *coup d'état,* but it fizzled out when President Svinhufvud, himself a member of the 1918 White Guard, appealed to the members in a radio broadcast to remember their oath to the constitution and told them that they were being hoodwinked by extremists who sought to overthrow the government.

If man had ten senses instead of five, he might be able to understand many deep truths of life that now are unfathomable to him. An additional sense, for example, might enable him to discern and understand which factors in crises determine the future course of human affairs. Lincoln's Gettysburg speech and Churchill's "blood, sweat and tears" exhortation reached human hearts, stirred human emotions and exerted a powerful influence on the people. Illustrations of this kind which filled a void in human hearts and thereby turned the course of events could be vastly multiplied. So it was with Svinhufvud's appeal. The rebel camps broke up, their members returned home, six thousand surrendered their arms and others dispersed quietly. Not a shot was fired on either side. The force of the tide of revolution had spent itself and was turned back to become a part of the deep ocean of trouble.

Another tide, gentle at first, soon left its bench-marks on Finnish soil. It was the tide of economic world recovery. Finnish exports and imports began to rise slowly in late 1932. The government passed a compulsory bill for lowering of interest rates. It placed farmer and other propertied interests in such a favorable position that it served to cancel their support of the Lapua movement. This, combined with loss of favorable public opinion, soon caused the movement to wither and then die. Its adherents lost 12 seats in the Diet in the 1932 elections. Finland's free government had weathered its worst political storm.

Finland's economic storm was still raging but now there was hope, since everyone was free to concentrate on solving other problems. Government and industrial leaders began to seek ways by which exports might be increased, restore balance of trade, arrange for the purchase of needed foreign goods and create full employment. Conditions improved everywhere except in Germany, where Hitler had imposed a variety of financial and fiscal restrictions on trade with Finland. This was the day of *Aski* marks. The result of Hitler's action was that Finland's trade with Germany, both export and import, dropped appreciably and also there was a lessening of cultural relations between the two countries.

Finland's expanding economy and stabilized government prompted her to seek new alliances. In 1931, she joined the "Oslo Group," which consisted of Belgium, Holland, Luxembourg, Denmark, Norway and Sweden. These nations sought to apply to the economic field "those principles which underlie the League of Nations."

Slowly, step by step, internal and external forces both political and economic brought Finland into a closer working relationship with democratic states. This new relationship had grown stronger by 1937, when Finland initiated steps which it hoped would lead to the formation of a group of small nations consisting of herself, Sweden, Norway, Denmark, Estonia, Latvia and Lithuania. These nations planned to bind themselves together by the infinitely stronger and more lasting ties of common interest, common ideals, common understanding and common purpose than by formal economic or political treaty.

Finland's orientation with the political, social and cultural ideals and customs and economic relationships of the west helped to stabilize her now eased political situation. It helped also to give the Finns a clearer conception of how best to find ways to express and perpetuate their social and cultural ideals and programs, and to harden the mold of their political methods and structures.

Finland's orientation with the west was not alone in helping her people to find their way out of the war's chaotic aftermath which hung like a pall over the world. The parallel development in another and important area, the economic field, accompanied and strengthened it. World economic recovery was making slow progress now that more and more people had again gone to work to produce food and materials. The patient was recovering. He needed more that palliatives if he were to regain his health and vigor. Sugar-coated pills in the form of governmental aid or stimulating narcotics in the form of temporary governmental substitutes could not take the place of individual initiative and effort. Over-all governmental planning and controls had been necessary and useful in the emergency as they are to a limited extent at all times, but they could not serve as a substitute for the released energy and determined effort of a whole people.

This new release of individual energy and effort in Finland, which was made possible by the beginning of world economic recovery, when spelled out in results showed an expansion of export trade by one half in value and one sixth in volume between 1932 and 1938. By 1937, Finnish exports rose in value and volume above her peak prosperity year of 1928. All Finland was working and the effort paid off handsomely. The new high volume of exports gave Finland a "favorable" trade balance, so favorable that it enabled her to reduce her foreign indebtedness by more than one half. This was all-important to Finns, far more important than buying badly needed supplies, because Finns seem to fear only God and debt.

Although they denied themselves luxuries they, being hard-headedly realistic, did not deny themselves new industrial equipment. They used all available foreign exchange, after debt payments, to buy new machinery for plant improvement and expansion. Unlike the middle western German farmer who was reputed to have said, "I raise more corn to feed more hogs to buy more land," and then asked, "For what?" the Finns knew their answer to "For what?"

They wanted to improve the standard of housing in order that their people might have better homes; to increase their output of electric power which would replace human energy and take loads off men's backs; and to improve railroads and highways so that commerce could move more freely in increasing volume. During this period Finland imported far more industrial equipment and other forms of capital goods than she did of goods for consumption or convenience, such as food, clothing, automobiles and the like.

Best of all, nature was treating agricultural Finland more kindly during these years by giving the farmer a succession of good crops—which in turn improved the lot of farmers and provided the whole people with more and a greater variety of food.

Other manifestations of improved conditions revealed themselves in balanced budgets, even substantial government surpluses, in the years between 1933 and 1937. This was during the period when the great United States government was annually showing a deficit of billions of dollars. What caused the difference between the fiscal condition of the two governments was that Finland had gone to work like a man and had discarded belief in the magic of mirrors and economic sleight of hand and America had not.

Unemployment in Finland was nil, whereas it was still in the millions in the United States where high-placed officials advanced the belief that America would always have millions of unemployed.

It was also during this period that the Finns began to realize clearly that, like American meat packers, they should develop ways to make a profit even from the squeak of the butchered hogs.

Wood was Finland's hog. Wood and wood products then amounted to 83 per cent of her exports. Now, instead of exporting only round or sawn timber, Finland began to manufacture wood products in increasing quantities. These new products included pulp, cardboard, paper, sulphate and sulphide cellulose. The annual value of exports in pulp board and paper products jumped from about one fourth in 1928 to nearly one half of all exports in 1935.

Finland's change from that of a national producer of raw products to that of a manufacturing nation carried many benefits as well as some problems in its wake. The advantages included larger and steadier markets for Finnish products, better prices, more employment and a greater need for skilled labor, which commanded higher wages. Among the disadvantages were the unbalancing of the old relations between town and country, since growing industrialization increased the factory population. Inevitably, this accelerated the drift from the land to factories in towns and cities. The government, while aware of the dangers in this transition if carried too far, nevertheless aided and encouraged it. At the same time, however, it made renewed efforts to help Finnish agriculture develop step by step with Finnish manufacturing. It did this by providing agricultural tariffs and subsidies and its efforts were effective in that the record shows an increase in agricultural products. In the 1924–28 period, Finnish farms produced only 60 per cent of the food stuffs needed for home consumption, whereas in the 1935–36 period, they produced 81 per cent.

One other disadvantage which came out of Finland's transformation from that of a producer of raw materials to that of a finisher of manufactured products was that the benefits from debt reduction and capital improvements favored the rich rather than the poor. The wealth of the industrialists and capitalists grew by leaps and bounds whereas the income of the workers increased only slightly. Wages in general, which hit a low in the 1930–32 period, had been increased very little by 1937, while those of farmers and timber workers in 1935 were below the 1928 level. Taking 1928 as the 100 base, Finland's real wages stood at 110 in 1930; 102 in 1932 and 109 in 1935.

What had happened was that debt repayment and capital improvement had tended to freeze the standard of living at a lower level than could be justified. Because the Finns believed so implicitly in the old adage that "you can't have your cake and eat it too," they overdelayed their time schedule for raising wages. Even today, Finland is still behind in their wage-raising schedule.

Good fortune, however, has favored the Finnish working classes in some other respects. Finland has no counterpart of America's big city slums, nor anything closely resembling them. Living costs in Finland were lower than in the United States in most particulars. Never having enjoyed luxury and a variety of foods, the Finns live frugally on simple healthy fare and thrive on it. The vast majority of the families cultivate a garden plot and many of them have either cows for milk or pigs for meat, or both. Fuel costs are comparatively low. All of outdoors with vast woods and large water areas provides places for wholesome and inexpensive recreation. The State maintains an excellent and inexpensive educational system for all children.

By 1938, Finland had achieved comparative prosperity, fascism was a dead issue, the government was supreme and *Lex Kallio* had almost satisfied the Finns' land hunger. The repeal of prohibition had served to bring about a decrease in alcoholic consumption and drunkenness. Foreign policy was hardening in the new mold to the extent that relations with the Soviet Union were satisfactory, even almost cordial.

The ancient power of the Swede-Finns was declining so rapidly that fewer of them held high places in government and Finland's policy of treating a minority with justice and generosity was serving to diminish the animosities of the Swede-Finn—Finn-Finn quarrel.

The Communists appeared to have accepted political extinction and the more moderate of them joined the Social Democratic Party, which then was and still is one of the dominant political parties of Finland.

Hard work, poise, realizable ideals, justice and honesty were now showing evidence of their irresistible power, a power that nothing short of an implacable force from the outside could halt and then only momentarily. Even generations or centuries are too short for such calculation purposes, since the qualities the Finns had harnessed and were using are timeless.

The significance of Finland's achievements is that human progress is attuned to the moral law. Social and political justice confirm the equality of men and guarantee their liberties. By adhering to these principles, Finland had succeeded between 1920 and 1939 in appreciably easing her growing pains.

Chapter seven

Finland's Exhaustless Green Gold Mine

Finland's forests are her inexhaustible green gold mine.

Unlike the mines that produce gold ore and are abandoned when all of the metal is mined, Finland's gold mines produce fresh supplies each year. Two hundred thousand lumberjacks during the fall, winter and spring seasons cut and handle one hundred million logs annually for Finland's timber products industries.

At the present time 85 per cent of her exports consist of lumber and other wood products. Twenty-five per cent of Finnish workers are engaged in forestry and forestry products.

It is natural, therefore, that the Finns and forests are soul mates to be separated only by death, an attachment that has been growing for twenty centuries. Finns and trees understand each other and seem almost able to converse together without using the device of man-made words. They feel as much at home in the woods as does a Texan in a ten-gallon hat and high-heeled boots, because they are either in or near woods but never out of sight of them.

Trees sprout, grow and die so that Finland may live. An observer quickly discerns that Finns and trees were made for each other if he is fortunate enough to see Finns felling trees in forests, guiding logs as they float downstream, operating sawmills, making a boat, building a house, or working in wood industries. In all of these activities the Finn is in his natural element.

Almost any Finn can, with a few tools, quickly build a good house without fuss or feathers. The only tools he finds indispensable for such a purpose are saw, hammer, small axe, square, plane and his *puukko*. The latter he must have. It is a sharp-bladed sheath knife that every male carries fastened to his belt. There is a rumor to the effect that he sleeps with it. He uses it for everything from fitting boards in a house, building boats, cutting bread, to carving a fellow Finn. Once, in answer to the question, "Which does a Finn consider more valuable, his wife or his knife?" Stade studied for a half a minute, then replied in all seriousness: "I don't know. They are both valuable."

The Finn possesses little of Kipling's Elephant Child's "insatiable curiosity" in most areas of human activity except with trees and their products. In these fields he is consumed with a curiosity which fires his imagination to such an extent that no one surpasses him in them.

One of Finland's major problems is that of adjusting the ever-present conflict between food and forests. She has only so much land, therefore if more is used for the food and livestock production that sustain the lives of her people, there perforce is less forest area.

In their effort to avoid robbing Peter to pay Paul, the Finns have initiated soil improvement and silviculture programs, and have developed and are using a vast body of available information on the chemistry of soil, fertilization, drainage and allied subjects.

Finland has about 54 million acres of forests. The species she largely uses for her wood products are pine, spruce and birch which, due to barren soil and a relatively cold climate, grow straight and have few branches. The quality of Finnish forest stock is believed to be further improved by the long hours of summer sunlight, since they grow only at that time of the year and that is when the pellucid light of "white nights" is almost as bright as daylight.

Another forest factor which serves Finland well economically is that of her large number of watercourses which the Finns use to float 70 per cent of their raw-material wood to the mills.

Finland gave little heed to silviculture, the art of caring for and producing forests, until recent years. Even today silviculture seemingly is an unfavored child in that, according to a recent National Forest Survey, only 14 per cent of her present forests are being managed on fully correct silvicultural lines. This does not imply that Finland's other 86 per cent of her forests are mismanaged but instead that their foresters still tend to follow the methods of primitive farmers who planted potatoes in the dark of the moon so that they would go to root instead of tops. Even so, primitive farmers whose knowledge has come down to them from father to son for generations know enough about soil care, seed selection, time of planting and cultivation methods to enable them to raise big crops. This has been the case with Finland's foresters in the past but today Finns are using both scientific and practical knowledge in the care of their forests.

In 1921–24, Finland became the first country in the world to conduct a uniform and simultaneous survey of its forest resources, and in 1936–38 she conducted a second one. The Finns gained from these two surveys a reliable picture of both timber reserves and condition of forests.

Taken as a whole, Finland's forests are middle-aged except in the north, where old forests are more abundant. The total annual growth of her forests is estimated at approximately 1,190 million cubic feet. Of this amount, at the present time 430 million cubic feet annually can be used as raw material for industry. The rest is exported unfinished or else is used as fuel on farms, in towns and cities and even in railway locomotives. The Finns estimate that in recent years they have cut nearly one fourth more than the over-all growth their timber would allow them to take out. They have learned, however, that by draining, selective seeding and other new methods they can double the present growth of their forests. All they need for that is work, hard but healthy work, in their green forests.

Finland's economy largely rests on forests. They are the fat on which she lives during these lean years of reparations, debt payments and huge capital investments in industrial equipment and human betterment.

A comparison of Finland's total forest area with that of Europe's shows that Finland's total area amounts to only 3 per cent of that of Europe, whereas her forest area equals 7 per cent of all of Europe's forest area.

Finnish farmers own more than half of their country's forests. The country's Forestry Act and Conservation Laws enable the Central Forestry Association through Local Forestry Boards (Finns like Americans are prone to organize and organize) to supervise forest exploitation and enforce the law, and through other organizations to place all private forests under expert supervision. This has been found necessary, since Finland's forests suffer heavy losses through fires and storms. Fire losses are minimized by observation stations and the Fire Law, which compels every citizen to help fight fires. Storm damage has been lessened by proper forest care. The trees of Finland do not grow to the great size that they do in many sections of America nor does Finland have a great variety of species as does the United States. The forest area in Finland in which pine predominates totals 53 per cent; spruce-dominating forests total 28 per cent; birch, 19 per cent and aspen about 2 per cent.

The state owns slightly more than one third of Finland's forests, the greater part of which are in the far north where climatic conditions retard growth and transportation problems are great. The communes, hundreds of thousands of farmers and individual land owners, hold title to approximately 58 per cent, the church about ⅕ of 1 per cent and woodworking enterprises own the balance. In most parts of Finland every farmer is a forester and his wood lots produce a sure cash crop.

The Finns hope to bring growth and cut more nearly into balance and thereby help reduce self-thinning losses by reducing logging waste, collecting small wood more effectively and encouraging more efficient home consumption use.

A majority of Finns are employed in one phase or another of forestry and woodworking activities. Because of its age and size, the first of these is the sawmill industry which has been operating in Finland since the sixteenth century. Some of the sawmills are comparable in output capacity with the great sawmills of the States but many of them are operated by crews of eight or less men and women. These mills hum throughout the long summer days: an observer saw one of them operating in the north country at midnight, without artificial light.

About the middle of the nineteenth century, before the Finns had acquired much scientific information about the growth and care of forests, the state, fearing the too-rapid exhaustion of standing timber, did everything it could to slow down the operation and expansion of the sawmill industry.

At that time, the iron industry in Finland seemed most promising and public policy favored hoarding the forests for the iron industry's use. It is not strange that they did, since man has ever looked to distant places for treasure while ignoring the gold at his feet. Time and wisdom gained from accumulated information have joined with circumstance and demands to clarify the Finns' forestry and to improve their judgment.

As the science of silviculture advanced, the Finns, while still believing that "only God can make a tree," began to see that man could help God by doing many things that would aid the safety and growth of the trees. With the dawning of the realization of this truth, they began to seek ways that would automatically guarantee the preservation and maintenance of forests. This new conception served to influence the state to modify its previous position, but in true Finnish fashion, it made the change so gradually that it did not free the sawmill industry of restrictions until 1861.

Thus it was that, as the pieces of the master jigsaw puzzle of life, about which man knows so little, slowly fitted into their places, the Finns readied themselves so that they might share in the swift growth of world markets for lumber.

Other factors also were working in the Finns' favor. One of them was the perfection and availability of the steam engine for power purposes. Heretofore, they had been forced to place their sawmills where water-power sources were available. This need had required them to bring the mountain of forests to the Mahomet of water power. The steam engine enabled them to take the Mahomet of the steam-powered sawmill to the mountain of forest. This new flexibility of operation carried with it a vast and rapid expansion of the sawmilling industry, because it lessened the problem of transporting raw materials by substituting manufactured goods and also could produce the kind of goods that export markets wanted near shipping facilities.

The final favorable factor in Finland's sawmill industry expansion was that Great Britain, which long had been one of Finland's best customers for forest products, substantially reduced customs duties on wood products.

Statistics clearly show the story of expansion in the first fifty-year period in the status of the change that had taken place in Finland's sawmill industry: in the decade ending 1869, Finland exported an annual average of 85,000 standards;[1] in 1879, 166,-000; in 1889, 247,000; in 1899, 357,000; and in 1909, 515,000. The year before World War I began in 1913, Finland's 600 operating sawmills produced 770,000 standards for export. The war abruptly ended its expansion period, but export was resumed in 1919 and in 1922 it had achieved the prewar figure. In 1947, Finland's volume of sawn wood free exports (this does not include reparations payments to Soviet Russia) amounted to 78 per cent of her total forest products exports.

The sawmill industry, which drove full speed ahead during the twenties, suffered a slowing down in the early thirties but speeded up until in the late thirties Finland led the world in the

[1] One standard equals 1980 board feet.

amount of exported sawn timber, with Canada, the Soviet Union, Sweden and the United States following in that order. Great Britain continued to be Finland's largest buyer, followed by Germany, Holland, Denmark, Belgium and South Africa. During this period, Finnish exports of unprocessed timber represented 17 per cent of this product's world trade with Finland supplying one fifth of the world's coniferous lumber, slightly more than one fifth of its plywood, four fifths of its bobbins and a large portion of its pit props.

One of Finland's largest new industries, that of manufacturing prefabricated dwelling houses, schools, stores, warehouses, transportable military barracks, etc., was born in 1939. It now has become a mass industry in Finland and over forty plants now use 10 per cent of Finland's sawmill output for this purpose. Their manufactured product can be divided into three main groups, precut houses, panel houses and cell houses. These manufacturers co-operate in their sales program. Their effective sales method plus the great need in war-devastated areas for comparatively inexpensive houses that can be quickly and easily built enable Finns to sell them like proverbial hot cakes. In 1945, they delivered 35,000 prefabricated houses to Soviet Russia—12,000 of them as war reparations—and sold Russia the remaining 23,000. Poland, Denmark, France, England, Holland and Belgium were among the countries which bought large numbers of these houses and thirty other countries bought smaller numbers of them. The United States has some of them and is still purchasing others.

Another reason for the rapid growth of Finland's prefabricated housing industry is that her manufacturers have given special attention to constructual improvements such as heat economy, which they obtain by extensive use of insulation. They usually include in the construction all necessary timber above foundation level, which includes walls, partition walls, insulating materials, windows, doors and necessary fittings. They do not, however, include inside fittings, sanitary arrangements, water piping and electrical equipment. One of the export advantages of the prefabricated houses is that they can easily be adapted to meet local requirements such as elimination of insulation for warmer countries and room arrangements to meet a country's customs.

Finland made the greatest advance in the value of her forest products when, at the turn of the century, she began to establish a large variety of woodworking industries. These included mechanical pulp mills, cardboard and building board factories, sulphite and sulphate cellulose mills, paper mills for paper and converted paper products. In 1938, Finland's mechanical pulp production totaled 750,000 tons, cellulose 1.5 million tons and paper 550,000 tons. In 1952, the Finns had nearly achieved prewar levels in the production and sale of these products.

Finland built her first plywood factory in 1912, but the growth of the industry was slow until recent years. Today, eighteen mills annually manufacture and export more than 200,000 cubic meters of plywood.

Birch logs, of which Finland has an ample supply, make excellent raw material for the manufacture of plywood. The industry had to overcome many obstacles but did so with the aid of new semi-automatic machines which make perfectly glued plywood. The glueing department, which is properly termed the heart of a plywood mill, uses a mixture of solution of albumin and caseine in water and lime and thereby creates a suitably resistant product for cold or temperate climates. Due largely to the superior qualities of birch as a raw material, because of its evenness and strength, Finland has developed with the help of scientific and technical research a plywood industry that ranks ahead of that of any other country in both quality and quantity.

Finland's spool and drum industries were the first to make industrial use of birch and thereby gained a unique place for itself in the international market, in that previous to 1939 it produced 85 per cent of the world's exports in these articles.

It was not until 1930 that Finland began the manufacture of

wood-fiber panels. A growing world demand for this product has led to the establishment of eight factories for its production.

Finland's woodworking industries furnish employment for an ever-increasing number of workers and bring her larger profits for a smaller amount of cut timber, including pulp and paper mentioned above, plywood matches, excelsior, bobbins or spools, pit props for coal mines, furniture and prefabricated houses.

The Finns' frugality prompted them to start the sulphate pulp wood industry. Since they hate waste, sawmill waste, which consists of slabs, odd lengths, uneven pieces of lumber, bark and sawdust, troubled them. There were quantities of this waste in every operating sawmill and it had little value other than as fuel or for purposes using only a small part of it. Their pulp-wood industry now uses all sawmill waste.

The Finns began to make paper in a small way out of rags as early as 1670. The method of paper manufacture from wood fiber was known in Finland in the early 1860's, at which time the Finns began to build pulp mills. The marked development of this industry, however, did not begin until about twenty years later, when the chemical or cellulose process was invented and perfected. Russia was then her principal market for these products and continued to be until the 1917 revolution. When the Russian market collapsed the Finns were forced to find new markets, but could not create these without the help of up-to-date equipment and new sales methods.

The chemical pulp industry, however, furnishes the most striking example of industrial progress that Finland has made. Today it has become what would be an enormous business even in a great nation. For little Finland, *enormous* is too frail and insignificant an adjective to describe it. It grew tenfold in twenty years. Between 1940 and 1946, it jumped from 253,078 tons of sulphite and sulphate pulp to 383,513 tons for free export and 78,292 tons for Russian reparations.

The manufacture of newsprint and other paper is another Finnish specialty in which she stands second only to Canada.

Aside from newsprint, Finland manufactures kraft paper, paper for printing, writing, art, cigarettes, etc. Her total export of these products in 1940 was 95,979 tons and in 1946, 317,633 tons, with an additional 25,576 tons going to Russia on the war reparations account.

The paper and board converting industry was started in Finland in the 1930's. It is now producing multiwall paper sacks, grocery and other bags and containers, fiber board, gummed and impregnated papers, stationery of all kinds, creped kraft paper, products of crepe paper such as napkins, tablecloths, handkerchiefs and curtains, facial tissues, sanitary towels, fancy papers, shelf papers, doilies, embossed papers and boards, spools—in fact everything that can be made of paper. During the war years the Finns made clothing apparel from it and used cellulose for cattle fodder. These, however, were emergency uses that have not been continued.

The late J. A. Cope, a graduate of the Yale Forestry School and for many years head of the Department of Forestry at Cornell University, a recognized top authority in his field, spent several months in 1950 lecturing on forestry at the University of Helsinki and other Finnish audiences. He was sent by the American Friends Service Committee to lend whatever helping hand he could to the Finns in the conduct of their one vital and all-important industry. He wrote the author that his feeling was that of carrying coals to Newcastle. As a master in his field he quickly recognized that Finns were even greater masters in it.

From what they have done with forestry and forest products, and from what they are doing with both, the record carries highly credible evidence that they know the business from A to Z.

The Finn is truly Mr. Woodworker. The national of no other country is a runner-up for the world's title.

Chapter eight

Additional Finnish Industries

From the viewpoint of numbers employed and income produced, forestry and agriculture dominate Finland's economic and industrial life but they are not all-inclusive.

Finland established many smaller industries either before or after she became a grand duchy of Russia in 1809. She started some of them to supply her own needs. Later, about a century and a half ago, when she discovered hungry Russian markets for almost anything her people could make she branched out widely in the manufacturing field.

Since the Russian standard of taste was not high and the need for low-priced products was great, the Finns, without especially skilled workmen or modern manufacturing equipment, were able to establish and profitably operate a variety of plants in the metal, textile, leather and pottery industries. Russia later placed a tariff on Finnish-manufactured articles in an effort to equalize the work of the sober, hard-working Finns who produced more and better goods than did the hard-drinking, easy-going Russian workman. The manufacturers of these goods received a crushing blow when the Russian market completely disappeared following the revolution in 1917.

Finland's manufacturers in the minor industries who had inadequate and old equipment and few skilled workmen soon discovered that they were unable to compete successfully with their highly specialized foreign competitors whose plants were equipped with the most modern machinery.

Despite these handicaps, the people of Finland continued to make a small amount of many kinds of articles needed for domestic consumption, because they had a small group of skilled artisans such as glass, furniture, metal and other workers who needed employment. They also continued to operate such plants because life blooms eternal in the human breast—this fact sustained their hope that they might eventually develop their industries and thereby be able to produce goods which could successfully compete in foreign markets. One other reason for this continuance was that the Finns had great need for self-sufficiency following World War I when international politics and growing tensions created trade barriers in many countries. This situation encouraged them to advance their program of strengthening both their minor and major industries. Their program was made easier by available and adequate capital at low interest rates from foreign sources.

One of their first major moves was to build many new hydroelectric stations, a basic need for any program of industrial expansion, since Finland has no black coal beds. That being the case, they were forced to depend upon either white coal (electricity), or wood, which would be wasteful of their number one export material; or to import black coal, which would drain their supply of the foreign exchange so badly needed for the purchase of new machinery. Finland now has 700,000 H.P. harnessed for industrial uses and is constructing plants which will make another 300,000 H.P. available. Estimates indicate that Finland has about 2,000,000 H.P. of water that can be harnessed.

Additional capital and cheaper power, coupled with better designs, improved machinery and the introduction of modern manufacturing methods soon enabled Finland's small industries to increase production, improve the quality of old products, manufacture new ones and thereby compete successfully with foreign concerns both in their home market and abroad.

During the 1928–38 period, the value of Finland's non-wood-working industries' output increased 50 per cent. The Winter War with Russia, 1939–40, checked their growth except for that of the metal and engineering industries, which benefited from army orders. The small industries' total output was further lessened following the war's end by the loss of territory ceded to Russia which contained 432 factories employing more than 25,000 workers. The loss of these factories was particularly heavy in that it included Finland's only soapstone factory, her only factory for producing rayon, one of her two raw sugar-beet refineries, one of her four Martin steel works, one third of her flour mills, and more than one third of her potato-flour and starch mills, half of her bolt mills, half of her candle, chlorine and bone dust factories, 96 per cent of her water-glass plants and nearly half of her roofing and other felt plants. Finland's greatest single loss to Russia in the ceded territory, however, was in available water power, which amounted to 232,000 kilowatts.

The metal industry of Finland, as described by government publications, embraces all branches of metallurgy, engineering and manufacturing which operate with iron, steel and nonferrous metals as raw materials. More than one thousand small and large concerns are engaged in it and in 1948 they employed 83,000 workers.

Finland's metallurgical industry, to use the term in its broadest sense, includes blast furnaces which process the products of her copper, nickel, iron ore and other materials, foundries, rolling mills, mechanical engineering shops, naval dockyards, the electrical industry, radio factories, etc.

The Finnish copper mine, the Outokumpu, the richest one in Europe, supplies all of Finland's domestic needs for copper and copper alloys as well as considerable quantities for export. Its annual output is now nearly 20,000 tons. Finland is also able to supply her own cast iron needs but has to import about 60 per cent of her sheet metal.

Finland created her metal-working industry in the sixteenth

century but developed it so slowly that at the end of the first
world war only about one seventh of her industrial workers
were engaged in it. Its great growth and expansion coincided
with that of the woodworking industry and the mechanization
of agriculture between 1920 and 1939. The development in these
two fields rested on an adequate supply of machines and equipment. This demand forced such an expansion of mechanical
engineering workshops that by 1940 fully one fourth of Finland's industrial workers were employed by the metallurgical
industry. Their products at the present time consist largely of
machines and equipment for the woodworking industries, locomotives, ships, electrical machines and equipment, cables and
machine tools, fittings for water and steam pipings, separators,
sports equipment, automobile spare parts and fittings, transport
and weight-lifting apparatus, laboratory equipment and nails.
Finland also has an automobile industry which manufactures
coaches, trucks and many kinds of motors.

This enormous expansion does not all represent a normal
growth since much of it must be credited or debited as it may
be considered, to Soviet reparation requirements. The war reparations comprise woodworking industry machines and parts,
railway engines and parts, and freight and passenger cars, electric
motors, complete woodworking plants and ships.

The first porcelain factory in Finland, the Arabia, was started
in 1874, in Helsinki. It produces every type of porcelain and
earthenware articles, such as refractories, sanitary ware, technical porcelain, china and earthenware, ranging from simple
household utensils to the finest dinner sets, designed and deco-
rated by Finland's top artists.

Arabia is now daily producing about 80 tons of ceramic bodies
and 65 tons for refractories. The highest award, or *Grand Prix*,
was conferred on Arabia's products at the World's Exhibition in
Barcelona in 1929, Salonika in 1935, and Paris in 1937. Arabia's
products are sold in more than thirty countries.

Arabia is the largest porcelain and china factory in Scandinavia. It is equipped with modern machinery, including three tunnel ovens which enable its 3,000 employees to make it one of the world's leading enterprises in that field.

One of Finland's most important secondary industries is that of clothing and textiles. These industries are able to satisfy most of the domestic demand for the goods they manufacture. The bulk of their raw materials is imported, and in the case of cotton, all of it is. A Scotchman launched the textile industry in 1820 by building a factory at Tampere which, through growth and mergers, by 1934 had become the largest textile manufacturing plant in the northern countries. These mills employ about 10,000 people, nearly all women, and annually use over 13,000 tons of raw material. They supply about two thirds of Finland's yarn and fabric requirements.

The wool industry and manufacture of linen fabrics also have been operating in Finland for more than a century. They together employ about 8,000 workers. The Finns have also a small knitting-goods industry and small silk, ribbon, hat, carpet, belting and net industries.

The most distinctive quality products which the Finns make in small quantities are the hand-knitted sweaters, mittens, mufflers and similar articles which are made in the homes mainly for family and domestic market purposes. These articles have distinctive excellence of design and quality, and with slight changes in form undoubtedly could find a ready market in the States. The Finns, true to their one-step-at-a-time habit, however, hesitate about making changes necessary to meet American buyers' requirements. The author learned this some years ago when he gave some samples of Finnish hand-knitted work to buyers of one of America's largest department store chains. These buyers recommended certain minor changes which they believed would create a large demand in the American markets. These recommendations were sent to the Finnish housewives through the handicraft association. Their reply, Finn-like, in effect was, "We are not going to change from the way we always have made them. Our people like them this way and we prefer to make them this way." This attitude is not much different from that which British handicraft makers and manufacturers held and stubbornly adhered to in the face of seeing their goods displaced in foreign markets by German-made goods whose manufacturers had followed the policy of providing the world buying public with what it wanted, not what the manufacturers wanted to make or believed it should have.

Finland's foodstuffs and related industries include flour mills, more than two thirds of whose wheat for grinding is imported; sugar refineries which import 85 per cent of their raw product; hundreds of dairies which annually produce over 30,000 tons of butter and 10,000 tons of cheese, most of which is exported.

During the first six months of 1951 Finland produced nearly 8,000 tons of cheese and exported 5,086 tons. The Finnish cheese industry concentrates its production mainly on Emmenthal cheese but also manufactures appreciable quantities of Edam and Roquefort cheese as well as various process cheeses which it boxes for shipment to foreign markets, mainly in England, Belgium, the United States and Greece. They also have factories for canning food stuffs and making sausage, breweries (nearly one hundred of them) and the tobacco industry.

Due to their centuries-long experience, the Finns take to dressing furs and leather as naturally as they do to forest care and woodworking. Generations of peasants practiced fur and leather dressing with such inherited skill that the industry began to thrive when manufacturing plants superseded handmade articles in the latter half of the nineteenth century. For a period, Finland had the largest leather works in Europe and established a large export market. At one time the leather factories supplied the domestic market with its sole leather needs and gradually also that of uppers and fine leather.

Seventy-five per cent of the leather manufactured in Finland is used for making shoes, and the balance for all other leather products. Finland's ninety shoe industry plants' output in 1948 totaled 4.8 million pairs. Most of these plants are small enterprises, each of which employs a few dozen workmen, for a total of about 5,000 workers. Her rubber industry, confined mainly to one plant, produces footwear, tires, rubber flooring, waterproof coats, etc.

One of Finland's most distinguished and distinctive industries is that of making glass. Its beauty and excellence are established by the large number of *Grand Prix* it has received in international exhibitions. The war, by its interruption of the import of necessary raw materials and fuel, served sharply to decrease Finland's production and export of glass products.

Although timber continues to be the dominating building material in rural areas of Finland, her cities and larger towns have turned more and more to the use of fire-resistant materials. This shift in materials for town and city construction now annually produces nearly a half million tons of mortar, cement and lime for building and agricultural purposes. Numerous small brick kilns meet the country's demand for bricks and the stone industry supplies a certain quantity for domestic building purposes. The stone industry concentrates its efforts in producing tombstones and stone for monumental purposes since Finnish granite is in demand in the world market.

As would be natural in a nation whose economy rests upon forests and wood products, the Finns make a great variety of the best and most up-to-date woodworking machinery which includes sawmills, gang saws, edgers, cutters, conveyers, etc.

Finland's metal and engineering industry, however, really specializes in manufacturing every kind of modern machine needed by the paper industry from the raw material stage to the finished product. These include labor-saving devices for handling and transporting felled timber, knife and friction barkers, chippers to reduce pulpwood to chips, devices for preparing cellulose cooking acid, diffusers and suction filters for washing sulphate pulp, pulp grinders and efficient equipment for bleaching. These industries make every type and kind of tool and machine that the timber and woodworking industries use.

Finland's metal and engineering industries also manufacture earth-moving and road-making machines, excavators, etc. They also make steam and diesel locomotives, wheel sets for railways, high-speed and tool steel and various steel castings and farm machinery.

Finland's shipyards are now busily engaged completing the last of 90 Russian reparation ocean-going wooden schooners of 300 tons dead weight. Her shipbuilding concerns also make ice breakers up to 10,000 H.P. as well as other types of ships.

Finnish mercantile marine companies operate ocean-going ships that run on regular and frequent schedules to important South American, North American and Levant ports. Many other Finnish freighters make frequent sailings to Scandinavian, European mainland and British ports.

Besides a vigorous and growing graphic arts industry, which employs about 10,000 workers, Finland has made a most distinctive contribution through its industrial arts and crafts productions. The movement gained its initial impulse following the founding in 1871 of the Central School of Industrial Art. Among other accomplishments this institution trained, inspired or sponsored the new school of Finnish architects and architecture which has gained imitation and respect throughout the world. It also led to the creation of the "Friends of Finnish Handicraft," an organization which, through its staff of artists and annual competition for design, among other activities, has helped to make Finnish furniture, ceramics and interior decoration products known and desired far beyond Finland's borders. This is especially true of Finnish glass for decorative and table use which, along with that of Sweden, is the equal if not the superior of any that is produced elsewhere in the world.

This brief and somewhat statistical recital of the efforts of 4,000,000 Finns to find ways to provide superior products for their own needs as well as for sale abroad helps to illustrate the wide range and variety of skills the Finns possess; emphasizes their qualities of vigor, initiative and resourcefulness, gives a glimpse of their well-rounded understanding, and at the same time reveals their inherent artistic ability which from time to time finds supreme expression through a Sibelius, a Saarinen or an Aalto.

Dry reading though such an account may be, its information shows the many-sidedness of the Finns, of interest to anyone who wishes to know them better. This is true because the best and most accurate index to what a people is like and the surest way to understand them is to learn how they live and work, what they produce and the quality of their products. A people with a limited amount of vigor and with an indifferent attitude about how much or what kind or quality of goods it produces is headed for the ridge of the horizon over which it will disappear. Individuals, as well as the peoples of a nation, can never lower their standards or restrict their efforts if their purpose is to "realize their glory and fulfill their promise."

Unlike the peoples of many European nations, who also are beset with difficulties that are seemingly too great to overcome, the Finns do the day's work and at night plan even more work for tomorrow. By so doing they are able to face life realistically and honestly, and as a by-product they have earned for their country the enviable recognition by all men everywhere as *Honest Finland.*

Every man who is proud of his national heritage tends to compare other peoples with his own people when they were at their supreme best. Many Americans believe that those qualities which have best served to make America great found their finest expression in the lives, work, actions and principles of our pioneers. They were a hardy, sturdy race, with all-around abilities, who believed in themselves and in their country.

The people of Finland today are much more like our American pioneers than any other people in the world, a people who believe in themselves and in their country. It is this unshakable faith that sets Finland and her people apart. Some people may not like the Finns, but nearly everyone respects and admires them.

Chapter nine

Finland's Food Sources

During recent years Finland has brought her food production and consumption more nearly into balance but is still in the red ink as a self-feeding nation.

The three factors which have most largely contributed to this favorable change are (a) diversified farming, (b) introduction of scientific agricultural and animal husbandry methods, (c) increase of the amount of tillable soil by draining marsh and clearing submarginal and forest areas, (d) the *Lex Kallio* land settlement law, mentioned in an earlier chapter, which enabled several score thousands of tenant farmers to buy and own land which, because they owned it, adopted long-range soil improvement programs.

The government also used the broad provisions of *Lex Kallio* in carrying out its resettlement program of the Karelian evacuee farmers, whose intensive methods of farming smaller properties helped swell the total of Finland's farm products.

All of these steps, combined with the introduction of a considerable amount of modern farm machinery, such as tractors and gang plows and other tilling equipment, harvesters, threshers, mowing machines and the like, have not yet served to modernize the major part of Finland's farming operation. Most of it still operates in the age of back and muscle.

American agricultural specialists who have studied hay-making methods have calculated that Finn farmers expend five times more man-hours in producing a ton of hay than do American farmers.

These same American experts have calculated, with the aid of pedometers, that Finnish farm wives walk an average of 20 kilometers daily (about 12½ miles) to perform their duties. Many small landholders continue to harvest their grain with a cradle, bind it by hand and thresh it with a flail.

These methods, which were discarded by American farmers two generations ago, indicate that a large section of Finnish farm life follows a course that involves drudgery and hard work —a procedure which drove many of America's farm-raised children off the farm.

The Finns do not seem to mind this drudgery and hard work as much as did the Americans, perhaps because of their fixed belief that hard work never has hurt anyone. While their belief may be well founded, it nevertheless is one of the surest ways known of discouraging young people raised on the land—the very ones most needed there—to leave it for other pursuits.

The migration from rural to urban areas which the United States has experienced during the past half century or more is now in full swing in Finland. During the 1926–46 twenty-year period, there were 687,723 Finns, approximately one sixth of Finland's total population, who moved from rural to urban centers; and women formed the majority in this migration movement.

Although still slightly more than one half of Finland's people continue to live in rural areas, not all of them are engaged in full-time farming. Some Finns who live in rural areas work for industrial concerns near their homes—in 1945, nearly 100,000 Finns were employed by more than 2,200 such industrial establishments.

In addition to these 100,000 industrial workers who live in rural areas are an estimated 200,000 or so part-time farmers who work their own farms and forest plots in the summer and during the remainder of the year find employment as lumberjacks, etc., or in woodworking plants. If this part-time forestry and wood-working employment is excluded, the production of food continues to engage the efforts of more than 40 per cent of all Finns.

Because they had more time than money, and more primitive than scientific information, the Finns continued until after World War I to produce their crops the hard way with simple, inexpensive farm machinery, and to farm as their fathers had. The result was that previous to 1917, Finland produced only 40 per cent of the cereals needed for human consumption. Twenty years later, with more foreign exchange and the benefits which they derived from the introduction of scientific methods, the Finns in 1937 produced 87 per cent of their own cereals. This slowly achieved near-balance of production and needs was thrown off following 1944 after Russia claimed as war booty about 11 per cent of Finland's highly productive agricultural area.

At the present time Finland's tillable farm area comprises five million acres that are operated by 348,000 farmers.

What do Finland's farmers raise?

Cattle breeding and dairying are their number one activity. This is emphasized by the fact that almost three fourths of Finland's tillable soil is used for pasturage, growing hay, oats and root vegetables with which to feed more than 1,000,000 head of cattle, and about the same number of sheep, 400,000 horses and an equal number of hogs.

After many generations of trial-and-error effort to become a self-feeding nation, the Finns began in a small way nearly a century ago to concentrate on dairying. Since their native breed of cows was not the most efficient milk and butter fat producer, they experimented in crossbreeding it with foreign strains during the next fifty years.

Their effort to upbreed their cattle was sharply halted by tuberculosis which began to decimate their herds. They were unable to determine which one of the fifteen foreign breeds was responsible, but they were certain that it was neither their domestic nor the Ayrshire. When they were sure of their facts the government decreed that henceforward cattle raising in Finland would be limited to these two breeds. Two results followed the government's decree: the first, that the disease was checked, then wiped out, and the second, that by 1948 nearly half of Finland's cattle were Ayrshire.

The government took the action about the turn of the century; since then dairying slowly but gradually has grown into importance in Finland. It began to expand at a considerably faster rate following Finland's independence. During the period when Russian grain supplies were plentiful and comparatively low-priced, butter, cheese and milk grew to hold an important place in Finland's economy. The Finns consider beef of secondary importance. In the thirties Great Britain, Finland's best butter customer, was annually buying more than 30,000,000 pounds of Finnish butter.

Co-latterly, while improving the strain of their cattle the Finns made great advances in specialized, scientific cattle feed. The most successful and best known of these is the A.I.V. method, discovered by the Finnish scientist and Nobel prize winner in chemistry, A. I. Virtanen, who perfected a method for preserving the proteins and vitamins in fresh grass.

Finland's present accent on dairying, which requires the use of a little more than seven tenths of her tillable acreage for the production of feed for cattle, divided a little more than half for hay and pasturage, 17 per cent for oats and the remaining 28 of the 70 per cent to the production of turnips, *mangelwurtzels* (a beetlike root vegetable), potatoes and other root vegetables.

Hay making in Finland is a picturesque sight. When the hay has been cut with mowing machine or scythe, the entire family helps rake and stack it in small, round rows of stacks on standing poles. They seemingly gather every blade. The hay is left in the small stacks until it is entirely cured, then is moved to small hay barns or sheds that dot the meadowside or to farm headquarters. Nature helps them by usually deferring rains during the haying season.

Finland's other farm crops follow in order: rye, barley, wheat, vegetables and some sugar beets that are used for human consumption. Finns also grow some flax and hemp which, with wool from the sheep that live mainly on hay and pasturage, supply part of their textile needs.

The Finns have failed to explore or develop the one crop, potatoes, which they can grow more successfully and with less effort and expense in cultivation and care than in almost any other place in the world. It is possible that they have neglected their potato potential because of their love of forestry and cattle. Whatever the reason for their failure to become potato raisers on a large scale, the fact remains that they have not done so.

The Lapland province of Finland, which now grows mainly forests and hay, can produce a greater per-acre potato yield than does high-priced potato land in the United States. Lapland has other important advantages as a potato-growing area in that it has practically no insect pests. Their absence eliminates the necessity for spraying. In addition, Lapland has few weeds, thus potato growers there are required to cultivate their crop not more than once or twice.

Since potatoes are one of the best and least expensive sources of human and hog food, aside from being fairly good chicken feed, it is strange that the practical Finns have neglected the development of potato cultivation. More potatoes would make it possible for Finland to grow more hogs and thereby provide hams, sausage and other pork products for foreign markets. Potatoes, processed through starch factories, would enable Finland to help supply the world's starch needs, of which there has been a shortage since Germany's downfall.

Since it takes from three to four years to produce and grow a milk cow, and two hundred years to grow a tree thirty centimeters in diameter, and only one year to grow a potato crop,

and also since one litter of pigs every six months reaches mar-
ketable age when six to eight months old, it is strange that the
Finns have overlooked the development of such a potentially
exhaustless silver mine.

Horticulture in Finland, like agriculture, and for the same
reason, has limited possibilities. Adverse climatic conditions in
the form of late spring and early fall frosts, which shorten the
growing season, serve to limit the variety of farm products,
fruit and berries that the Finns can grow. Apple trees, which
produce well in southern Finland, are killed every so often by
an occasional hard winter. The Finns know and expect that this
misfortune will strike them about once every decade—despite
this they replace the winter-killed apple trees with young ones.

Strawberries, lingon and cloud berries thrive in Finland. Finnish strawberries, like those grown in Norway and Sweden, are
unsurpassed in flavor and firmness and are good to the last
morsel. Unlike many United States types of strawberries, those
that grow in the northern countries are small and firm and
really wonderful—strawberries at their best. Finland's blueberries
grow wild, but like the cultivated strawberries, they are smaller
than American blueberries and more pleasing to the taste. The
Finnish lingon berry is somewhat like the currant in size and
color and makes excellent jellies.

Although these jam types of berries constitute an important
part of Finnish diet, neither individuals nor the government
has expended much effort in research and plant breeding to
increase their production.

It was Dr. Arthur Morgan's opinion[1] that the Finns might
well follow the successful course with these berries that the
United States has taken with blueberries and cranberries. Dr.
Morgan stated in his report that until about thirty years ago the
American public depended upon wild blueberries as their source

[1] Presented in a report to the American Friends Service Committee, which
had sponsored his survey of Finland's industries and organizations for the
purpose of aiding the Finns in development of their total resources.

of supply, but this was changed when a government technician and a private horticulturist began to study the question of blueberry cultivation. They selected and raised the best wild plants, then crossbred the best offspring until they succeeded in developing a berry that was five times larger, better flavored and with better keeping qualities than the wild ones. America's cultivated blueberries have now nearly driven the wild ones out of the market, while at the same time they have become a valuable cash crop which annually grosses about $300.00 per acre.

The Finnish lingon and the American cranberry are somewhat alike; therefore, in Doctor Morgan's opinion, the Finns might well undertake to experiment in the development of the lingon berry, which bears as well in the forest as in open ground. America at one time relied on wild cranberries to supply their needs in the same manner that Finns depend upon wild lingon berries, and horticulturists in the States began to upbreed the blueberries. While the initial investment for purchasing the new plants, preparing the land so that they could grow best, and buying harvesting equipment ran into substantial sums, the net profit of today's American cranberry growers has been greatly increased above that of wild cranberry growers. Dr. Morgan believes that Finns could have a like experience with cultivated lingon berries since, as he stated, one person "with a picking machine probably could gather twenty to forty times as many berries in a day as a person working by hand."

Heretofore and until the past few years, with a plentiful supply of cheap labor, Finns gathered wild lingon and cloud berries. They also gathered lichen moss, of which there is a large available quantity, for export to Germany. The disappearance of the German market, plus Finland's demand for workers to supply Russian reparation payment materials and to help hasten economic recovery by producing greater quantities of timber and woodwork products for free export, has furnished work for all able-bodied Finns, young and old. This situation has brought to a halt the gathering of lingon berries and moss for export. Only time and circumstance will reveal whether or not the Finns will initiate and carry out a long-range agricultural and horticultural program which eventually will help to bring their food production and consumption situation into balance. Now, in the spring of 1952, they are working with desperate determination to complete the Russian reparation bill in full next September, and at the same time, to produce enough goods for free export and thereby provide sufficient money to repay loans when due and to purchase necessary mechanical equipment and food. They have little or no allowance for luxuries in either their individual or government budgets.

Their experience in forest products—established markets and well-planned sales organization—necessitates their concentrating on those activities which will enable them to meet obligations and provide necessities.

It is possible, also, that the slow dragging feet of tradition, custom and method, which live largely in by-guess-and-by-God grooves, will make Finns hesitate to blaze new agricultural and horticultural trails. Another factor in the situation is that the Finns understand and have a liking for trees and cattle. These are good reasons for their clinging to both. Joe Louis illustrated this point once in an interview while being persistently questioned by a reporter about why he had purchased so many drugstores. Louis finally answered by saying: "Ah likes drugstores."

So it is with the Finns. They like trees and cattle. Perhaps they feel that they are entitled to this much from a hard life.

Fish is an important item in the Finns' diet. Because the supply continues to be abundant and can be produced without feeding or care or cultivation costs, Finns eat fish generally and regularly. The cost of catching, dressing and marketing is not great, thus the cost to the consumer is within his reach.

Finland has three rich fish sources, sea, river and lake. Since, however, the sea waters of the Baltic and the Gulf of Bothnia contain only a small percentage of salt, which runs from .2 to .5 per cent at the surface, it serves to reduce the number of sea fish.

The most important species of fish in Finnish waters is the Baltic herring. The Finns catch these in great quantities with fyke nets around the Turku archipelago in the spring and summer seasons, and with seines in winter. The total annual herring catch in recent years has approximated about 20,000 tons. This is nearly four fifths of Finland's total catch of sea fish. Neither their cod nor sprats catch is great. These species, along with flounder and turbot, are mostly confined to the archipelagoes of southwest Finland.

Pike, perch, turbot, roach, bream, ide and pike-perch are caught in the lakes. The most important of Finland's migrating fish is the sea-salmon, whose feeding and growing grounds are in the Baltic but which spawns in Finland's rivers.

Much of Finland's fresh-water fish supply is caught in the river mouths while on their spawning trips. The species so caught or trapped include salmon, sea-trout, lavaret, river trout, brown trout, grayling and ide. Next to strawberries, the most tasteful of Finnish foods is smoked salmon. There is none better.

Lake fishing in Finland is of chief importance as a domestic source of supply for those who live near or beside the country's many lakes. The quality of lake fishing varies according to the lake site, size, depth, nature of the water, lake bed, etc., as well as the species in the stock. Bream and pike-perch abound in the lakes of southwest Finland and those of the east have *muikku*, a small fish related to salmon. The lakes in northeast Finland and Lapland have the lavaret and salmon in addition to the pike, perch, roach and ide which are common to all of Finland's lakes. Finland's lake catch averages an estimated five million kegs of fish. The river catch—including the crayfish, which the Nordic people believe is a particularly succulent morsel—is about one million kegs smaller.

Chapter ten

How Finland Moves and Buys

Methods of transportation and marketplaces help to reveal to an observer some of the characteristics, habits, standards and purpose of a people.

In the American Southland, and in many South American and European countries, those driving through will meet hourly a large number of people who are walking along the roadside, always moving slowly, on their way to a neighbor or to the village or town. They are the unfortunates of society both because they possess no easier or faster method of transportation and because time, the precious essence of human life, is of so little importance to them. Their ambition is slight. They seemingly lack the ability to cope with life and its problems. To the end of time they will walk the roads of the world wearily, slowly, with drooping shoulders and aimless steps that graphically reveal lack of hope—defeated men whose bodies tell their tragic story.

Many people in other nations also walk the roads but do so with a movement of their bodies, purposeful steps, swinging arms and a heads-up way of carrying themselves, giving evidence that they know where they are going and why, and furthermore, that in time they will find other means than their feet to carry them on their errands.

The Finns are that kind of people. Their roadside walkers (who may plod, but shamble never) give observers the impression that they are thinking, I may be down but no one can keep me there for long.

None of the above comment is open to the interpretation that walking in itself is subject to criticism. No such suggestion has been implied. Walking, either for pleasure, exercise, or as direct, independent means of getting somewhere, has great merit. The late Henry Ford, who went a long, long way in his life, once remarked to the author, "I like to cut across lots alone on my own feet." But aimless, shiftless walking for little purpose is something in which Finns never seem to indulge.

Just as individual man, to compete successfully in the swift-moving twentieth century, must use some faster means of travel than his legs provide, so must a nation change its commerce transportation methods from horse-drawn vehicles to that of railroads and motor vehicles.

During the first twenty years of life as an independent nation, the government of Finland increased its state-owned operating railroad mileage by 50 per cent. In spite of this, train and track capacity today are far short of national needs. Passengers hauled by trains jumped from 22.4 million in 1938 to 55.6 million in 1946, but movement of goods has not shown a comparable increase.

Timber and forest products (although the greater part of logs are transported either by river floating or lake hauling) come first among the railroad commodities hauled, agriculture second and paper and pulp third. Normally, passenger revenues exceed total freight revenues by about 8 per cent. The locomotives, freight and passenger cars of Finnish railroads, like those of many other European countries, seem like toys when compared with those of American railroads. Their wood-burning, small locomotives, with big bulges at the top of their smokestacks, take the observer back to picture books of American railroad locomotives in the Civil War period.

The government also constructs and maintains the country's highway system, consisting of approximately 35,000 kilometers of main highways (a kilometer is about five eights of a mile), 3,500 kilometers of parish roads and 25,000 kilometers of village roads. A small percentage of Finland's highways are hard surfaced. The state operates some bus services, mainly to help mail transportation, but most buses, a fleet of more than 2,000, are operated by individual companies.

River traffic is comparatively small aside from that of floating logs, a fascinating sight in the north country where lumbermen guide logs with pikes through runways in the swift moving water. This dearth of river traffic is due to the many existing rapids and shallows. Lake traffic, which is still handled by steamers, and nowadays more and more by Diesel boats, is an important part of Finland's transportation system. It would grow to large proportions except for the narrow channels and swift waters which connect many of the lakes.

Finland's mercantile marine, which was large for so small a country, suffered heavily as a result of World War II. The number of its vessels was reduced from 857 with a net register of 378,749 tons, to 549 ships with a net register of 187,600 tons. Fifty-two of these ships were lost in the war and Russia claimed as war booty 104 of them, including the newest and best ships of Finland's mercantile marine.

Finland's other means of transportation, aside from the faithful horse in rural areas and the automobile and streetcar in urban areas, is the airplane. Operated by a state-owned company, domestic airlines reach nearly all parts of Finland, while Finnish and foreign-operated airlines maintain direct service to Helsinki between European centers and the United States.

Their means of transportation, which helps to keep the Finns from being a stick-in-the-mud people, serves also to keep them in touch with the world. In 1946, for instance, they delivered 181.7 million letters and parcels, and 409 million newspapers and periodicals to Finnish citizens. In addition, mails from abroad brought the people of Finland 22.7 million letters and parcels. When they do not wish to read letters, more than half a million

Finns who own licensed receiving sets listen to the programs of any one of the ten standard or four shortwave broadcasting station programs.

Among the first impressions of Finland's stores that a visitor gets is that they are orderly and clean and their goods are displayed in much the same way as those in American stores. The shops, taken as a whole, are smaller and the variety and size of stocks carried are not great. Although Finland's stores are modern in many respects, they nevertheless have an old-world atmosphere.

Some of their stores are distinctive if not unique. Finland's largest store, the Stockmann's Department Store in Helsinki, has, for example, a book department that sells a larger number of new books than any other single bookstore in the world. Row after row and shelf after shelf contain great quantities of books in many languages, but mainly in Finnish and Swedish. One noticeable thing about these books is that most of them are paper bound. This is the case both because it serves to keep them in lower price ranges and because the Finns, whose first interest is in true values, prefer to pay for the message carried in the book's pages rather than for the minor values in hard or fancy bindings, all of which greatly increases the price. The meat of the coconut, not the husk, is what they want.

Lahti also has a unique store. It sells only dolls, most of which are Finnish, that are dressed in native costumes. Small girl visitors who visit it give expression to breathless "oh's" and sighs of desire. Stockmann's bookstore and the Lahti doll store help to create the conviction that the Finns make reality of the principle that "whatever is worth doing is worth doing well."

These two stores, while unique in one way, are not in many ways different from the other stores of Finland. Village stores in Finland, apart from the kind of goods they carry, are not greatly unlike village stores in America. This is true also of the stores in Finland's towns and cities, except in one respect: their American counterparts carry a greater variety and larger stocks of goods than do the Finnish stores. This difference is not as noticeable now as it was a half a dozen years ago when the shelves and showcases of Finland's stores were pitifully bare.

One of the influences which helped to bring about the uniform high quality of Finland's retail service is that of the Consumers Co-operative Movement. This movement has enjoyed remarkable success in the northern countries where hard living conditions have trained the people to co-operate in their effort to make life easier or even possible. Without neighborly co-operation they could not live comfortably, if at all. Thus they have been conditioned through many centuries to co-operate. Limited incomes also serve to make them seek ways to cut corner costs in living.

Finland was fertile ground for the co-operative movement in the changed economic and social conditions that were brought about by the growth of industry as well as the foreign competition in agricultural products. The swift growth in numbers of the industrial workers and the country's small agricultural output, the ever-increasing need combined with other difficulties, were among the factors which encouraged farm producers and worker consumers to collaborate. Consumers wanted quality goods at a moderate price; farmers needed better seed, fertilizers, machinery and suitable credit to produce more and better products. One other factor in the situation that helped to launch the movement so favorably was that it served in a measure to combat the Russian czarist government's oppression of the Finns. All classes joined in helping to promote it in the belief that it would develop into a movement in which all classes could co-operate. This it has become.

The co-operative store movement which began in Finland about 1880 was borrowed from the corresponding English movement. Its real progress followed the adoption of the government's Co-operative Act early in the twentieth century. Co-operative societies began to be formed soon thereafter in towns and boroughs throughout Finland, as well as in country areas. Friction began to develop, due to the difference in commercial interests of the rural population from those of the worker in the towns. Mixed with this commerical interest difference, but minor in importance, was that of a difference in political outlook. The outcome was a split in 1916 when each group went its own way and created an organization of its own. Since then the movement has developed into two separate parallel organizations, each with its own stores and central organizations and factories. All stores of both organizations sell to nonmembers. Taken separately, the central commercial organization of the two bodies, SOK and OTK, are the largest wholesale dealers in Finland. They own wheat and rye flour mills, bakeries, brick, macaroni, match, margarine and nail, underwear, bedding and chemical technical factories, tailoring and ladies' dresses establishments, coffee-roasting plants and meat-processing establishments.

Each of the two distributive organizations operates insurance companies to provide insurance for stores, members and nonmembers.

The products of the factories and establishments which the two central organizations own and operate and the supplies they import are sold by the stores, which are a part of their distributive organizations and amount to approximately 40 per cent of Finland's grocery retail business. The corresponding figures for Sweden are about 10 per cent, and for England about 12 per cent.

The co-operative stores, especially those in rural areas, perform a twofold service for members and customers by carrying consumer goods for sale, but they also buy and market such agricultural products as grain, eggs, meat, vegetables, etc., which they either sell in the towns or export. Nearly all of Finland's grain, for example, is handled by these stores.

Finland has also a central agricultural supply society which provides agricultural machinery, seeds, concentrated feeds and fertilizers for members and non-members, and trades in agricultural products.

Finland's purposeful spirit of co-operation, manifested in her international relations in which she understands, sympathizes, and gets along with Soviet Russia as well as the free nations, is largely because of her co-operative attitude. The Finns' co-operative spirit also expresses itself through a large number of co-operative societies. These include co-operative dairy associations, under whose guidance Finnish farmers have increased the amount of butter production and upgraded its quality. Its farmer members own nearly 40 per cent of Finland's cows. The Co-operative Butter Association exports about 90 per cent of Finland's butter and 70 per cent of its cheese.

Other Finnish co-operative movements include those of credit societies, the sale of livestock and eggs, exploiting the forests, and in a smaller way there are co-operative societies for harvesting and threshing grain, sawmilling, etc. At the end of 1946, Finland had 599 electricity, flour mill and sawmill co-operative societies. There also are animal-breeding, dwellinghouse and telephone co-operative societies.

The firm strength of Finland's co-operative movement rests on the useful and wise services it performs for both farmers and industrial populations. Its record of performance has made it the most comprehensive and popular movement in Finnish society.

The individual Finnish farmer, for example, raises small crops and is restricted by limited and local markets. He could not sell his produce to advantage if he operated alone. By banding together with other farmers, and thereby widening his market so that trained co-operative salesmen may sell his goods, he gets better prices for them; nor could he without co-operation be able to find export markets for his surpluses. Failing that, he would be forced either to reduce production, which would mean economic disaster for him, or else to call upon the government for help, which he is loath to do. Because he prizes his freedom and independence, he tries to avoid too much government control and direction of his affairs.

One other aspect that comes to light upon one's recognition of the great scope and remarkable success of the co-operative movement is that it strikingly reveals the Finn's free, independent spirit and his desire to co-operate with his own and other peoples. He will go to the farthermost limit in his efforts to get along with other governments and their nationals, but he wishes to be left alone and permitted to live his own life.

In addition to the great variety of helpful economic services which Finland's co-operative societies and stores (there were 492 co-operatives with many thousands of stores in Finland in 1947) provide for their 1,132,200 members, and non-members as well, they have served the people of Finland effectively in other ways.

One is that through member participation in the conduct of their management they have widened the scope of the members' interest in affairs outside the immediate community in which they live and thereby in a measure not only helped to keep the people of Finland in closer touch with the outside world but to give them a better understanding of it.

Another by-product of Finland's co-operative movement is that the strong and well-staffed central organization of the two larger wholesale co-operatives has helped to introduce better methods of display of merchandise, and in various ways has upgraded the methods of merchandising of stores other than their own member co-operatives. The co-operative organizations and stores of Finland have served to introduce improved merchandising as well as better business methods into the retail business of the country. By so doing they have performed an indirect service, similar to that performed by American food chain stores in the States. Since Finland has no food chain stores to introduce improved methods, rural Finns, but for the co-operatives, would still be doing business with the old-fashioned country store which operated on hope and guess.

The third important by-product contribution which the co-operative movement in Finland has made is in the form of educational and information work. This has been a decisive service in helping in the initiation and development of better agricultural methods, of national economic conditions as well as of education of the people as a whole, and in the improvement of the farmers' living conditions.

The central organizations of Finland's co-operative societies conduct for their officials, staffs and members a continuous source of instruction on questions which relate to co-operative activities as well as the everyday routine work in the operation of all phases of the business.

The educational work for agricultural co-operation is carried on by the Pellervo Society which maintains legal, market research and correspondence departments. A bacteriological and chemical laboratory which conducts scientific research mainly for one member co-operative, Valis, is directed by Nobel Prize winner, Professor Artturi I. Virtanen. The Pellervo Society publishes several periodicals which deal with such subjects as cattle breeding, slaughterhouse operation, and dairy techniques. The research and information departments study and report to the members, through the publications, on the best methods and procedures that the peoples of other countries have created and developed. Were it not for the leadership and educational activities that the co-operative societies provide, a large segment of the Finnish population would not have been able to perfect and advance their social and economic programs either so rapidly or effectively. The significance of the educational worth of the co-operative societies is emphasized by the realization that the people of Finland, situated as they are on the distant fringe of western civilization, would be unable individually to secure such useful information.

The success of the movement in Finland serves also to give fresh emphasis that free, vigorous peoples, not governments, are the source and inspiration of civilized progress. In all countries where the character and good will of citizens flourish, it will be found that the people themselves create and advance movements whose goal is social progress and human betterment. Private citizens uniting together and co-operating in an effort to improve their own lot as well as the lot of other citizens hold in their hands and hearts the hope of a more stable and better civilization. This is the slow way. Its unquestioned merit is that it is the one way by which a people may control its own destiny.

Internally, at least, as judged by co-operative success, the Finns are determined to continue the control of their destiny.

Chapter eleven

Labor and Management Organizations—
and Woman's Place

The penchant of the Finns for voluntary organizations, which up to now has helped them to keep control and management of their affairs in their own hands instead of permitting the government to gobble up everything as governments tend to do everywhere today, is emphasized in a striking way by the existence and effort of their labor and management organizations.

Voluntary organizations in these fields, when one leaves the government out, are second only in importance, both as to size and influence, to the co-operative societies in helping to determine Finland's economic growth and social advancement.

Both organizations are comparative newcomers in Finland's life and both have had a stormy existence. This is especially true of union labor organizations. The trade union movement started in Finland in 1894, fourteen years after the co-operative movement was launched there. Typesetters were the first group to organize. One reason for their leadership may be found in the nature of their work. It seemed to keep them well informed of the trade union movement's progress throughout the world. The idea of organizing nation-wide trade unions soon spread to other trades. It was not, however, until 1907 that the Finnish Trades Union Organization was formed. It began with a membership of 26,000 that in ten years had grown to 160,000.

Its stormy days appeared following the Russian Revolution in 1917, when the Communist element gained control, and as in some American unions, created dissensions which almost hamstrung the movement. The turning point for the better came in 1930 when the Democratic members, who had a preponderant majority, walked out and left the Communists with the empty husk of the organization. The Social Democratic members next created the Central League of Finnish Trade Unions (SAK), and in doing so divorced it by regulation from political parties.

The SAK began with seven trade unions and 15,000 members. It today is composed of 38 trade unions and more than 350,000 members, about 60 per cent of whom are Social Democrats and 40 per cent, Communists. The Paris Peace Treaty had specified that Communists could not be excluded from membership. The Communists were defeated in one decisive union battle, but despite this defeat they continue with adroit manipulation and fierce determination to win control. Victory for them is not apparent in the foreseeable future.

The rules and regulations of the Central League, of which the individual unions are a constituent part, are that their activities must not be contrary to the aims of SAK; and that the member organizations must secure permission to strike from SAK's executive committee.

The main aim of SAK is to secure the adoption of an adherence to the principles of collective agreements. Such agreements are now actually in force in almost every trade that exists in Finland.

Aside from railroads, air service, liquor and a few other similar activities, which the government controls or owns and runs, and a minority interest in the bus lines, Finland operates almost entirely as a free enterprise nation. Ninety-three per cent of the gross value of Finnish industrial output is produced either by individuals, joint stock or other privately owned companies, and three per cent by co-operative societies. Excluding the companies in which the State owns a majority of the shares, it produces the remaining three per cent.

The employers of Finland have created the Central Federation of Employers, the purpose of which is to deal with all labor questions, other than those fixed by the state, which arise. Neither the employers' organization nor those of the workers, with a few exceptions, had made collective agreements prior to the outbreak of the winter war with Russia in 1939. The hardships from which both groups suffered during this war served to bring them closer together, and from this new-found unity their organizations announced on January 24th, 1940, that henceforth they would discuss in a spirit of mutual confidence ways and means of amicably settling all questions which related to their respective spheres.

This January agreement, as it is called, exerted a great influence on labor relations during the war in that all questions relating to general standard of wages, labor legislation and the like were discussed and negotiated between the two organizations. The influence of this agreement carried over into the period of peace which followed the end of the war when both groups continued to co-operate loyally.

The spirit of unity and co-operation between the two groups carried over and through the years that followed even after a third party, the government, assumed a dominant role in labor and industrial affairs. The brief January 1940 statement of agreement had emphasized the purpose of the employers and labor to consider their problems in a spirit of harmony and mutual trust. The practical results which flowed from this new concept, combined with war-wrought changes, created a need for spelling out in more detail the brief January 1940 statement of purpose of employer-labor relationships. After protracted discussions the two groups, the Finnish Employers Association and the Central Association of Trade Unions, did this on April 28, 1944.

The new agreement defined negotiation terms between the two groups, their relationship to each other, procedures in labor conflicts, terms of work and time of studies. It regulated employer welfare work as well as terms on which workers may give notice. The one question which was left to the central organizations to decide was that of collective agreements. Provision also was made for joint acknowledgment of the existence of prerequisites for the conclusion of collective agreements.

This agreement created a new and greater field of activity for the employers' organization in that previous to the 1940 agreement it had concerned itself mainly with eliminating or lessening any causes which could give justification to conflicts with labor which were outside the scope of the government's body of highly developed social legislation. The government had enacted laws which regulated hours worked, holidays with pay, safety, sanitary conditions, social insurance, factory rules, training, pensions, factory inspections, etc.

In addition to enabling acts, the Finnish constitution contains many admirable features, one of which is the provision that any citizen has the right to form or join an association, provided that it is not contrary to the law and good custom. The citizen also is given the right to abstain from joining an association.

A labor agreement, under the Finnish law, provides that one party, the worker, undertakes to work for a second party, the employer, in return for remuneration and under the direction and supervision of the latter, and covers both labor and intellectual work. A public service employee is not, however, subject to the provisions of the Labor Agreement Act of June 7, 1946. Finland's collective agreements largely deal with wages, working time, intervals of rest, order of work and termination of agreements. They may also include other provisions. When concluded they are binding on associations and member-associations of both employers and workers who were affiliated with them when the agreements were made. The government created a special Labor Court in January, 1947, with duties to sit in judgment on collective bargaining disputes except those of penal character. A new mediation law passed in 1946 makes both the employer and the involved union liable to attend the mediation conference called by a government-appointed mediator as well as to supply him with all necessary information pertaining to a basis of settlement. In case of failure the mediator is required to report the status of the dispute without delay to the minister of social affairs.

The Finnish record shows that between 1931 and 1938 inclusive, there were 418 work stoppages with 163,612 workers affected, who lost 1,035,706 work days. The government sought to halt this unfortunate trend because the attendant economic loss was unfavorably affecting the entire national economy, stirring up animosities and creating human misery. Its first remedial efforts consisted largely of using its good offices to promote better co-operation between employers and workers on a voluntary basis. Later, in June, 1946, it enacted a new law which required industrial concerns with about forty or more employees to create a special labor and management factory committee, specifying that it must meet at least three times annually to deal with such questions as related to output capacity of the enterprise, factory labor conditions, supervision of effective utilization of fuel and raw materials and marketing of products, as well as to plan measures which served to facilitate the supply of food and equipment for the workers. Here indeed is the entering wedge of worker participation in the management of industry—a much mooted question in the United States. These factory committees are charged by law also with the duty of promoting the professional skill and technical education of the workers, and to find ways that will enable them to use their leisure time to best advantage. The factory committees in addition are directed to act as a first instance in the settlement of disputes between employers and workers and staff personnel. In a nutshell, their real job is that of promoting the maintenance of industrial peace.

The realistic Finns know that once a law finds a home on the statute books it operates on the principle that possession is nine points of the law and cannot be easily evicted. Knowing this, the new law provided that its provisions would exist for only three years. Americans are reminded from time to time of how difficult it is to repeal old laws by having brought to their attention the hoary-aged blue laws that belong to a forgotten age.

At the end of 1947, there were 811 factory committees in operation, most of which had held more than the statutory three meetings per year. They had dealt with all questions which the law prescribed for them, but the one most frequently considered was that which concerned social conditions for workers and staff personnel.

The golden thread which run so clearly through the entire design of the Finnish government's labor laws is the one of guidance, stimulation—in a word, freedom of action by the concerned parties, or better still, *liberty*. The government is the umpire who urges the players to obey the rules, suggests ways by which they can do it. It is not a policeman with a club. Co-operation on a voluntary basis is its aim to the end that every Finn laborer and employer may be accorded just treatment in order that Finland may produce the maximum amount of food and goods which are the foundations of a good society.

The government's *hands-off* policy except in crises, its endeavors to place or keep the responsibility for industrial peace and justice where it belongs—in the hands and hearts of the individuals concerned—has paid large dividends in helping the community of Finland at large to achieve a remarkable record of working its way out of its difficulties.

This does not mean that Finland has neither labor-employer disputes nor strikes. On the contrary, it means that legal machinery exists by which the concerned parties are enabled to settle their own differences under the watchful eye of the government. The Finnish way is better than the American way, but it is inferior to Sweden's system, although the Finns have borrowed generously from the Swedes. One reason why the

Swedish system is the better of the two is that the Swedes have been working at it longer and therefore have been able to improve it more. The Finns, following the Swedish example, have narrowed the field in which disputes may arise by placing on the statute books many aspects of working conditions such as safety measures, etc., and thereby removed them from the field of bargaining.

Both countries have enacted laws which seek to make both labor and employer organizations stronger, more responsible and less dependent upon government ukase. They have done this because out of their experience they had learned that government-dominated arbitration efforts usually fail for the obvious reason that the public has small confidence in the justice of arbitration findings which were the joint work of government, labor and capital. The kind of relationship between capital and labor that both governments sought to bring into being was one in which an agreed-upon policy for adjusting differences would make legislation on the subject unnecessary.

Both governments have said in effect to labor and employee groups: "Grow up, shoulder your own responsibilities, get together, adopt mutually satisfactory negotiation procedures, reform your organizations, co-operate with and trust each other, so that friendly understanding and peace will exist throughout the nation."

The record shows that Finland's way of encouraging, even forcing labor and management to grow up is infinitely better than the American way of coddling, both parties constantly running to teacher for help to settle differences.

One possible reason why Finland's methods lag behind those of Sweden is that the Finns, having less with which to experiment, are slower to adopt new ways than the Swedes. Another reason is that the Finns are a little more set in their ways and, if that is possible, a bit more stubborn than the Swedes.

The Finnish government's "hands-off-as-far-as-possible" policy in the labor field in no way indicates its lack of interest or concern about what happens there. Its Labor Exchange Act of 1936, for example, requires communes to found and conduct, free of charge, labor exchanges or labor markets. The government did not, however, undertake to direct the formulation of wages until 1942, when it sought to meet the conditions growing out of the war crisis. In 1945, it issued a new order for the regulation of wages which established the principle that wages were to be raised commensurate with the cost of living.

By 1948, the combined influence of the labor shortage and the consequent demand for labor, the scarce supply of rationed foods and essential articles, plus additional factors caused wages to rise above the level established by the wages regulation orders. Government regulation despite these runaway factors served to slow down the tendency of the ever-increasing wage level.

In carrying out its policy of limiting the basis for possible differences between labor and management, the government adopted a Labor Protection Act. Its officials were authorized to formulate and issue detailed regulations for the safety of workers in eighteen different industries in which some element of danger is attached.

The government also regulates the hours of work in every field of human effort in which men, women and children work for pay. Overtime and night work, special protection for women and children workers and length of annual holiday are also regulated. A Finnish worker who has served the same concern for five years is entitled to an eighteen working days holiday with pay.

Among other steps the government has taken to protect workers was that of adopting an Accident Insurance Act for industrial accidents, as well as for occupational disease. The cost of the insurance is borne by the employer. Finland also has old age and disability insurance, the costs of which are borne by the insured themselves, employers, municipalities and communes. The employer bears half of the cost of those he employs. Finally, the government has established an unemployment fund which comes from the public treasury. No benefits are paid to members engaged in a strike or under lockout or who are sick or have left their employment for no valid reason, or have been dismissed for a valid reason, or who have refused to accept offers of suitable work.

The savings to American taxpayers should the government of the United States create and operate similar provisions is nearly beyond calculation. It is idle to raise the point, since only a whole people dedicated to the principles of justice and public well-being has the fortitude and courage to place justice and public well-being ahead of pressure group demands.

Finland's commonsense realistic labor policy, as expressed in the terms and purpose of its government's labor laws and regulations, serves to require shiftless, lazy or irresponsible citizens to improve their ways, rather than to reward them as do many American labor laws and regulations. This policy has expressed itself in production results so effectively as to cause the outside world to wonder about and admire Finland for its ability to work its way out of its difficulties.

Those men who operate on the principle of "getting theirs" are inclined to hold the view that Finland's labor laws and policies are weighted against the worker, whereas in reality they are weighted against the drones and irresponsibles. Life still is hard in Finland as it was at Jamestown, Virginia, in 1607, when Captain John Smith issued his dictum: "He who will not work, cannot eat." In America, due to pressure group demands and public funds provided by taxation or loans, drones and irreponsible workers are able to live comfortably even if they will not work. In Finland, where principles take the place of American ballot-box timidity, where wealth from natural resources is insignificant when compared to America's enormous horn of plenitude, where war's ravages have destroyed so many sections as against its destruction of none in America, the Finns have far smaller per man profits to divide than do Americans. In Finland, because there is such a great amount of work to be done by such a limited number of workers, those who do work refuse to carry the additional load of those who loaf.

The inevitable result which comes from a Finnish-American comparison is that both real and actual wages in Finland are lower than in America; the margin of profit is less and the need for industrial equipment greater. This is true because of war's destruction, war reparation penalties, and Finland's late entry into the industrial age. The life of the Finnish workingman is hard and grim, but it is in keeping with all of the rest of Finnish life.

Woman's Place in Finland

Finland stands high in the list of enlightened nations that have emancipated their women, establishing equality of the sexes in rights, opportunities and honor. While external influences had their place in Finland's emancipation program, the real influence was truly a native one.

The most noticeable deficiency in the Finnish labor policy and program is the inferior position in which it places women, particularly as concerns pay. The 1945 government's wage decree remedied this to an extent, but the wages Finland's women receive are still about 30 per cent lower than the wages men receive. Assuming that women workers perform as much work and do it as well as men, it would indicate that Finnish industry is profiting greatly by employing women workers, since nearly one half of the industrial workers of Finland are women.

This situation seems as much out of place in the Finnish picture as would a Polar bear on a South Pacific atoll for the reason that in Finland's long history her women have walked by the side of her men, not trudged behind them as men and customs in many countries still forcibly demand. The Finns were the first country in Europe to grant women the full rights of citizenship, including suffrage, as well as the right to hold seats in the

Diet. They did this in 1907, thirteen years before what many people believe to be enlightened America followed suit.

In 1907, the same year that Finland gave women official recognition of their equality with men, the voters of Finland elected nineteen women to the Diet, which consists of two hundred members. In the intervening forty-five years the voters have continued to elect about the same number as Diet members. Despite the belief to which Väinö Hakkila, long-time Speaker of the Diet, testified, that "the women have promoted matters advocated by them in the Diet with a success greater than their numerical strength gives reason to expect," the Finns have failed to give her an equal place with men in Finnish industrial life.

The women of Finland who have held office have made an excellent record. Finnish women also have displayed marked abilities in many other fields such as medicine, social work and education. The male Finns, acting in perfect harmony with the males of other countries, have been slow, however, about naming women to fill high positions in public life. Nor is Finnish industry's record in regard to giving women well-paid, highly responsible positions wholly commendable.

Finnish women demonstrated during the Winter War that they could carry on the work of the nation's industries while the men went to the battlefields. The women filled their places not only in industry, but also in education and agriculture, and revealed that they possessed to an unusual degree, energy, brains and initiative. The manifold services they effectively rendered the entire nation during that supreme crisis brought something new, fine and big to Finland from which there is no turning back. The people of Finland recognize what has taken place, but with true Finnish caution they are prepared to take only one step forward at a time, and that one only as the way opens. This is revealed by the statement of Diet member Müna Sillanpää, who said in regard to women's place in Finland's life, "Something new has to be created, but it must be laid on a solid foundation."

It would be wrong to place the entire blame on the males of Finland for their failure to bring women to a full level with men in every particular, because this is a man-operated world. Men have run it, and most ineffectively, for a long time. Despite their constant failures, this has given men a sense of superiority over women. Their failures should make men humble. That they do not is partly the fault of women. This is true because women, perhaps inspired by their intuitive purpose and in order to gain the upper hand before civilization disappears, tend to feed men's vanity by playing up to them. Whether they do so in an effort to catch or hold husbands, or whether they have learned that honey catches more flies than vinegar, only a woman can answer. The fact is that they do, and in many subtle ways. Listen carefully, for example, to the beautiful harmony and the lilting melodies of *The Merry Wives of Windsor*, and you will discover that the musical instrument which dominates its production is the male-sounding "bull" fiddle. It is the instrument that inspires the Wives of Windsor as they make merry. Countless other examples could be cited which illustrate the same point concerning the way women play up to men.

Even in the face of all of them, the males of Finland need to look to their laurels, such as they are, because the day of complete equality of the sexes in Finland is on the verge of dawning. When it dawns, Finland will be entitled to another credit mark in the book of civilization.

Chapter twelve

Education

Today's generation universally and more firmly than any previous one believes that education offers the most certain way to make reality of civilization's ideals of justice, liberty, peace, plenty and progress.

Its belief may be well founded. Time alone can give the final and full answer. Evidence in support of the belief is not too favorable in the important particulars of justice, which has lost her hearing as well as her sight in large areas of the world; liberty, which everywhere moves with leg irons; and peace which in either shooting or cold wars—seems to have gone from the earth. An increasing number of social misfits and the appallingly increasing numbers of what have been called "educated fools" appear to support Pope's belief that "a little learning is a dangerous thing." Plenty is unknown except in a few free countries, and progress, except in the development of physical sciences, moves at a snail's pace.

Many people who hold deep religious convictions continue to pin their faith on man's regeneration through spiritual experience and growth.

All informed men and women to an extent do agree that when education is fused with sound character values it becomes a powerful force in speeding the useful and wholesome growth of man. They are agreed, too, since man is a combination of spiritual, emotional and intellectual qualities, that the individual who has been exposed to or acquired education but does not possess the ability to evaluate and relate liberty, justice and the undeniable rights of man, which are "among the inescapable facts of the world," may easily become the prey of demagogues. Many millions of uneducated men and women who lived, labored and died during the past centuries, however, did have the ability to evaluate and relate these values to life. Had not this been the case, man still would be living in trees and caves.

This is not the place either to list or discuss the deficiencies of the educational systems and procedures of advanced nations. They exist. That is certain, otherwise we would not have with us the wide and deep differences in theory and practice that exist among educators, and the quality of the product of their efforts—graduates of our schools—would not be so uneven. Such discussion and listing would, however, be beside the point, if for no other reason than that all concerned citizens are supporting educators in their efforts to eliminate the weaknesses that exist in this youngest and perhaps greatest of all man's efforts, to bring light and learning to the world's masses in the effort to enrich individual lives and to stabilize and thereby strengthen the whole of society.

One possible reason why little Finland has been able to create such an enviable place for herself in the world is that her educational system is designed to emphasize both learning and values. No claim is made that the Finns were sufficiently prescient to realize the importance of combining the two. Circumstances brought about the fusing. The values part came first through the Lutheran Church. The Sweden-Finland Church Law of 1686 prescribed that every Finn should read and write, and the church conducted the schools. The Finns did not undertake to enforce the provisions of the law with compulsory attendance at school—compulsory school attendance had not even been dreamed of at that date—but they encouraged school attendance by penalizing everyone who failed to learn to read or write. An illiterate person, for example, could not marry, nor could he enjoy civil rights. This early Finnish bow to the freedom of the individual, by leaving to him the decision of whether or not he learned to read and write, is significant in that it reveals that the desire for liberty rested in Finnish hearts nearly three hundred years ago.

The father of Finland's basic system, the folk schools (public schools) was Uno Cygnaeus. The significant, vital service he rendered his fellow countrymen by his formulation, creation and direction of an educational system which brought the Finns' best qualities into full flower and tended to suppress their bad ones requires that some information be presented here about the origin, training and experience of this flaming sword of a man. Cygnaeus was born in Hämeenlinna, October 12, 1810. He was a grandson as well as a nephew of bishops of the Lutheran Church. He was raised by parents in a home where education was "a living and vital part of the family circle." He became a pastor of the church and taught a church school for two years during his ministry. Finland was then a grand duchy of the Russian Empire, of which Alaska also was a part. The Russian governor of Alaska persuaded Cygnaeus to go to Alaska to serve as minister and teacher. He did so in 1845 and later returned home by way of Siberia. Shortly thereafter he was made a bishop. The church transferred him to St. Petersburg where he served as director of Lutheran Church schools and religious instruction in the Finnish schools. His experiences in educational work and other observations of the way it operated inspired him to learn more about what other countries had done in this field.

He made further studies of foreign educational systems in the twelve months between October, 1858 and October, 1859, of both the schools and schoolroom procedures in Sweden, Denmark and Germany as well as in Finland. He did so as the representative of the government committee which had been appointed to study both the advisability and possibility of establishing a modern system of public education in Finland.

In his study of the Finnish schools he discovered too much mechanical reading that lacked comprehension of what was read; lack of cleanliness; varying standards of teaching quality and inadequate provisions for child health and spiritual training. Switzerland's schools seemed to him to offer the best possibilities for insuring the pupil's growth and culture. Teachers there were held in high esteem, and school administrators were responsive, active and competent. He returned home convinced that school and church should be operated separately.

Among his recommendations were (1) Provide educational facilities for the poor. (2) Continue to emphasize religion and religious teaching, but give increased attention to other subjects. (3) Send Finnish educators to other countries to study their educational systems. (4) Improve Finnish teachers colleges. (5) Stress health education. (6) Give special emphasis to instruction in everyday life needs, such as handwork and home gardening. (7) Provide women with opportunities for both cultural and practical training. (8) Above all else, emphasize right living and honesty.

In 1860, following his return home, Cygnaeus presented his findings and recommendations. He followed this with an energetic effort to get them adopted. He met with many difficulties, but in 1861 he overcame his first hurdle when the Finnish Senate appointed him inspector of all of Finland's schools and teachers colleges. Here again was one of those junctures of affairs that appear in the history of every nation where the man, the need and the hour meet.

Before Uno Cygnaeus died in 1888, his name and that of the Finnish folk school system had become synonymous. He was a wise, thorough and industrious man who was far ahead of his time. He completely changed, expanded and strengthened Finland's public educational system and in so doing, built the firm foundation on which it rests today. Present-day educators have developed to their fullest use his ideas concerning universal education, thus bringing within the reach of every youngster instruction in religion, cultural subjects and handicrafts. He elevated teaching to an important place in national life; strengthened and improved teachers training colleges; introduced higher standards of cleanliness in the schools and provided medical care and lunches for the pupils, all to the end that Finland as a nation might grow strong and purposeful through the strong and purposeful individuals who had been pupils in her schools.

The hard inner core of Cygnaeus' conception of the purpose and service of public education was first, that it should discover and develop all of the pupil's God-given aptitudes, and, secondly, that it should direct and train the pupil both for his own good and for the good of Finland as a whole. He insisted that the school should be separated from the church, and brought this about. At the same time he believed that the public school should retain the Christian foundation of the educational procedures of the church. He accomplished this also. To these he added instruction in subjects that would serve to train the eye as well as the hand.

This innovation was especially important at that time because Finland produced by hand in the home or on the farm nearly everything her people wore, used or ate. Therefore, he held that education must teach the youth to use his hands. This is the beginning of the manual training which today in the United States is called industrial education. But first and last, over and above all else, he insisted that the schools should emphasize right living and honesty for the good of the individual pupil and the nation as a whole.

Cygnaeus built the foundation on which Finland has erected her admirable educational structure of today, nearly all of which has been built during the past twenty years. She made her first important move in this direction in 1921 by enacting a universal compulsory attendance law. This law provided that all Finnish children who do not pass on to a secondary or a trade school must complete elementary school work and two years of school work above the elementary school. Compulsory education under this act covers eight years of school attendance. The courses taught in the two-year continuation school which follows elementary school deal mainly with the requirements of practical life. The additional subjects include literature, history and civics.

The pupils are divided into two groups after they have completed their elementary school work; one group enters the universities and scientific colleges through the secondary schools, and the other attends extension classes and trade schools. Since the first group consists chiefly of children of well-to-do parents (this is necessarily the case, since the cost of higher education in Finland is heavy) the Finns consider the system as one that is unfitting to a democracy.

The decisive factor in creating a path to learning, as defined by the government's 1946 School Reform Committee, was to be that of natural endowments, talent and ambition rather than the financial position of the parents of the pupils. Although social differentiation was not great, the Finns sought to eliminate it completely. No social differentiation existed in the folk or elementary schools where the state provided free textbooks, meals and medical service for all pupils. The state previously had provided some slight grants-in-aid for gifted pupils in the secondary schools, but these were not substantial enough to provide such pupils with food and lodging. This situation was remedied to an extent with larger grants-in-aid by the state.

Unlike America, whose communities created a school system one layer at a time, the government of Finland has created a national system of elementary education and arranged for its operation in communities. In both countries, however, elementary education is under the direction of local government. Finland's system is different in one respect, in that the national government subsidizes the schools and its educational authorities maintain general supervision over them. Secondary schools in Finland are maintained either by the national government, local governments, individuals or private organizations.

The overwhelming majority of pupils in Finland attend folk

schools, all of which provide an eight-year course, and a few of them nine years. At least the more recently built ones are quite similar to and as attractive in every way as are the best of the so-called consolidated schools in America. They are superior in some ways to their counterpart American schools in that the usually unimaginative Finns have revealed a capacity to make them attractive to children by using such devices as placing clay replicas of a variety of animals and birds in the outside cement walls. Aside from classrooms and science laboratories which are all well proportioned and well lighted and have rows of glass windows, some buildings contain swimming pools, gymnasiums and other youngster delights. In the 1948–49 school year, 15,741 teachers taught 483,000 young Finns in these schools. Finland's expansion of her elementary school system is revealed by giving the 1945 figures, when 4,061 teachers taught 143,577 pupils.

In addition to her elementary schools, Finland has 314 secondary schools with a total enrollment of over 82,000 pupils, of which 99 were state schools and 215 were private or commune schools. These 314 secondary schools included coeducational schools, boys and girls schools, classical lyceums, etc. The state school's fees were considerably lower than those of private schools. About three thousand of the graduates of these secondary schools continue their studies at universities or colleges of university rank, and the remainder either enter trade schools or go to work.

Superimposed on the Finnish secondary school system is a layer of what is called Peoples Colleges and Workmen's Institutes, the first of which was established in 1889. Except for the latter, these are residential institutions. Their adult pupils, for the greater part, have attended both elementary or middle schools. They have had some experience in life and possess a thirst for knowledge. These schools place emphasis on such courses as civics, history, literature, the Finnish language, and practical subjects in a one- to two-year course. The majority of these institutions are directed by special organizations, but the state foots from 60 to 75 per cent of their bills. At the end of 1945, Finland had 71 Peoples Colleges with a pupil enrollment of 4,299 and 76 Workmen's Institutes with 32,259 pupils.

Paralleling the work of the institutions to an extent, but with different training provided, are Finland's 314 trade schools, many of which offer agricultural courses. These include farming, dairying, cattle farming, domestic economy, forestry and gardening. There are 149 of these schools. In addition, Finland has 49 commercial schools, 4 navigation and 112 technical schools. These 314 schools have an average annual enrollment of about 26,000 students.

The top layer of Finland's educational system consists of three universities, teacher training colleges and a technical institute. The University of Helsinki was founded in 1640 in Turku and later, after a disastrous fire, was transferred to Helsinki. It is to Finland today what Harvard University was to the United States a century ago. Its faculty, headed by 184 professors with 251 other teaching staff members, conducts faculties of agriculture and forestry, law, medicine, philosophy (which is divided into the department of history and languages and the department of mathematics and physical sciences), political sciences and theology, as well as institutes for pharmacy and physical education. Its total student enrollment exceeds 10,000 students. Finland has two other universities which are located at Turku: one, a private Swedish university, was founded in 1918, and the other, a Finnish university, was founded in 1922. They are much smaller than the University of Helsinki.

There are twelve folk school teachers training colleges in Finland, two of which offer a two-year course, one a three-year course, four a four-year course, and five have a five-year course. Some of these are for training teachers of Finland's Swedish schools, but the majority of them are Finnish.

Finland also has five schools for deaf mutes and two schools for the blind which the state supports, and in 1946 had 2,027 state-aided study circles at which more than 42,000 people studied.

These study circles are the most important part of free folk education that is not fixed by law. They usually form a part of some educational system or institution. Their strength lies in the close co-operation and spontaneous contributions of their intellectually hungry adult members. The membership in one of these groups, all of which have a leader, is preferably kept to thirty or less. One of the central aims of the organization is to stimulate and foster a desire of the members of the circle to be able to read Finland's best literature in many fields to the end that it would help them become better citizens.

The circles offer a large number of study courses. They include religion, reading, arithmetic, singing and musical instrument playing. The lecture method of teaching is generally used, combined with general discussion by the members.

Working side by side with the study circles are those of the Workers Cultural Union—which was established in 1919, and carries on educational work with all its variations that deal with workers—and the Union of the Youth of Finland, founded in 1897.

The universities of Finland, teachers colleges and the Social High School of Helsinki help to supply the lecturers for these groups. Nearly 2,300 public libraries serve to help satisfy the Finn's thirst for knowledge. More than twenty scientific societies that cover as many different fields act as useful aids in rounding out and extending opportunities for the growth of the people of Finland.

Finland has also built one of the most modern graduate schools of business administration, with facilities for 900 students. Even the university students have started building their own dormitories, and 582 students of Helsinki University live in three *Domus Academica* which are managed by the students themselves.

Two other important educational institutions deserve special notice.

The first of these is the Institute of Technology in Helsinki, a state institution with 283 faculty members and an enrollment of 2,227 students. If the dreams of the faculty and students are realized it will, in time, become the equal of the older and well-established great technical institutions of Europe and America. The Institute formerly was located in the heart of Helsinki. Its new home is on a large tract of land on a peninsula about six miles from Helsinki where the new buildings peep at each other and the nearby sea through pine forests.

There are many remarkable things about Tech Town, but one of the most remarkable is that its own students have brought it into being. The circumstances back of its origin were that many of its older students were soldiers or women workers in munitions factories during Finland's 1939–45 wars with Russia and Germany. They returned home to a spiritual vacuum when the wars ended. Their country had been defeated. Ten per cent of its territory had been ruthlessly claimed as war booty by its mighty aggressor. It staggered under the crushingly heavy reparations burden. Human and economic crises had been tremendous. Peacetime values had been either forgotten or disclaimed. Student as well as other life in the nation was completely disorganized. The future was almost too dark for even Finns to contemplate.

The nation faced the alternative of either sitting down and wailing "Oh, woe is me!" or going to work to better the situation. Tech students chose the latter. Their first need was an education. To get it they required buildings and rooming facilities for the students. One of the Institute's old buildings had been damaged by Russian bombers and Helsinki was filled to the last extra room with evacuees. Some genius came up with the idea: Why not build a Tech Town?

The idea quickly spread, grew, and soon it was feeding on its own merit. Then it flamed into a great cause. Finland's spirits

needed a great cause then. The older generation soon became
infected by the inspiration of the plan. They backed the effort
with something of the attitude: If you youngsters, who are
going to carry the greater part of Finland's heavy load, have
hope for the future, we can do no less. The oldsters helped but
it was the youngsters who made the plan a reality.

They drew up and presented petitions to government bureaus.
Their enthusiasm cut miles of red tape, and officialdom soon was
wholeheartedly supporting the effort. The government provided
a site for Tech Town. The students enlisted industrial, financial
and business leaders in the effort. They did not overlook the
Olympic Committee—the competing women athletes in the 1952
Olympics will be housed in the new dormitories. They appointed
building, finance, and money collecting and sports committees.

The building committee held an architects competition for
plans. Finland's world-famed architect, Professor Alvar Aalto,
won the competition. He designed the buildings which fit so
perfectly into their surroundings that they seem almost to have
grown with the forests, hills and sea. Aalto's plans sketched every
detail of the new community. They show where every road and
street will lie, the location of every dormitory, laboratories, classrooms and other buildings as well as athletic fields and facilities.
These will include running tracks, grass and hard courts, an
outdoor stadium, a football field and a swimming pool. He also
included plans for transforming the wooded landscape into parks.

Meanwhile, the other committees were equally busy. One of
the problems they faced was that of finding building material.
Fate, which carries evidence that "God works in a mysterious
way His wonders to perform," came to their aid in a strange
way to help them solve part of this problem. Fate's part—and a
peculiarly just and fitting part it was, too—consisted of having
had a Soviet war bomber drop his bombs smack on the Soviet
Legation in Helsinki, completely destroying it. The Bank of
Finland had later bought the lot on which the Soviet Legation
stood, and planned to raze the ruined walls preparatory to erect-

ing a new building on the site. Tech students, in return for doing the razing job, were given the bricks—800,000 of them.

Every foreign visitor to Finland who wishes to see concrete evidence of Finland's indomitable spirit should visit the inspiring and beautiful new Tech Town, since it so clearly explains what makes Finland, Finland.

The people of Finland are giving expression to the practical, realistic part of their nature by building Tech Town in that they are providing training facilities for future engineers, chemical and electrical experts, architects and leaders in other material fields who tomorrow will invent better machines or improve old ones; unlock more of nature's secrets for man's use; develop new ways to transfer loads from men's backs to power; and build better homes to the end that all men may live more securely and comfortably. This represents an important and necessary part of Finland's effort to improve and strengthen society as a whole.

The ideal and spirit of the students soon fired all Finland with such enthusiasm that money-collecting teams met with increasing success. The students did not, however, rely on contributions alone. One of their most successful activities was that of importing and selling some of the "luxuries" postwar Finland did not have, such as coffee and American cars. The Finnish public was willing to pay high prices for them; coffee, for example, sold for five dollars a pound and even more. Because the proceeds went to the students, Finnish consumers gladly paid these prices for their "luxury" imports, and everybody gained.

We have been dealing, however, with material forces. The other part of Finland's purpose, that of spiritual growth and the determination to create amicable relations with all peoples, also has found expression in a most unique way. This newest and possibly finest expression of the deeper purpose which the people of Finland seemingly never cast aside or forget consists of the recent establishment of an International College at Hauho, in south central Finland.

The purpose of the International College is to find and develop ways that will establish and maintain harmonious human relationships on both a national and international basis. To that end its international student body, whose members come from different walks of life and have different religious, social, ideological and political beliefs, has an opportunity to know each other and together study subjects which concern human life and relationships in an effort to find deeper and more creative ways to bring peace to the world.

The founders of this unusual institution hold a deep conviction that it could render a real and significant service by helping to build and foster a growing understanding and co-operation through the education of people who want to dedicate themselves to the task of molding a society of whole human possibilities. Their conviction was made stronger by the existence throughout the world of the large number of individuals and groups who are striving to create better international understanding as well as a more harmonious co-operation between social groups. Their question was: What can we do that will be helpful to advance this great human purpose?

The Finns are almost direct in action. There is little of the "God-sake" (for God's sake, let's do something about it) in them. They soon came up with the idea for an international college which would serve to build bridges over which everyone might cross who wanted to help create better human and international relationships. Finland seemed to be the ideal geographical place for such an institution. It is permeated with a free atmosphere in which honest endeavor to create better relationships may be readily advanced. It is the world's most strategically placed buffer zone of the free and the Communist world.

The founders of the International College at Hauho, Finland, which stands in pine woods on the shore of a beautiful lake, sincerely believe that they will be able to create some bridges and open some new roads to peace and unity by bringing (through its students from many countries) the causes of tension, suspicion and misunderstanding to an unpolitical platform where they will be handled in an atmosphere of understanding and co-operation.

Finns themselves provided all the necessary funds for the purchase of the land and the buildings, for the staff and for the opening of the College. They did this before June, 1951. In its first year ten students from five nations were in attendance. When more funds become available, they will erect new and greatly needed buildings and increase the teaching staff and student body.

The spiritual, church, government and other leaders who had the daring, vision and understanding to establish and support the International College have estimated that an additional $270,000 will provide it with its necessary new buildings and take care of the operating expenses for two years. After two years' operation, the government of Finland will annually contribute between 70 to 85 per cent toward its entire operating cost. The remainder will come from student fees and the Christian-Social Settlement Federation of Finland. The founders are raising $70,000 of this $270,000 in Finland. From what source and in what way the remaining $200,000 will come, the founders of the College do not know. But they have faith that it will be provided.

This sum of $200,000 is an infinitesimal pittance when compared with the billions of dollars that the United States Government is now annually spending in its efforts to create a strong, free, and peaceful world. It is possible that one hundred years from now, when men appraise the course of events and the influences which have contributed most effectively to the establishment of amicable international relations on which peace rests, they will find that the tiny and insignificantly less expensive seed Finland has planted at Hauho will outweigh in results all the billions of dollars that we are spending. If that should be the case, it will be because, even in our material world, the things of the spirit alone are durable, lasting and decisive.

One of the most inspiring things about Finland's new International College is in the way the people of a small and poor nation demonstrate their ability to dare so big.

Could it be that the Finns have discovered the way to live forever? It is possible, because the things of the spirit live forever, whereas perishable material things crumble to dust.

Who today but a small number of the most erudite numismatists knows the value of a *Yek Hazar dinar?* Who will know what the value of today's dollar is in 2052?

Everyone in 2052 or in 10052 will, on the other hand, know what the value of common understanding, and co-operation, and amicable relations means.

It could be that Finland's International College will help her people to fulfill their mission.

Chapter thirteen

Music, Literature and Press

The cultural life of Finland has not lost its close contact with western civilization since the eleventh century, when the Finns accepted Christianity. The Roman Catholic Church, and a few centuries later the Evangelical Church, served as powerful links in the chain which bound the Finns to the west.

The statement was made earlier that the culture of Finland in certain respects lacks the "depth and grandeur" illustrated by that of some other lands. This is true provided culture means the enlightenment of taste acquired by intellectual and aesthetic training, and also provided Finland's majestic, incomparable Jean Sibelius is excepted—universal though his genius is, it is also distinctively Finnish. To his ear, each note of nature in Finland has an especial musical value. He heard, caught and transferred to musical scores the sights, atmosphere and natural harmonies of Finland's forests and fields.

Many parts of Finland are places of great silence. In them the visitor seems to be moving in a void that is apart from the earth, where absence of man and the pervading power of nature creates strange fancies in his mind. There is an archaic loneliness in her vast virgin forests that casts its magic spell on pigmy men. Many Finns feel this magic which runs through the music of Sibelius.

Magic and wisdom are identical according to Finnish mythology. Even today, living as they do so close to nature, most Finns have an uncanny gift of second sight which, like the American Indian's sixth sense of caution, enables them to see and understand many of nature's secrets that are beyond the comprehension of the majority of people, nor has the Finn neglected the development of his sense of hearing. His ear is attuned to nature's sounds. He hears the music of the spheres, which so often is a somber music, and it has entered his soul.

Jean Sibelius is the Finn raised to the *nth* degree in these respects, rather than a spontaneous deviation or variation from type. He has heard, seen and understood the soul of nature in Finland as well as having glimpsed the soul of her people, and with exceptional genius he has portrayed in timeless creations their spiritual relationship. His music, rooted deep into "the unchanging landscape of Finland," is supremely Finnish. Better than any pictures or words, it expresses the depth, height and quality of the soul and purpose of Finland and a sympathetic understanding of his people's earnest endeavor to contribute towards the progress of human civilization.

His compositions are strong because nature in Finland is strong, even granitelike. Finland's great novelist Alexis Kivi wrote about "a strong will that carries its man even through gray granite." This spirit and conception runs through Sibelius' compositions. Only his "Finlandia," which he composed early in the century when Russian oppression was at its worst, has a purely nationalist character in that it expresses in music what the Finns were prohibited from saying in words; namely, their unyielding opposition to foreign domination.

One of America's great music critics has written of Sibelius' music, "This is music that everybody would have liked to write. But neither the theories of the whole world nor the most skilful definitions are able to create tunes like this. Only a great spirit can raise and exalt these melodies to such a perfect power as this."

One of the most deeply satisfying aspects of human life is that when the light of a great genius flashes across the sky above the reach of most men it inspires other men to follow the path it has lighted. This has happened in Finland. It has brought about a change in the character of Finnish music from which a kind of national musical language has emerged.

Järnefelt, a brother-in-law of Sibelius, interprets the lyrical side of Finnish nature in his melodies.

Toivo Kuula (d. 1918) composed rugged, wild music that is full of pathos, whereas the music of a Sibelius pupil, Leevi Madetoja, is gentle, soul-stirring and devout.

Many other equal or lesser Finnish composers are carrying on their chosen work of giving fresh and beautiful interpretations to the international language of music, which of all the arts has given to the world their messages about the national culture of Finland.

All Finns love music, and in annual song festivals one can sometimes hear a chorus of many thousands of male and female members singing in perfect harmony. At least two famous Finnish male choirs visited the United States after the war and achieved success among the American music-loving public.

Neither in quality, distinction, nor variety does Finland's literary output equal that of her music. A striking quality of their music and literature is that both deal largely with the beauty of nature, the serious phases of human experience and the spiritual aspirations of men.

A distinguished American scholar who was born in Finland, Dr. John Wuorinen, has written that the symbols Finns revere, the ones that quicken their hearts, "appeal to their loyalties and command their love, have to do with the life and work of men who helped them to achieve the miraculous thing they have desired most, their freedom and independence. The roster of Finland's honored men is headed by poets, pedagogues, scholars and other patriots who never donned a uniform or fired a gun. While it includes men who fought for their independence in 1918 and later—it includes, for example, a hero-child of twelve who died in the war of 1918 and Marshal Mannerheim who

served his country as a soldier in 1918 and again in 1939–1944—
it is composed overwhelmingly of men of the pen and not of the
sword."[1]

Finland's men and women of the pen, if we accept Dr. Wuorinen's penetrating summation, have expressed in song, story and
treatises the philosophic faith and the yearning of the people.
Their simple faith in a divine author and authority and the
destiny of man's soul continues unshaken, as it does in stable
institutions and automatic progress. This is not true today in
many places where doubt, insecurity and alarm have destroyed
a like faith.

Neither the Finns nor their writers devote much time or
effort to reading or anticipating the plot of life—when they
accept something as true it means that they believe it. They fit
William James Bull's statement that "the most interesting and
valuable thing about a man is his ideals and over-beliefs, which
include basic assumptions about God and religion, and the home,
marriage, life, death and what constitutes happiness."

Unlike the American philosophy of life, which is far too diverse for a synthesis to be made of it, Finnish life, lacking such
diversity, is easier to understand and therefore can be characterized and interpreted by writers.

Mikael Agricola, who compiled the Finnish alphabet book so
that the people might learn to read, also translated into the
Finnish language a catechism of the reformed doctrines, a
prayer book and in 1548, the New Testament. To Agricola
belongs the credit of making Finnish literature possible.

Its growth was barely appreciable until nearly two centuries
later. The factors which largely were responsible for its slow
development included foreign domination, since Finland remained a homogenous part of the Swedish Empire for another
160 years, during which time Swedish was the language of

[1] John H. Wuorinen, Ph.D., *Finland and World War II* (New York, The
Ronald Press, 1948).

government and the ruling classes even after Finland became a
grand duchy of Russia in 1809. Her affiliation, first with Sweden
and later with Russia, served to make her people feel that they
were a subject race. This tended to check the growth of what it
would mean to them to become Finns.

Thus time passed in quietude until Ivar Arwidsson, angry
about conditions, flared, "Oh, to have a real Fatherland, to be
a citizen of a State, and not a squatter on a mangy ground governed by sly foxes and stupid asses." Arwidsson is credited with
having said: "Swedes we are no longer; Russians we can never
be; therefore we must be Finns."

The Finns themselves realized but dimly the brilliance of their
light. Sir Edmund Gosse wrote in his *Northern Studies* that it
was interesting to note how much that was notable in Swedish
history had come from Finland in the annals of statecraft,
church and war, and added, "The names of Finns are singularly
prominent" and in literature, he stated, "Some of the leading
writers in each century have been natives of Finland."

Arwidsson's clarion call aroused all Finland. Swedes they no
longer were, Russians they never could be, so they emerged as
Finns and with them emerged Finnish literature.

Johan Ludvig Runeberg, a teacher, led the way with a collection of poems which appeared in 1848, and tell the story of
humble Finnish heroes in the wars against Russia. It has been
written that "The book rings with a note of national pride that
had not been heard in Finland before."

A contemporary of Runeberg's, Elias Lönnrot, Finland's successor to Homer and predecessor of America's Burl Ives, wan-
dered through Karelia, living in peasants' homes and learning
their songs while he entertained them with his flute. After he
had discovered a vast oral tradition of "magic rhymes and riddles, legends and festival songs," he was inspired to weave them
into a poem as did Homer after he had "heard men sing by land
and sea." Lönnrot called his book *Kalevala*. This great epic is
based on stories from the lips of popular bards. It reflects the

beliefs and wisdoms of generations of Finns and contains the essence of national character and also serves as the origin of Finland's distinctly national cultural life.

Lönnrot began his epic with the Finnish legend of the creation of the world. The narrative recites the triumph of Finnish legendary heroes over their foes and is interspersed with bridal songs and dirges, but its central theme is the triumph of Kalevala, Finland. Research has provided incontestable evidence that the poems of Finland's epic *Kalevala* had been carried for centuries by word of mouth from the west of Finland to the east. By transferring them from memory to paper, Lönnrot proved Finland's right to be recognized as a distinctive nation.

According to Andrew Long, *Kalevala* differs from other folk-legends in that it carries no trace of aristocracy.

There is scarcely a mention of kings or priests, the heroes of the poem are really popular heroes, fishers, smiths, husbandmen, medicine-men or wizards; exaggerated shadows of the people, pursuing on a heroic scale, not war, but the common daily business of primitive and peaceful man. In recording their adventures, *Kalevala*, like the shield of Achilles, reflects all of the hopes of the race, the feasts, the funerals, the rites of seed-time and harvest, of marriage and death, the hymn and the magical incantation.

Lönnrot's *Kalevala* was first published in 1835, but it was not until after an enlarged edition was published, in 1849, that his epic became widely popular. A point of interest to Americans is that Longfellow copied its meter and used some of its theme in "Hiawatha," which he published in 1855.

The following fragment of one of Lönnrot's poems, as translated by Sir John Bowring, establishes this point:

> Song was then by song repeated,
> Rapture was by rapture echoed
> Not a tenant of the forest
> On his four feet hurrying forward
> On his little patties tripping
> But came hastening then to hear him.

Runeberg's poems, which sounded the first note of national pride, and Lönnrot's *Kalevala*, which transformed what heretofore had been an oral tradition into a written tradition, advanced the Finnish people's groping efforts to strengthen their spirit of nationalism and their purpose to make the Finnish language a written language. The writings of these two men exerted a powerful influence in the shaping of Finland's destiny by helping to keep Finns' eyes and purposes fixed on the simple virtues of daily life.

Runeberg and Lönnrot were the forerunners of Finland's Renaissance movement in the romantic idealization of this small nation. Other able writers followed them, and as always happens when a worthy idea or movement comes to the attention of men, it begot other ideas and stimulated the launching of other movements.

One of their contemporaries, Johan Vilhelm Snellman, became disturbed by the fact that although Finnish was the language of the vast majority of the people, it also was true that hardly a single educated family in the middle of the nineteenth century spoke Finnish. What to Snellman was even worse was that they had no means of learning it. Swedish was the language of the secondary schools, of the teacher, pastor, magistrate and official. Snellman held that if proper relationships were to be created between the classes and the masses, and Finland thereby to become a united country, the Finnish language must be taught in the schools. When Snellman brought this about he turned "romantic nationalism" into a movement for "education" out of which came a substantial body of literature.

Alexis Kivi, one of Finland's brightest literary luminaries, first wrote *Kullervo*. A later book, *Seven Brothers* (1870), has been translated into several languages.

The writings of Sally Salminen, author of *Katrina*, are well known outside Finland, partly because she is an American-Finn; but those of Eino Leino (d. 1926) never achieved the international recognition to which his genius as a lyrical poet entitled him. Educated Finns who rank Leino as Finland's greatest lyrical poet hold that he approaches Goethe in his delicate, expressive style. Another reason why Leino stands so high in Finnish estimates as a lyrical poet is that temperament is its normal habitat. Finns who either possess little temperament or have a high boiling point seldom give evidence of this. Their dramas and short stories deal in the main with the children of sorrow, who pervade Finnish life and literature; thus lyrical poetry is not a natural expression for them.

Kaarlo Sarkia is another present-generation Finnish lyrical poet whose work is widely known. According to the Finnish critic Kauko Kare, Sarkia's "colorful, glowing descriptions, rich, mellow and poetic measure and his youthful worship of beauty, like that of Keats, have carried him to the height of great lyrical poetry." In his last work, *The Scale of Fate*, Sarkia also reveals himself as "a burning ethical, social poet to whom the ideals of peace, humanity and brotherhood have become obligatory."

The generally acknowledged greatest of living Finnish writers is F. E. Sillanpää, who was awarded the Nobel Prize in Literature in 1939. He is the poet of the light-blue summer night, his people are almost physically luminous, those maidens and young farmers who generation after generation have lived the good summer months almost without sleep. Another Finnish writer, Unto Seppänen, describes these same people with deep, glowing humor.

To prevent this from becoming a catalogue of the names and works of Finland's host of able and promising writers, I will close with mention of one present-day Finnish author's name that is well known to the American reading public—that of Mika Waltari. G. P. Putnam's Sons have been the fortunate American publishers of Waltari's last three novels, each of which held a place in all best-seller lists for long periods, with total sales of approximately nearly one half million. Their titles are: *The Egyptian, The Adventurer,* and *The Wanderer.*

The Tilkka Military Hospital, Helsinki. This dramatic building was designed by architect Olavi Sorrka and was built in 1930.

A scene in a Finnish *sauna* or steam bath.

Children's Castle, Helsinki.

An elementary school in the working-class section of Helsinki, named after Aleksis Kivi, the poet.

The Main Building of Helsinki State University on the Great Square.

The School of Forestry, Helsinki State University.

Two views of architect Alvar Aalto's Helsinki Stadium. The 1952 Olympic Games were held here.

Sweden's King Gustavus VI, during a visit to Finland in April, 1952, salutes the impressive cross at Field Marshal Mannerheim's grave. Situated in the center of the military cemetery, the cross honors the tombs of the plain soldiers as well as that of Finland's national hero.

A bust of Jean Sibelius, by the eminent Finnish sculptor Mauno Oittinen.

The Scandinavian Airlines System maintains daily flights between New York and Helsinki.

Finland's Press

The first sentence of Article 10 of Finland's constitution states: "Finnish citizens shall enjoy freedom of speech and the right of printing and publishing written or pictorial representations without any previous authorization." This provision explicitly guarantees freedom to the Finnish press. No restrictive legislation has since been enacted regulating who is permitted to found, own and publish a newspaper.

There was a period when the Russian Empire undertook to muzzle Finland's press, and for a time largely succeeded in doing so. In 1930, members of the Ku Klux Klan-like Lapua movement tried to prevent the publication of periodicals by its opponents. On July 1, 1930, Premier Kyösti Kallio on his own responsibility ordered the suppression of all Communist newspapers, and on July 2nd asked the Diet to authorize his action. He resigned when it failed to do so.

Aside from these two instances, the press of Finland has, in most respects, been as free legally as the American press to print what it wishes.

There are five Communist-edited newspapers in Finland. Except for these, the editors of the preponderant majority of Finnish papers accept government suggestions concerning international affairs on what is best to print for the good of the nation as a whole. Their editors keep in close touch with national policy and well-being and are somewhat governed in what they publish by official suggestions. This applies particularly to relations with Russia because of Russia's inferiority complex, which some Russians have admitted has every possible reason to exist.

Although until recently, except for morality, honesty, courage and industry, Finland has trailed behind civilized progress, her people in many areas of human activity have kept abreast of the times. This applies to the publication of newspapers. Their first one was founded in 1771 in Turku. America had few newspapers at that time.

Finns today are as avid newspaper readers as their American friends. This is shown by the fact that Finland's 120 newspapers have a combined circulation of 1,600,000. Since there are only 4,000,000 Finns, this means that nearly one out of every two people in Finland—this includes children—is a newspaper subscriber.

Even to those who are unable to read Finnish, the general appearance of Finland's newspapers shows that Finland is a paper-producing country. Compared with many European newspapers the Finnish small town *Sanomat* is well printed and illustrated and often carries pictures from the United States. It contains six or eight pages even on weekdays. The smallest papers nowadays have at least two or three American comic series, and the heroes with Finnish names—Jiggs is "*Vihtori*," Mickey Mouse "*Mikki-hiiri*" in Finland—are as beloved in Finland as elsewhere in the Western World.

Chapter fourteen

Art, Architecture and Sculpture

Finland's fine and applied arts contributions are distinctive partly as a result of the innate good taste of the people, partly because of their love for beauties of nature and partly from their aspiration for human well-being. Their artistic creations have a bold, strong quality that is tempered with beauty. Their pictorial art has a medieval tradition of unpretentious sorts and a national character which had its revival in the early part of the nineteenth century. Their present-day art did not begin to make virile progress until after 1870, when Finnish art students began going to Paris for study.

Young Albert Edelfelt (1854–1905) was the forerunner of the group. Edelfelt continues to stand as the great background personality of Finland's modern art. The trend toward realism at that time touched him but it failed to detract from the atmosphere of intrinsically classical idealism of his work. This was fortunate in that it gave a certain nobility and refined dignity to his portrayals of national characteristics.

A younger compatriot of Edelfelt's, A. Gallen-Kallela (1865–1931), is revered by Finns of today as the great spirit of the national trend in art. Gallen-Kallela followed Edelfelt to Paris where in addition to his art studies he developed his growing interest, of which he was a product, in the complex new forces that were then moving in the world. His highest goal became that of portraying the national characteristics and original beauty which he sought among the people, from nature and finally from the imaginary of the national epic, *Kalevala*. In addition to attaining a position as one of the greatest fresco painters in the history of modern art, Gallen-Kallela was and still is "a powerful source of inspiration to his surroundings."

Finland made her greatest progress in pictorial art under the inspiration and guidance of these two men in the two decades which followed 1890. The Finnish art movement, coming as it did during a period of fierce oppression by Russia, naturally became a part of the growing spirit of nationalism. Younger Finnish artists were inspired to interpret the inner character and the benevolent dignity of their peasant subjects.

Finnish art in the decades following 1910 became marked by a trend towards greater expression in feeling and color as well as in a more constructive application of form. While color art, which carries evidence of French influence, continues to be popular with Finland's artists, it has gained few adherents there of cubism, new realism or surrealism. Finnish painters, true to their national characteristics, continue to strive to attain professional skill and unaffected direct expression of what they see with both their physical and minds' eyes. An increasing number of Finns are becoming painters and some of them have achieved international distinction.

Interest in sculpture began to be manifested in Finland about the same time that interest in pictorial art became evident, seventy-five years ago. These two movements were an indirect outgrowth of the Literary Study Circle which had helped to stimulate Runeberg, Lönnrot, and others of the group who brought the Finnish nationalist movement into existence. Those early interpreters of Finnish life, qualities and characteristics of the Finns lifted the eyes of everyone above the routine round of births, marriages and deaths, and gave Finns a new and fresh conception of those inner qualities which give life a purpose and explain its highest meaning. When Finnish eyes caught the beauties and the strength that existed on this higher plateau they saw a whole new world opened up, one of purpose and meaning which had many inspiring facets: music, poetry, painting, sculpture and a host of other mediums by which man expresses, portrays or interprets his aspirations and hopes.

This period was truly the one in which Finland's soul awakened, and once awakened, the Finns, true to character, undertook to do everything they could to make the most of their new understanding and vision. Runeberg, Lönnrot, Edelfelt, Gallen-Kallela and a host of others soon began to use their talents in their efforts to express or portray the beauty, strength and quality of Finnish life. Because they were honest workmen who treated basic, universal and timeless subjects, the product of their efforts had great significance.

Sculpture came to Finland about 1870. One of the first Finns who achieved distinction in this form of art was Ville Vallgren (1855–1940). It has been authoritatively stated that his masterly execution of small statuettes and other art objects gave him world renown. This new expression drew its inspiration from natural motifs.

Professor Onni Okkonen of Helsinki University believes that Wäinö Aaltonen (b. 1894) is the greatest of Finland's skillful sculptors, not only in the history of Finnish sculpture but also that of Europe in recent times. His art is unique in its personal character, according to Dr. Okkonen, and it is "intensely strict in its monumental force, and possesses a graceful vitality. Its racial characteristics are clearly evinced." Aaltonen has completed "an imposing series of monumental and intimate works in hard Finnish granite, marble, bronze and ceramic materials." In a factory town like Tampere the central bridge over the rapids is adorned by four large Aaltonen figures which give a new beauty to the whole town. The Finnish parliament members also sit under Aaltonen statues in their great modern congress room.

Sweden has gained a great sculptor, Jussi Mäntynen, from Finland by offering him silver as material for his wild animal groups. But Finland has a young generation of sculptors coming up, and at least two of them, Kalervo Kallio and Mauno Oittinen, have recently gained a high reputation in the United States by the portraits they have executed here.

The decorative arts, textiles, ceramics and modern glass are high on the list of creative achievements in Finland. Contributions of textile artists, such as Laila Karttunen, Dora Jung and Eva Anttila have become known outside Finland.

Ceramics and the Arabia factory must be mentioned, since the group of artists working with Arabia has produced some of the highest quality, most artistic creations in their field. Their designs have exerted considerable influence in the ceramic art world. Young men like Kaipainen and Schilkin now are heralds of a wholly new school of color and form in this old art.

Beautiful and practical wooden furniture is part of the tradition-bound peasant culture of Finland. On this sure ground the Finnish home decorators have built a modern type of furniture. Aided by technical advances in plywood manufacture they have developed designs which the continental and British art centers have accepted. The most modern Finnish furniture is designed by the genius Alvar Aalto, whose work in this field we will include in the discussion of his architecture at the end of this chapter.

Second only to the music of Sibelius in bringing Finland acclaim for creative work in the field of art is that of her architects. Sibelius' majestic compositions have given peace and inspiration to countless millions of men and women and brought to being the latent musical talents of some of his fellow countrymen. This service of inspiring and stimulating other men to improve their talents and realize their potentials is one of the most important contributions that men of genius can make. It frequently is more important than their own creative works in that it helps convince aspiring men of the truth of the statement, "What man has done, man can do."

History is replete with illustrations of this nature. Contributions of the Finnish architects E. Saarinen and Alvar Aalto are a case in point. Their styles, forms and techniques have revolutionized Finnish architecture and—of greater significance—have influenced architectural design throughout the world.

Finland's historic architecture was characterized by artistic restraint, simplicity, dignity. Until about the middle of the nineteenth century, which in Finland could be called the Great Awakening, her architects still clung to the classical ideal but were beginning to make less and less use of its false, redundant forms.

One of the greatest Finnish figures in this period of dawning rationalism was Eliel Saarinen. About 1900, he and his colleagues created the new Finnish school of rational architecture. They soon discarded the romantic ideals of their youth and showed a tendency toward more severe treatment that aimed at a balanced composition of form. The principles they formulated in their efforts to define architectural truth led to the emergence of functionalism. They sought to create new forms that were better suited to modern materials and constructional methods which were not straight-jacketed by tradition. The homes, schools, hospitals and industrial buildings they designed were made to suit the purpose for which they were to be used. They retained beauty in their design but made it depend upon rational use and modern construction methods rather than upon superimposed decorations. They largely avoided exaggeration. The modernity of the design of their buildings is composed and conscious in style. Saarinen's town hall in Lahti and the impressively beautiful and useful railway station in Helsinki are excellent examples of his work.

Great as was Saarinen, Alvar Aalto is to Finnish architecture what Sibelius is to its music and Mannerheim was to its arms and statecraft.

Aalto is Finland, and he is also universal. Wherever he goes he absorbs like a sponge everything available that will contribute to his artistic development. Aalto's active professional life coincides with the greatest period of agitation in Finland's history—liberation, independence, a brief period of peaceful freedom and then wars. War's waste and destruction left little money for rebuilding. Simple designs which used the smallest possible amount of available building material had to be created. Wood is Finland's chief crop and Aalto, who grew up in a family of foresters who loved wood and understood its uses, was inspired to find ways to make more flexible the use of wood in constructions and decorations. His efforts to imbue things with an almost organic flexibility has its source from the nature of his country. He uses this talent to create designs for ceilings and partitions and walls, then he attacks the outer walls. The dormitory he designed for the Massachusetts Institute of Technology in 1947 is a striking example of his abilities.

A description of this dormitory and its setting by Sigfried Giedion states that Aalto employed all means in his efforts to avoid the ant-heap atmosphere often emanated by such buildings. Aalto gives the individual his personal rights through a great variety of means such as the way he arranged the staircases by the blending of spaces, by alternating the capacity, form and arrangement of bedrooms. He dared to free the façade in an undulating wall so that every student has a free view of the Charles River without being made aware of the large expanse of the building.

Mr. Giedion quotes some first impressions from a letter of an English observer:

It is itself so full of life that it literally makes one feel oneself more consciously alive. The great curving walls are made of small bricks and these too he brings to life. A small brick can go this way or that way, or it can be laid very smoothly as though it were poured concrete. It has variety in colour and also, within the limits of its function, in size and shape.

Then the great curve is no sudden anachronism . . . just down the road is a row of rippling Boston bay windows and Aalto has kept the same semicircular curve, only projecting it into the twentieth century. Perhaps the three most exciting aspects of the building to me were the half-glimpsed end view where the windows, projecting as a series of buttresses, form a wonderfully rich linen panelling in the foreshortened view; then, the great main entrance (past a Maillart support) when one sees immediately, transparently, through the whole building: through to the great playing fields to the right, to the sweep of the river in front, the curve of the interior space and the (future!) hubbub and life of the students. . . . The third is the view from the great hall to the dining room below, where space flows up and through and around, and one realizes that life really can be like this: whole.[2]

Aalto has exerted a marked influence on world architectural design, use of materials and institutional settings, despite the fact the greater majority of his buildings are in his homeland. Among them are sanatoriums, office and public buildings, but the majority of them are industrial plants which include both buildings and resettlement of entire industrial areas. It has been written of him that "he knows how to raise a plant from a purely professional instrument up to a piece of architecture in which the site, the use of different materials, and the organization of volumes in space are given as much attention as the production line."

While Aalto ranks high among the world's contemporary architects and community planners, he also used his genius in furniture designing. Furniture manufactured from Aalto's designs today has become one of Finland's most distinctive products in that he uses wood which he has made flexible. Aalto knows wood through and through. His latest major accomplishment has been the development of a suction process for treating wood by which it is made so supple and flexible that it may be twisted or turned with ease. Chemists have made this new process practical by discovering methods to form a cablelike structure from a number of small rodlike pieces of wood that are tapered at both ends. Aalto calls the new creation "woodmacaroni." It opens up a great field of possibilities for the use of wood in making furniture as well as other products.

[2] Sigfried Giedion, *Space, Time and Architecture* (Cambridge, Harvard University Press, 1941).

Chapter fifteen

Social Welfare and Sports

The democratic people of Finland who believe in the principle that all men are created free and equal have abolished hereditary and established equal rights for every citizen. Finland has no hard, stratified class lines such as exist in many European countries, serving to keep the individual in the classification of society or calling into which he was born. As in America a man's place in society is fixed by his character, ability and attainments.

In democratic countries such as Finland and the United States, the welfare of the individual is of paramount importance. Finland's laws are designed to serve and protect the individual. Finland was one of the first countries in the world to adopt an eight-hour-day law, paid holidays, accident insurance, old-age pensions and strict provisions concerning the employment of women and minors in industry. At the present time, due in part to her limited financial means, the Government of Finland's social welfare activities largely center on resettlement of war-displaced citizens, care and training of war widows, orphans and disabled ex-servicement, child allowances, maternity grants-in-aid, vocational training, poor aid, public health, social insurance, labor protection and housing.

During 1949, the Government of Finland, the communes (local governments), employers and private agencies, expended slightly more than $120,000,000 on these and other social welfare activities. This sum represents an expenditure of an average of $30.00 for human care and betterment by each man, woman and child in Finland.

Child allowances is the largest item in Finland's social welfare budget. This item is followed respectively by social insurance costs, loans to promote dwellinghouse construction, family allowances, vocational training and maternity benefits.

Finland's wars, between 1939 and 1945, with the Soviet Union and Germany, greatly increased the scope and size of her social welfare work. This new and increased burden was placed on her during the period when her economy and productive capacity were at their lowest ebb.

One of Finland's major tasks after the cessation of hostilities in 1945 has been feeding and caring for—and finding work and building homes for—425,301 evacuees from the areas which the Soviet Union wrung from Finland.

The Soviet government agreed to permit the Finns to remain in their old homes if they would become citizens of Soviet Russia. Nineteen Finns accepted this offer and 425,282 refused it. The Finnish government faced a gigantic task of finding new homes for its displaced citizens since they equaled approximately 10 per cent of Finland's entire population.

No war-devastated nation, when percentage of the involved population and available land and financial resources are considered, had as stupendously great or more difficult a resettlement program to carry out. That of itself is important to remember. What is more important is that Finland is the only stricken nation to complete the job, down to the last family.

Taking first things first, the government undertook to provide food and shelter for the evacuees, the great majority of whom came from Karelia. Rationing and increased food imports at that time supplied all Finns with what was barely a subsistence diet. Shelter was found by enlisting every Finnish owner of a home with less than two persons per room to allot one or more rooms to displaced families. An expanding industrial program, which was necessary to meet Soviet reparation demands and increase the production of materials for free export to provide Finland with foreign currency, helped to absorb the industrial workers. Extensive legislation was enacted to provide land for the farmer evacuees who totaled about 55 per cent of Finland's displaced citizens. This program of resettlement was completed by July, 1950. New fabricated houses have also been built for industrial workers thus completing the resettlement task. At one time Finland had 245,000 displaced persons who were dependent on relief in the form of daily allowances. In September, 1948, this number had shrunk to 12,058.

At the end of 1945, Finland had 24,000 war widows and 50,000 war orphans under seventeen years of age. The great majority of orphaned children were under school age. In 1947, more than 10,000 of her 50,000 disabled ex-servicemen were still suffering from a 50 per cent or greater disability.

The Finnish Law, which pertains to social welfare in the widest sense of the term, comprises three different legislative groups: ordinary social welfare, social insurance and public assistance.

Finland's aid-for-poor legislation makes it unnecessary as well as unlawful to beg in that it requires local government authorities to provide a living and care for the destitute, for minors without supporters and for all other individuals who either are unable to care for themselves or are not cared for by others. This legislation goes even further in that it provides the recipient with aid that will enable him to become self-supporting. Finland's poor aid is handled chiefly by the local communes, which provide nearly all of the funds. This procedure helps to hold waste to the minimum, prevents the padding of relief rolls for political favor and tends to help the shiftless, lazy or shameless from becoming an unnecessary burden to the public treasury as has become the shameful case in America. Finland's poor legislation also provides that, within certain limits, the communes are entitled to claim partial compensation from either the recipient or from such of his nearest relatives as can give it. The state, in some instances, repays the communes for a part of their poor aid expenditures. The state also provides, through annual Diet appropriations, direct responsibility for certain poor aid expenditures of a preventive character, especially for disabled persons.

The chief aim of Finland's child welfare laws is to provide care for those of her children and young people who, without such aid, would not receive proper upbringing and thereby be more susceptible to moral corruption. The Finns center their child welfare activities on the theory that children should be brought up in the atmosphere of the home. If the parents fail to co-operate, which seldom is the case, the state places the children in one of its institutions. The child welfare act provisions include regulations which forbid the employment of children and young people in unsuitable work. The Act's provisions pay special attention to the conduct and operation of child institutions.

The author visited one of these state-aided institutions in 1946, at Kannaksen Ammattikoulut—not far from Helsinki. The institution's former home in Karelia had been destroyed by the Russians. In a description of it I wrote:

The new school had been built, under the guidance and with the help of two or three men, by fifty as fine-looking sixteen-year-old boys as anyone has ever seen. The government gave the school a ninety-seven-acre farm on which fifty sons of veterans and war evacuees are beginning two- to three-year courses in agriculture, blacksmithing and carpentry. This fall the number of students will be increased to seventy.

Private and state funds support the school, the cost per year per student—they raise most of their own food—is about $200. The headmaster told us that the families of these boys had lost everything but their courage, and that with this they were building anew in the hope that all of the boys would become good, useful Finnish citizens. . . .[1]

[1] *An Experiment in Friendship* (New York, G. P. Putnam's Sons, 1947), p. 136.

The memory of those fifty boys, intelligent, healthy, as their sun-tanned and bright faces reflected their depth of feeling while they sang "Finlandia" for us with beautiful voices, continues to be heart stirring and inspiring. They personified the courage and purpose of Finland, the aspiration and the life of their land which are the hall marks of the Finns as well as of the recognized and the obscurely great of the world.

One of the unique phases of Finland's poor laws—the country is unique in so many admirable ways—is that they do not classify vagrancy as a criminal offense. The legal consequences of vagrancy deal not with acts or offenses committed but instead with the way of life of the individual concerned. No one under Finnish law may be classified as a vagrant without the facts having been established that a way of life characteristic of vagrancy has become habitual with him. The categories to which vagrancy measures are applied include tramps, persons who shirk work, beggars and prostitutes. When a vagrancy charge has been established against an individual, the state institutes welfare measures which are aimed at reforming him as well as safeguarding society from the detrimental effects of vagrancy. In 1946, Finland confined only forty vagrants in workhouses.

Welfare work designed to improve the situation of individuals in need has long been in operation in Finland. It has its genesis in the co-operative, humane and helpful spirit of her people. The church had carried on many welfare activities before Finland became a part of Russia in 1809, but Finland's first real poor legislation was promulgated in a government decree issued in 1852, which related to the joint guardianship of destitute persons in the grand duchy. It entitled every needy parish member lacking means of livelihood to have his living provided by poor aid, but if he were able-bodied, he must work to earn what was given him. Under the terms of the poor aid act of 1922, the local government authorities are held responsible for support and care of the destitute, minors without legal providers, as well as all other persons who are unable to maintain themselves out of their own means or their work or who are not cared for by others.

Above all the Act provides that aid must be given in a form that will enable the recipient, if capable of working, to provide for his own needs. Communes are required to possess a communal home in which due regard must be paid to the inmate's age, habits, stage of moral—how frequently the word *moral* and all that it connotes appears in the individual and governmental life of Finland—development and manner of life.

The 1922 Act provides, for example, that a child over two years of age may be placed in a communal home only on a temporary basis while a more suitable place is being sought.

Sick persons are to be provided with medical and also hospital care if needed. The commune is required to establish work centers in which work is provided for all men who are under obligation to repay with labor the poor aid that has been given their wives and children.

Finland's labor laws are on a par with international conventions concerning working conditions, but she has no compulsory sickness insurance law. The worker, however, is entitled to full wages provided his sickness is not of long duration.

Because the larger part of Finland's industries are situated in parts of the countryside which were uninhabited, the enterprises found it necessary not only to provide homes for these workers but to shoulder other social responsibilities that usually are the responsibility of local authorities. They, therefore, have assumed voluntary welfare responsibilities. One of these was either to build or finance homes for their workers. A 1948 survey of 462 industrial plants showed that 25 per cent of their workmen lived in company-owned houses and 181,730 persons (including families) lived in their own homes, a great percentage of these financed by companies.

The companies provide medical care, including doctors and nurses, clubhouses, libraries, assembly rooms and sports grounds for their workers, and day nurseries for the children of their women workers. The day nursery maintained by the Arabia Company in Helsinki is a model of its kind.

The distinctive qualities of Finland's welfare activities are (a) its humanity—the Finns strive to provide food, shelter and care for every needy citizen, (b) its concern for the moral as well as the physical wants of the needy and (c) its insistence that the needy individual, whatever the cause of his need, shall be given training such as will enable him to become a producer, not a drag on society.

It is evident both from the specifications contained in their social welfare legislation as well as by how they implement it with what they do that the Finns act in the belief that no chain can be stronger than its weakest link. The source of their sense of national respect, which has won international respect, is the individual self-respect of the individual citizen. They seem to realize that when enough individuals lose enough of their own self-respect they will taint the spring which feeds the national sense of self-respect. When self-respect—God's most precious gift to man—goes, all else that is worth while in helping to set and keep man on a plane above the animals of the field will soon disappear. To Finns the attainment of the good life is a hard struggle which can be lost if too many members of society weaken in their purpose. Can it be that Finland's strength has been developed to the point it has by helping and encouraging every citizen to carry his own load and a little more?

Is such a purpose and a policy worth while?

It is not worth while to those individuals who believe that civilization is headed for hell in a handbasket. It is worth while to every individual who believes in God's enduring purpose for man—whom He made in His own image.

The Finns are a sports-conscious, and particularly an out-doors sports-conscious, people. Their language, for example, contains at least twenty words which express the action of running. Every eighth person in Finland, meaning 500,000 people, is a member of a sports or athletic club, and Finland has more than 500 competition grounds.

It is possible that the Finns owe much of their proficiency in outdoor sports to the fact that as soon as a child there can toddle it learns to ski. Entirely apart from its being an exhilarating sport, skiing is an important ever-necessary means of getting from one place to another during the deep snow period of winter.

Unlike that of Latin people, who have a compelling fascination for sports contests which entail bloodshed and death, such as cockfighting and bullfighting, Finland, except in a few sports, does not have the American concept of sport as exemplified by football, in which skill and body contacts are enlisted. The Finns' sports interest centers in contests in which skill and stamina are all important. This is borne out by their amazing Olympic record. In the 1951–52 Oslo winter Olympics they won several prizes while previous to the 1952 Olympic Games, Finland's athletes had won 80 Olympic Gold Medals, 172 Silver Medals and 76 Bronze Medals. Their successes have been confined to a relatively small field: long distance running, javelin throwing, gymnastics, skiing, skating and wrestling. This group includes only one sport, wrestling, where human body contests with human body.

Since this book is being written before the Olympic Games are held in Helsinki in July and August of 1952, it is impossible to predict how many Olympic winners she will have produced by the end of the year. It is probable that Finland's records of wins will not be greatly increased, since fourteen of her best athletes, all of whom placed first or lower in previous world contests, were killed by the Russians in the Winter War of 1939–40 alone, and it will take another few years to develop a new group of top Finnish athletes. Perhaps it would be better not to make predictions about how well the unpredictable Finns will do.

Had Russia held off her attack of Finland another year, it is possible that Finland's skilled athletes would have increased the number of victories in the Olympic contests, scheduled to be held in Helsinki in the summer of 1940 but postponed by the war until 1952.

Other reasons why the Finns do not indulge in a wider variety of sports are unfavorable climatic conditions, limited population and limited economic resources. Just as they have made courage and honesty driving forces, so they have overcome the restrictions of climate, small numbers and slight means with a concentration and driving force which has brought their athletes victories in competition with the world's best athletes.

One other determining factor in their selection of sports for competitive purposes is that throughout their history the Finns have been interested in sports that require force and stamina.

The hold that sports contests have on the Finns is revealed in the walking match between Sweden and Finland in 1941. This event was open to the entire populations of the two countries. Finland's 1,507,181 entrants completed the march whereas Sweden, with double the population of Finland, was unable to get as many as one million entrants. Finland's oldest entrant was ninety-four years old. But of the names of all Finland's world champions, that of Paavo Nurmi is best known. Sibelius, Mannerheim, Nurmi and Aalto—all Finns to the core—are the Finnish trademarks the world knows best.

Chapter sixteen

Finland's Hospitals

The people of Finland have many commendable qualities, among which is mercy. It stands high in the list. They have made it a reality in the way they care for the poor in body through their public health service, their many fine hospitals and the excellence of their doctors and nurses.

Unlike the first American hospitals, which were started and operated by groups of private citizens who banded together to work for the common good, the Finns have followed America's later procedure of placing a considerable part of hospital construction and operation cost on the government. In both countries, however, doctor groups and private philanthropy continue to participate in the cost and direction of hospital work.

Populationwise, Finland has a larger number of first-class hospitals than any other country, with the possible exception of Sweden. Finland's general and specialized hospitals can compare favorably with the best hospitals of their kind in the United States. The number of them and their high standards serve to emphasize three significant qualities of the Finnish people, namely:

1. The ever-menacing Soviet Russian threat to Finland's continued existence as an independent nation does not deter Finns from giving expression, through their hospitals, to their conviction that their nation and civilization will live forever.

2. Finland's hospitals, in structure, arrangement and equip-

ment serve to highlight the striking organizational, aesthetic and practical activities of her people.

3. The effort and expense which the Finnish government and its people expend in the care of their sick and wounded demonstrate that Macaulay, if he were alive today, could not find in Finland what he once described as "the most frightful of all spectacles, the strength of civilization without its mercy."

Finland bases her organization of health protection and medical care on a close co-operation of state and municipal authorities and voluntary associations. Her modern medical care is mostly a large-scale operation; thus, in instances where municipalities are small, a group of them or the state arranges the most economical and efficient hospital and other units. The final results, however, depend always on individual effort based on co-operation. The Finns have thus found that a small commune is the best organizing unit in that everyone feels he has some direct influence on the health of his community. The Finns, who always have been clean, are now also health-minded. The end result is that they have done some exceptionally fine work in their hospitals, which they call "health houses."

The Finns have conquered their worst national disease, tuberculosis. This plague, due to their cold climate, was especially prevalent during the war when they had neither adequate clothing nor food, plus the forced large-scale displacements of the population, spread at a terrifying pace.

Fortunately, in the 1930's Finland had already started her tuberculosis sanatorium program by the enactment of a law which required every commune to provide as many beds in a central sanatorium as the number of annual deaths from tuberculosis in their area. This administrative provision made it economically advantageous for the communes to fight T.B. in their areas. The happy result was that the sanatoriums in the communes now own about two times the number of beds than the minimum originally specified. The Finnish sanatoriums—as well as mental hospitals which have been built by commune federations on the same basis—are nearly all large, modern institutions. One of the most beautiful of them, the one near Turku, was designed by Finland's architectural genius, Alvar Aalto.

The Finns also used general BCG vaccinations, compulsory mass X-ray examinations and the new biochemical medicines. The success of their effort shows what can be done in a few years with a well-organized campaign in which an entire nation participates.

The Finns have tackled their other war-caused medical problems with the same characteristic *sisu*. One of the largest of these was the rehabilitation of fifty thousand or more disabled veterans, supplying them with artificial arms and legs and educating them for new vocations. They built permanent institutions for these purposes, and with their primary task completed are now able to care for their crippled children as effectively as does any other nation in the world. There is no more moving sight than that of seeing crippled children and veterans together, busily preparing themselves to live again with the light of hope in their eyes at an institution such as Invalidisaatio in Helsinki.

One other group of diseases for which the Finnish climate is responsible are rheumatic ills. The Finns have built a large special hospital for their care at an old spa at Heinola. Its upkeep is provided for by contributed funds. It is a characteristic of the people of this small and poor country that when the state or municipal funds are lacking, they do not ask taxpayers to pay more taxes but instead support with voluntary contributions the causes they themselves believe useful and necessary. Finland acquired a "radium home" to aid in the medical care of cancer patients in this way and a small group headed by an extremely able and energetic lady M.D., Dr. Eriksson-Lihr, is now engaged in building a modern institute for allergy treatment, the only one of its kind in the world. Dr. Eriksson-Lihr and her colleagues have made some important discoveries about the causes and treatment of allergies.

Finland's most ambitious development in the hospital field

is that of a new group of University clinics in Helsinki, located in a wooded area two miles from the center of the city. Recently, in its effort to picture an ideal city in which to live, a large British magazine selected the best features of every metropolis in the world. For the clinics' part of its ideal city, it selected Helsinki. Helsinki's clinic area already had a children's hospital which is visited by hospital builders from every part of the world, maternity wards where many babies are born every day, eye-and-ear clinics and a nursing school. Today the Finns are preparaing for the completion of an eighteen-story general hospital.

Characteristically enough, across the street from the University children's hospital the Finns have built a voluntary institution called not very appropriately "The Children's Castle." This fine institution cares for children not actually ill but in need of medical care for some reason or other. Another of its purposes is that of training young women to be child nurses. Both the University hospital and the private educational institute are headed by a famous Finnish pediatrician, Dr. Arvo Ylppo, who is well known in the United States.

Under the combined efforts of the voluntary and municipal organizations almost every commune in Finland now has a "health house," 650 of them altogether. A public health nurse inspects the babies of the community there at least once a week, and spends the remainder of her time traveling in the community. Midwives receive expectant mothers at these commune health homes at least fortnightly to educate them for the coming events, and a doctor visits each center at least once each month even in the remotest communes to care for the medical needs of patients.

While the cost of their health program is great, Finnish communities and the people consider the investment well worth what it costs. Since much of Finland's health protection work is done by voluntary workers, the actual cost in rural communities is about two and a half dollars per person annually, or about

6 or 7 per cent of all municipal expenses. Since 1950, the province of Uusimaa with the exception of the capital Helsinki, which is located in the area, has been under development for purposes of a health demonstration and education area. This project is being supported until the end of 1953 by the Rockefeller Foundation.

Finland's vital statistics already indicate the great good that can be gained by a whole country with the help of an efficient health protection program. It indicates also that the strength of Finland's civilization goes hand in hand with mercy.

Chapter seventeen

War and Disaster

The free world can well examine and ponder over the moves Soviet Russia made to intimidate Finland and, failing that, to crush her.

Communist leaders, with their conception of and fiery zeal for the creation of a world-wide mechanistic society which excludes God, the moral law and man's spiritual purpose, can and do justify what they did. This is possible because to them there is nothing wrong in making virtue out of duplicity, threats, false accusations, broken treaties and ruthless acts, provided these are employed in advancing their great cause in which they have unshakable faith.

The free peoples of the world who believe in a Supreme Being, try to follow the moral law and hold an abiding faith in man's spiritual purpose are profoundly disturbed by the things Communists do that are at such complete variance with every article of their faith.

To the Communists truth, except as they interpret it, has only one facet. It is not eternal. Truth is reflected to them in the facet of it that they see at the moment; therefore, right to them can be whatever they want. It never is an abstract principle.

The inevitable result that flows from their belief and outlook constitutes a case history of their relations with a given country —Finland, for example. It reveals no trace of honesty, fairness, justice or consideration of the rights of other peoples.

Soviet Russia's Finnish record from 1939 to 1945 is replete with dishonest and unjust accusations against honest and just Finns. The Communists shouted to the world their charges that the Finns were guilty of criminal acts, whereas it was the Communists who were the criminals.

The incontrovertible evidence of Soviet Russia's Finnish record carries a fateful warning to the people of other nations who may be inclined to believe in the good faith of Communist fair words without searching for their well-concealed motives; who accept Communist charges of bad faith at face value and fail to recognize their endless record of bad-faith dealing, or who are inclined to believe the Communists have some basis for their reiterated charge on every occasion when their sins are pointed out as "Lies! Lies! Lies!"

A study of Finnish-Russian relations between 1809 and 1938 reveals, except for the final period when Finland was an autonomous part of the Russian Empire, that the relations between the great and small power were friendly. This friendly relationship ceased to exist at the turn of the century and was not revived until after Finland had established her independence.

The following skeletal outline presents the highlights of Finland's foreign policy and her relationship with Soviet Russia between the time she became an independent nation and the Soviet's undeclared war against her in November, 1939.

It is necessary here, because of later complications, to add as background information the fact that some of the old Finland-German ties, religious, cultural and commercial, were still in existence. The Finns had continued to remember with gratitude Germany's military help when, in 1918, her White Guard was fighting Russian Communists and Russian troops who had remained in Finland despite Russia's recognition of Finland's independence. Germany's collapse in November, 1918, however, had carried with it the end of Finland's pro-German orientation.

Finland's next problem was: What was to be her relationship

with the Soviet government system? One alternative was that
of co-operation with the White Russian forces. This Finland
did not do since it would have meant her interference in Russia's internal affairs. That decision marked the beginning of
Finland's new policy. It was neutrality. Finland declined to join
France's sponsored *cordon sanitaire*, whose object was that of
blocking Russia off from the rest of Europe.

During the 1922–39 period Finland looked hopefully to the
League of Nations, of which she had become a member. A
direct result of her League membership was that Finland adhered more closely than before to her policy of neutrality. She
refused to join any bloc or group of major powers.

When the League of Nations proved powerless to check Germany's, Italy's, and Japan's policies of aggression it became evident that the League's economic sanctions, when not backed
by military force, could entangle small nations in distressing
situations. Finland, still adhering to her policy of strict neutrality, sought contacts at the end of 1935 with the Oslo group
and helped to form the Scandinavian neutrality bloc.

Despite Finland's policy of strict neutrality she was unable,
because of the Soviet Union's suspicious and two-faced policies,
to establish good relations with Russia. In 1927, the Soviets
refused to sign a nonaggression pact with her because Finland
insisted upon including arbitration procedures for settling disputes. In the meantime, the Soviets, through the Comintern,
continued to interfere in Finland's internal affairs. Finland did
everything she could to establish good relations with the only
nation that was capable of threatening her security. The Soviet
government did get around in 1932 to signing a nonaggression
pact with Finland, and in 1934, renewed it for ten years. The
renewed pact had five more years to run, when in 1939, Russia
attacked Finland without a declaration of war.

On November 2, 1936, the Commissar of Leningrad, A. A.
Zhdanov said in a speech:

We people of Leningrad sit at our windows, looking out at the
world. Right around us lie small countries who dream of great
adventures or permit great adventures to scheme within their borders. We are not afraid of these small nations . . . we may feel forced
to open our windows a bit wider . . . call upon our Red Army
to defend our country.

The Scandinavian states made a joint statement on May 27,
1938, which called on the great powers to refrain from using
force to settle their differences and urged them instead to use
arbitration. At that time, Finland's relations with all the western
European nations were good with the exception of Germany.

Her relations with Soviet Russia had been worsening during
this period. In 1938–39, Russia arbitrarily closed Finnish con-
sulates in the Soviet Union and, in violation of the Dorpat
Treaty, ended Finnish traffic rights on the Neva River. In the
spring of 1938, the Soviet government sent a special emissary,
Yartsev, to Finland to point out secretly that if a German force
landed in Finland for the purpose of attacking Russia, the latter
would fight them on Finnish soil. The Soviet, therefore, demanded the right to aid Finland. The Finns stated that they
would defend their own neutrality. It is possible they have the
gift of second sight, and having it, they realized that once Soviet
troops were allowed by treaty to enter Finland the treaty would
be forgotten, but the Russian troops would remain.

Yartsev continued to insist that Finland accept Soviet aid.
Once, during the discussion, Yartsev threatened Finland with
aggressive measures. The Russian Bear began to show its teeth.
This presaged war.

Shortly after Soviet Russia and Germany had signed the
Molotov-Ribbentrop nonaggression and arbitration pact on August 23, 1939—one of history's most insincere and futile agreements—the two brigands dismembered Poland. The ominousness
of what had happened and was going to happen escaped the

Finns. Ribbentrop later admitted that in this pact Germany had assigned Finland to the "Russian sphere of influence."

The German-Soviet plot began to unfold when, on September 18, 1939, Stalin summoned one by one to his presence, by invitation tantamount to a command, the foreign ministers of the little Baltic states of Estonia, Latvia and Lithuania. When they were in his presence he used a combination of honeyed words and wrist twisting to secure Soviet Russia's right to establish air and naval bases on their soil. Could it be that he realized that Hitler's word was as worthless as his own?

Finland's turn came on October 5th, when the Soviet government "suggested" that it send a representative to Moscow as soon as possible since "with the change of the international situation caused by war, the Soviet government now desires an exchange of ideas with the Finnish government regarding certain concrete political proposals." When the Finns did not jump at this crack of the Soviet whip, Molotov, two days later, urged speed. Finland sent as her emissary Juho Kusti Paasikivi, now President of Finland. His instructions were to stress the fact that Russo-Finnish relations had been regularized by the 1920 Dorpat peace treaty and, further, that Finland's Scandinavian orientation gave assurance of her desire for peace and her unqualified determination to remain outside all conflicts.

Moscow proposed a mutual aid pact and territorial concessions at the first meeting with Paasikivi. It was at the second meeting, however, that Molotov began to pull face cards out of his sleeve. Russia demanded, he said, for the security of Leningrad, that Finland close the Gulf of Finland. Finland, he added further, should give guarantees that she would give Soviet Russia a year's lease to certain harbors, a bay for anchorage of the Russian navy and certain islands on the Gulf of Finland; shrink Finland's Karelian isthmus territory north and northwest into Finland; give up the Shredin peninsula in Petsamo; and refrain from joining nations or alliances that were inimical to Soviet

Russia. Molotov insisted that Finland make more land concessions as aids to Soviet Russian security.

Russia refused to discuss the statement of Finnish military experts that no great power could invade Russia by way of Finland.

Paasikivi returned to Helsinki to report and get further instructions. He was delayed there by the absence of President Kallio and Foreign Minister Erkko, who were holding conferences with the Scandinavian countries' chiefs of state in Stockholm. Here Erkko was given to understand that in case of conflict Finland could count on no aid from Scandinavia.

At Paasikivi's insistence the chief of the Social Democratic party, Vaino Tanner, accompanied him to Moscow for the next meeting with Molotov, which was held on October 23rd. In their efforts to maintain peace and good will with Soviet Russia the Finnish representatives made concessions to Russia which their government considered far-reaching. She rejected some of Soviet Russia's proposals as prejudicial to Finnish neutrality but expressed a willingness to amplify the nonaggression pact by having both parties bind themselves not to aid any countries that had undertaken an attack on the other.

Stalin replied that Finland offered too little and that the Soviet's demands were so minimal that they were not worth bargaining about, "since someone might attack Leningrad." Like the little girl who, when her mother urged her to eat the crust of her bread, saying, "There are hundreds of little girls who would like to have it," countered, "Name one," the Finns asked who might make this attack: France, England, or Germany? But the Communists would not discuss the point.

The Finns next called attention to the Dorpat Treaty and its nonaggression pact which still was in effect. The Communist answer was that this had been signed when the circumstances were different.

When it seemed impossible to reach an agreement, the Finnish representatives returned home for further instructions. These were agreed upon in conference with representatives of the parliament, but no word of them became public. The Finns kept the discussions secret because they were sincere in their desire to find a satisfactory answer to Soviet demands without any interference from emotional public opinion. Since the Communist purpose was the exact opposite, Molotov used the Supreme Soviet as a sounding board to herald the entire discussion to the world. He did so in a speech while the Finnish representatives were en route to Moscow for the purpose of carrying the negotiations forward. He asserted in one part of his speech that Soviet Russia "not only had the *right*, but the responsibility to take serious measures to increase her security." (Italics are the author's.) He charged also that Finland was under influences which emanated from some third state.

As printed in an edition of ten million copies, the official version of Molotov's speech carried the phrase "laughter in the hall" after the above quotation. This "laughter in the hall" comment of the publisher indicates that the Communists did not fool themselves about the real reasons for their demands on Finland.

The Finns correctly interpreted Russia's publication of her demands to signify that a serious change had taken place in the nature of the negotiations. Their reasoning was that having made her demands public, Russia's prestige was at stake, therefore she could not retreat from this stand. Finnish Foreign Minister Erkko announced, on November 1st, that Russia's publication of her position made it more difficult to continue negotiations in a spirit of confidence. This statement failed to soften Moscow's hard demands for the reason that the Communists had been *telling*, not *asking*, the Finns.

The Finnish delegates presented a memorandum to the Soviet authorities in Moscow on November 3rd in which they stated that since Finland still adhered to and insisted on her inviolability and neutrality she could not, therefore, lease either Hanko or Lappohja Bay to Russia but would agree to cede to Russia the small Gulf of Finland islands in exchange for other territory.

Molotov replied: "We civilians seem unable to accomplish anything more, now it is up to the military to have their say."

Since the Finns are unafraid of the devil himself, Molotov's statement failed to frighten them into yielding. Stalin tried his hand by stating that no other government except that of the Soviet would tolerate Finland's independent attitude. Even so, he added, his government would not continue to tolerate it unless the Finns showed a willingness to meet Russia's reasonable demands and cede it such areas as would guarantee its security. That, he stated, could be done only by the Finns turning Hanko over to Russia. If they did not wish to call the action *ceding*, he said, they could call it what they wished. The language they used to clothe their transfer was unimportant, he added, but the transfer was all-important. The Soviet wanted Hanko, whether or no.

The Finnish negotiators asked for time in which to get further instructions from their government. They reported to Moscow on November 9th that their government was unable to accept Molotov's terms, for the identical reason that Stalin himself had once stated to the world when he said, "We neither desire to gain a single foot of foreign soil nor are we willing to lose even an inch of our own."

The Finns found the Soviet's professed "peace policy" incomprehensible, since it rested on territorial demands upon a weaker neighbor. The Finns, who know the Russians from long and unhappy experience, also realized that if they gave them an inch they would take a mile. The negotiations had reached a standstill when Molotov revived them with the argument that Finland's refusal to grant a foreign power military bases in her own territory was unrealistic, in that it was a falsification of Russia's real attitude. He attempted to make her proposal realistic by advising the Finns to sell to Russia or exchange the Hanko area or at least the islands. In this case, he "realistically" pointed out, they no longer would be Finnish territory. The Finnish representatives replied in writing to Molotov's magic and mirrors proposal that their government honestly desired to strengthen its relations with the Soviet Union and was prepared to make extensive concessions to satisfy Russia's wishes, but that it could not go so far as to surrender its lifelines, which the granting of military bases to a foreign power at the mouth of the Gulf of Finland would mean.

The Finnish reply ended the exchange of negotiations views. The delegation expressed the hope on November 13th, before starting home, that future negotiations would lead to satisfactory results for both parties. Moscow neither directly acknowledged this note nor took advantage of Finland's expressed willingness to try to find means that would satisfy her great neighbor.

The Soviet government did make an indirect reply. It was a vociferous, bitter press and radio reply which launched a propaganda campaign against Finland.

The western nations, particularly France and Britain, at first were dissatisfied that Finland had not accepted the guarantees which Russia had given it in the summer of 1939. However, they did respect the reasons for the small country's position and they did not pressure Finland into meeting the Soviet demands. The Ribbentrop-Molotov pact had served to change their attitude to the extent that they had become cautiously ready to give Finland moral support in case of a crisis. At a meeting in Stockholm, Britain expressed to Russia the hope that her demands on Finland would be reasonable and not lead to complications between the two countries.

According to *Finland and World War II*,[1] the United States was considerably more active since, although at one time she had seen a potential ally in Russia, after the Molotov-Ribbentrop pact she realized Russia to be same kind of a dictatorship as Nazi Germany. Following that discovery, the United States offered moral support and diplomatic aid to Finland. In a letter dated October 11, 1939, to Soviet President Kalinin, President

[1] John H. Wuorinen, *Finland in World War II* (New York, The Ronald Press, 1948).

Roosevelt expressed his concern for Finland and the hope that the Soviet Union would make no demands on Finland which would be inconsistent with the maintenance and development of amicable and peaceful relations between the two countries and the independence of each.

Kalinin replied that the Russo-Finnish negotiations had taken place on the basis of their former relationship, and that the aim of the negotiations was to further the relationship and to strengthen friendly co-operation for the purpose of consolidating their mutual security.

Molotov now appeared on the scene, and in explaining this exchange of notes on October 31st, ironically suggested that after all Finland was in a better position than the Philippines and Cuba, who had vainly petitioned the United States for freedom and independence. President Roosevelt sought to give Finland still stronger moral support by sending a telegram to the King of Sweden on October 18th, on the occasion of the meeting of the Scandinavian states in Stockholm, in which he announced his support of neutrality and those fundamentals of law and justice which the states that were being represented in Stockholm also had ever upheld. Later the United States Secretary of State thanked Finland for her firm stand in the Moscow negotiations.

In addition, the representative of the Scandinavian states all separately submitted identical notes to the Soviet government on October 10th, each expressing the expectation that Russia would demand nothing of Finland that would prevent her maintaining her independent position of neutrality. These statements were allegedly not accepted by Russia, on the presumable grounds that third parties had no business to interfere in matters which did not concern them.

It is thus easy to see that the influence of third parties on Finland's behalf, which Molotov mentioned in his famous speech, was of a purely moral nature.

Molotov's remarks at the negotiation conferences with Finland's representatives, as well as his October 31st speech, had made Russia's position clear. Finland's rejection of Russia's demands, he said, "naturally would cause Finland great damage." This statement and the reference that they leave their differences to the military to settle were pointed up by *Pravda's* comment on November 3rd, when it declared:

We are embarking on a road of our own, let it lead where it will. We will guarantee Russia's security, without caring for anything, breaking through all obstacles, of no matter what sort, to gain our goal.

Russia Substitutes Bullets for Demands

When Stalin and Molotov decided that neither threats nor bullying could make the courageous Finns yield to their imperialistic demands, they created an "incident" as the basis for a Soviet attack on Finland. The Soviet government itself shelled Mainila, Russia—near the Finnish border—on November 26th, and following their habit of making false charges claimed that the Finns had done the shelling. They alleged that seven shells had been fired, killing or wounding thirteen Russians. The Finns denied that they had done any shelling and requested an impartial investigation, or if Russia preferred, one in accordance with the provisions for settling disputes as defined in the Russo-Finnish boundaries convention. The Soviet government rejected the Finnish proposal.

The fact of the case, according to the Finns, was that Mainila was beyond the range of the Finnish artillery. Despite this fact, the Soviet press and radio used the incident as a springboard to start a huge propaganda campaign for war against Finland as well as to make new demands on her.

Two days after Soviet artillery had fired seven salvos in the air at Mainila on November 26th, and then accused Finland of having shelled the village, the Soviet Union unilaterally renounced the 1934 nonaggression pact with Finland and did so in direct contradiction to its specific terms. Working fast to clear the decks for a shooting war, the Soviet government, on November 29th, broke off diplomatic relations with Finland. It did this before Finland could forward an additional note which proposed that the two countries arbitrate the incident. In it Finland offered, as a further evidence of her sincere peaceful desires, to withdraw Finnish forces so far in from the Russian boundary that it would be impossible for them to become a threat to Leningrad.

Russia ignored this note.

The Soviet's armed forces were making reality of Molotov's words: "Now it is up to the military to have their say."

A Soviet armed force pushed across the Finnish border at Petsamo and made prisoners of Finnish boundary guards on November 29th. The Red war machine began to roll on November 30th, when Soviet planes made a full-scale bombing attack on Helsinki and several other cities and industrial centers.

Concurrently with these military attacks the Soviet radio branded Finnish reports of these raids as "lies" and explained that the Russian planes had dropped only bread to the starving poor people of Helsinki. The Finns, who have a keen but well-controlled sense of humor, called the Russian bombs "Molotov's bread baskets."

War with the Russians as one of the participants, which had been desolating Finland for a thousand years, had now come again with far less announcement than spring uses to herald her coming. The Soviet government not only attacked Finland with great force on a wide front, but did so with lightning suddenness. The attack extended along the entire Russian-Finnish border from Karelia in the southeast to the Arctic Ocean in the north.

The great size of attacking military forces which Soviet Russia had massed near the Finnish border proved that the Reds had been carefully planning over a period of several months to attack Finland. Another evidence of guilty Red intent consists of the military roads they had built, in uninhabited waste areas along the Finnish border, whose only conceivable purpose would be that of facilitating a Soviet attack on Finland.

Shortly after the swarms of Red soldiers had begun to pour into Finland they found their way blocked with fierce Finnish resistance. The Finns soon stabilized and held their lines until later when severe winter came to their aid; then they attacked. Russia staggered and gave ground while the world applauded the valiant Finns.

Finland's men and women meanwhile joined the army or began to work in munitions plants. In an effort to draw the teeth of Russia's vilifying propaganda, which was violently attacking high Finnish officials, the Finnish government resigned despite Parliament's unanimous vote of confidence. Risto Ryti, who was known to have a friendly feeling toward England, became Premier. The new government, which Finland named on December 1, 1939, stated that its main objective was the re-establishment of peace, but added that it would wage war as effectively as it could until peace could be established.

The sole question was: How long could Finland hold out? Russia had fifty soldiers to her one, and food and war material supplies in like proportion. It was a foregone conclusion that even superior courage and intelligence could not long withstand the crushing weight of an army which outnumbered Finland on a fifty to one rate.

The Reds did not rely solely on their weight advantage. Lacking as they do the western world's moral standards and sense of justice, they tried to becloud the issue in other ways in an effort to weaken the Finn's spirit. One of their tricks was to set up a puppet government for Finland. Their quisling hireling and leader was O. W. Kuusinen, a Comintern officer. Moscow then advanced the claim that its own created puppet government had requested the Soviet government to "stop by force" this war which Finland's "former rulers" had forced upon the unsuspecting, unprepared and reluctant Russians. Moscow heard its puppet government's plaintive appeal for help before it was uttered and had a mutual aid pact ready to sign with its own creatures.

Everyone who has followed the activities and watched the methods of the Kremlin's leaders realizes that they are crafty, wily chess players in the international chess game. They play with small nations and human beings which are to be sacrificed as one would a pawn. Their cleverness and ruthlessness are not, however, free from blunders. In the instance of recognizing their Finnish puppet government they blundered in the same way an old lady who had killed her husband was reputed to have done when she artlessly said, "The saying that murder will out ain't so, because I killed my husband forty-four years ago and nobody has ever found it out." The Stalin government revealed its criminal guilt when it formally recognized its own "established" government for Finland in the following statement:

Since the Finnish people have formed their own democratic republic, which is totally dependent on the people's support, the time has come to establish good relations between our countries (Russia and Finland) and to guarantee together the centuries-old desire of the Finnish people to have the people of Karelia rejoin their compatriots, the Finnish people, in a united Finnish nation. . . .

This statement reveals that the Soviet government's objective was that of conquest of all Finland in its having publicly admitted that "*the people of Karelia* [meaning those in the eastern Karelian province] *rejoin their compatriots, the Finnish people, in a united Finnish nation. . . .*"

Equally impressive and significant in its revelation of the Soviet government's true reason for attacking Finland is one other fact; namely, that on November 13th, the Soviet government offered the post as the leader of the shadow Finnish government to Arvo Tuominen, a former Comintern official who later left the Communists and joined his Finnish brothers. It made this offer to Tuominen on the same day that the Finnish negotiation representatives left Moscow after having expressed in a formal memorandum the hope that future negotiations would lead to results that would be satisfactory to both parties.

Moscow made no reply to this Finnish note. The reason was now clear. The die had been cast. Finland's future was to be Russia's future. Since the Finns, through their centuries-long experience with the Russians, had trained their eyes to be quicker than the Russian hands, they were able to discern which shell covered the pea. They knew that Russia's purpose was to make their free nation a Communist puppet state. Arwidsson's 1821 statement, "Russians we can never be," sounded the same spiritual overtones for the Finns that Patrick Henry's "Give me liberty, or give me death" had sounded for the American colonists.

It was their conviction that "Russians we can never be" which had enabled the Finnish government leaders to withstand Russia's plausible arguments, blandishments, intimidations and threats and finally to defend, with a tiny army, their country from a crushing Russian attack.

The Finns, as do wild mothers in the forest and field, or civilized mothers in the home, defend with their lives that which is dearest to them. Finns fought to protect their homeland, their dearest possession. Because their leader's intelligence was far superior to that of their invading enemies, because they were led by a military genius, Field Marshal Mannerheim, who had served for many years in the Imperial Russian Army, and because they are a composite of raw courage and deep piety, a small number of Finnish soldiers stopped the Russian armies at Finland's border. But the realistic Finns knew, as did the rest of the world, that Russia's massive weight and the Red leaders' practice of continuing to send "fresh troops in as a butcher pushing raw material into a mincing machine," eventually would crush the Finnish army. This conviction spurred the Finnish government to continue its search for any honorable way to end the war. Finland's leaders were impelled to do this also because of the desire which lives in Finnish hearts to maintain peaceful relations with every people.

A universal sympathy was quickly manifested for Finland, one of the world's smallest nations which, isolated and alone, was fighting a defensive war against the world's largest country. Another factor working in Finland's favor was that the antipathy which the western nations felt for Nazi Germany now also included Soviet Russia, since Nazi and Communist dictatorships were cast from the same mold, and Germany and Russia had further proven their kinship of purpose and method through the Ribbentrop-Molotov pact.

The resourceful Finns tried to capitalize on this sympathy by having their Parliament appeal to civilization on December 10th not to desert Finland while she fought her mighty enemy alone. Because they needed more than sympathy, the Parliament stated also that Finland needed active help.

Previously, on December 3rd, Finland had called the League of Nation's attention to articles Ten and Fifteen of its covenant and requested the League's Council to stop Russia's attack on Finland. The League Council met on December 5th to consider Finland's request and Soviet Russia's statement. The latter perfectly conformed with Soviet dialectic inversions. It began with the fiction that since the Kuusinen government represented Finland, Russia, therefore, was not at war with Finland and accordingly its officials would not attend the League Council meeting. The League Council on December 14th adopted a resolution which stated that since Soviet Russia's activities were contrary not only to general treaties but to its specific signed treaties with Finland as well, the League's members should give Finland all possible aid. The resolution declared further that because of her calculated violation of the Covenant of the League, Soviet Russia had disqualified herself as worthy of membership in the League of Nations. The League Council followed immediately with a similar action, and for the first time in its history it branded a nation unworthy of belonging to it. This was the League of

Nations' last as well as its most unusual and important decision. Its Council in effect paraphrased Carlyle's dictum by indicating to Soviet Russia through its action: "How can we hear what you say your purpose was when what you are doing keeps thundering in our ears?"

The League's action epitomized the nontotalitarian world's conscience. Winston Churchill expressed the feelings of honorable men about Finland's tragic situation in a radio address on January 20, 1940, in which he said:

Finland alone—in danger of death, superb, sublime Finland—shows what free men can do. The service that Finland has rendered to humanity is magnificent. . . . We cannot say what Finland's fate will be, but nothing could be sadder to the rest of the civilized world than that this splendid northern race should at the end be destroyed and in the face of incredible odds should fall into a slavery worse than death. If the light of freedom which still burns so brightly in the frozen North should be finally quenched, it might well herald a return to the Dark Ages, when every vestige of human progress during two thousand years would be engulfed.

Unfortunately for Finland in her supreme crisis she received little more than words and diplomatic help from the free world. What she needed was war matériel, soldiers and food. Sweden, almost alone, gave Finland substantial help. The Swedish government and its citizens provided Finland with more than $100,-000,000 worth of goods and food. Sweden sold Finland war matériel and permitted large numbers of her soldiers to serve as "volunteers" in the Finnish army in time to participate in the fighting. Sweden's war matériel was most substantial, and because easy and quick delivery was possible, it was of decisive importance to the Finns. England in like manner permitted the public recruiting of volunteers. Volunteers also came from other countries, but none of them except the two Swedish battalions and one company of Finnish-Americans reached the front lines before the winter war was ended.

One of the reasons why American sympathy for Finland was

so general and genuine, apart from her respect and admiration for the Finns, was that both the American press and broadcasting companies had sent a number of their most able correspondents and broadcasters to Finland. The reports of these men on the ground kept the entire nation fully informed of what was going on. One of the broadcasts, made by the author's lifelong, intimate friend, W. L. White, and entitled "The Last Christmas Tree," moved all America to tears. It is printed in full as the Epilogue to Part One of this book.

American help came in the form of a thirty-million-dollar loan, but it was limited to the purchase of civilian goods. The American government's policy of neutrality did not permit it to sell or allot old weapons to Finland—although two months later it gave them to England.

Germany's attitude toward Finland in this trying period was inimical. Her government-controlled press and radio showed hostility rather than sympathy for Finland and sought to minimize Finland's position. Hitler banned the transportation through Germany of Hungarian volunteers and of Finnish-bought arms in Italy. In addition, on December 12, 1939, and February 28 and March 4, 1940, the German government "advised" Sweden not to participate in the war on Finland's behalf.

The western nations were aroused by sympathy for Finland but they feared that she would be defeated quickly, until something miraculously happened to change their thinking. The something miraculous that appeared was Finland's naked soul. Her handful of soldiers succeeded in halting Soviet Russia's mass attack and then held it for two months on Finland's main line of defense. The Finns' able and heroic stand transformed Russia's offense into a costly warfare of holding her position. The Finns surrounded and destroyed several Russian divisions in the Lake Lagoda region to the north. The war took a new turn in February after the Red army had concentrated thirty divisions in the Karelian Isthmus on the southeast of Finland and reinforced them with strong artillery and armored units. The Finns held these new Soviet forces between February 1st and February 13th, before they succeeded in breaking through.

Finland's remarkable showing, combined with another important factor, prompted France and England to offer Finland direct military support. The other important factor was that Germany had seized and published French High Command documents which had expressed the belief in early 1940 that the Finnish front had the same significance to the Western Powers as the Macedonian front had held for them in World War I. The purpose of this objective analysis was to point out that the Western European Powers should blockade Germany on all sides and thereby limit her sources of raw materials. The Western Powers believed, also, that by helping Finland they might be able to induce Sweden and Norway to join in the blockade. Another possible reason for their wanting the Finnish war to continue was that, thus occupied, Russia would be unable to continue her oil and other vital exports to Germany. France announced herself ready to break off diplomatic relations with Russia, but England hesitated.

The British interests in Finland notified Finnish officials on February 24th that the British and French governments' plans called for sending a force of from 20,000 to 22,000 men to Finland. On March 1st, Finland asked them to send at least 50,000 men and have them reach the front by the end of March. The Western Powers, on March 7th, agreed to do so. Since these forces could reach Finland quickly only through Norway and Sweden, the Western Powers asked Finland to present an official request for such transit facilities to the Norwegian and Swedish governments by March 8th. Finland did so, but the two governments refused to grant this request on the grounds that it would violate their neutrality.

The small but troublesome word *if*, which so continuously obtrudes itself into the lives of individuals and nations, did so here in a dramatic way.

The question which arises here is *if* Norway and Sweden had granted transit facilities for the British and French troops, what might the consequences have been?

Would the new forces have enabled Finland to defeat Russia? Would they have fought on Finnish soil and destroyed all of Finland? Had Norway and Sweden's answer been in the affirmative, would their decision have involved them in the war at that time and thereby made them and Finland the battleground of the great Powers? Would military aid have bound Finland to the great Powers indefinitely? Would the great Powers' enlistment in a war against Russia have enabled them later to fight with Russia against Germany?

Finally, the most important question of all: Would free nations today be in a stronger position if they had been enemies of Russia instead of allies?

Only inscrutable fate can answer these questions, since the Western Powers sent Finland no tangible aid in her great emergency.

Finland Seeks Peace

Recognizing their country's limited and ever-decreasing supplies of man power, materials, money and food, Finnish government officials began to put out peace feelers. Neither the German nor the United States governments seemed willing to act as an intermediary. Germany did sound out Moscow but was rebuffed, as also were the individuals Finland enlisted. On January 25th, when Swedish Foreign Minister Gunther offered Sweden's mediation, the Soviet Union first intimated that it would be willing to begin negotiations with the Government of Finland, whose legality it had denied two months earlier. Two factors helped the Soviet government to reach this decision. The first was that she had learned of the intention of the Western Powers to help Finland. The second, that her leaders determine their policies not by principles but by expediency. This enables them to believe at any moment what they wish by accepting

John L. Sullivan's favorite aphorism as gospel: "If you believe it, it's so."

What road shall we take? Finnish government officials came to grips with this all-important question in early February, 1940. Will it be peace with the Soviet Union, if obtainable? Will it be military aid from the Scandinavian nations, if obtainable, thereby localizing the war? Will it be aid from the West, which would involve Finland in the World War?

They simultaneously explored all three of these alternatives openly in a spirit of fair play in their efforts to save their country.

Molotov sent word to Finland by way of Stockholm that his government did not consider it impossible to reach an agreement with the Finnish government, therefore Finland should begin negotiations by making concrete proposals of what territorial concessions she would be willing to make. He added significantly that since blood had been shed *against the Soviet government's wishes and without Russia's being to blame*, the territorial concessions Finland offered would have to be greater than those proposed by Russia in Moscow in October–November, 1939.

Premier Ryti himself delivered the answer to Stockholm. He stated that the Finnish government was prepared to negotiate. When Sweden's decision was made public in early February that her government found it impossible to give Finland military assistance in any form, the Soviet government considered Finland helpless, therefore ripe for acceptance of even harsher terms. This proved to be the case when Russia made her demands known through the Swedish government, to which Russia attached the time bomb that if Finland did not accept them Russia would make additional demands in the future. *Might* was riding high and *right* was helplessly bound. Finland now made one final appeal to Sweden for military assistance. Sweden refused. Finland then asked for Swedish economic aid if she accepted Russia's terms. Sweden promised it.

The Soviet government, which never overlooks any bet, although it had the mouse in its claws, now tried to use Britain as an intermediary. It asked the British government to transmit its peace terms to Finland. Lord Halifax, British Foreign Secretary, considered the terms too harsh and refused to transmit them. Moscow, using Sweden, next demanded, on February 28th, that Finland give her answer to its demands within forty-eight hours. Finland countered by asking for a more specific definition of new boundaries. She also inquired of Moscow what Finland would receive in return for territorial cessions.

The Western Powers in the meantime had increased and made more definite the extent of their proposed military assistance. Finland in considering the two alternatives, western help or peace, continued to place peace first. Accordingly, the Finns notified Moscow through Stockholm on March 5th that they would accept its terms in principle as a basis for peace negotiations.

When negotiations began on March 8th, in Moscow, Russia made new and even greater demands. These new and greater demands changed the premises on which the negotiations began. The Finns now reconsidered the Western Powers' help. French Prime Minister Daladier's following message, which had reached Finland on March 8th, stated that the Western Powers had waited several days for Finland to ask them officially for help, and added: "We know Russia fears you will appeal to the Allies, because she fears that an Allied intervention will lead to a Russian catastrophe. To avoid the catastrophe, Russia is now ready to negotiate in order to be able to destroy you later."

A decisive factor now entered the situation and caused Finland to negotiate for peace. It was Field Marshal Mannerheim's statement that the Finnish military position on the Karelian Isthmus was untenable and further, that since foreign forces could not reach the front within five weeks, these forces would be too few and too late to save the Finnish situation. Mannerheim's estimate of the situation induced the government to give its peace negotiators full powers.

No one who knows the meaning of and holds regard for justice, fairness and honesty could consider Moscow's peace terms reasonable. She demanded one of Finland's richest and most vitally important farming and industrial areas. She made no effort to defend the grab on the basis of security. On October 31, 1939, less than five months earlier, Molotov had branded as "groundless lies" the charge that Russia sought this area. The Russians, who normally are insensitive to their government's immoral acts, tried to justify and explain its hoggish appetite by Molotov's attempt to prove, in justification of his government's unreasonable demands, that Finland could continue to exist on what Moscow's forced-down-Finland's-throat peace had left her.

While the entire population of Finland believed the Moscow-dictated peace terms to be a gross injustice, they considered them conclusive and final. With characteristic honesty, they tried to fulfill the terms without thoughts of revenge. Even so, the good grace with which they met Russia's demands failed to create better relations. This in all likelihood may have come from the Communists' troubled consciences.

One illustration of the Communists' ungrounded complaints and suspicions is furnished by the Russian Minister's protest, when he returned to his post in Helsinki, over the fact that the Finnish flags were flying at half mast. It was true. But they were flown at half mast to express the Finns' mourning for their dead. The Soviet Minister asked no one the reason. He assumed that they were so flown because of his arrival. On March 21, 1940, Molotov stated that all questions with Finland had been settled once and for all. On August 1st, he stated that Finland had satisfactorily fulfilled the peace terms. He added, however, the clear threat that "certain elements of Finland's ruling classes" must stop using force to restrain the Communists. "Otherwise," he stated, "it is understandable that Russo-Finnish relations might deteriorate."

Considerable difference of opinion was expressed in the Finnish Parliament about whether to accept Moscow's peace terms or to make a supreme effort to continue fighting until the proffered help from the West might eventually reach Finland, and the question is even yet being argued in Finland. However different the result might have been the fact is that the Finns had demonstrated that they would fight against any odds to keep their country free. That the West understood why Finland submitted to Russia's peace terms was made clear in Lord Halifax's message to them in which he expressed admiration for their bravery and added that *it would bring its own reward in the future. He also gave assurances that when the Allies achieved victory Finland would participate in the advantages which a true and just peace would bring.* The reader is asked to remember Lord Halifax's promise and check against what eventually happened, as it is revealed in following chapters.

New Orientation

Since the Finns realized that they could not defend their country without help, they tried to establish new relationships. The West still wanted to help her, but the fall of France changed western policy. The western European nations needed Russia to help re-establish a balance of power. They, therefore, would risk no complications that might place Russia more fully on Germany's side. Even the American government's former good will toward Finland began to disappear in thin vapor.

Finland next turned to Norway and Sweden. The Soviet Union frowned on this move and Finland abandoned the contemplated tri-partite pact. It seemed evident that Soviet Russia's opposition to it came from Moscow's desire to hold Finland firmly in her sphere of influence.

Finland now directed her efforts toward widening the basis of her co-operation with Sweden for the purpose of increasing the likelihood of maintaining peace on the basis of existing treaties. Moscow looked upon these proposals as some kind of secret conspiracy against Russia.

When Finland's Scandinavian proposals failed to materialize, the desperate Finns turned to Germany, which had begun to show an increased interest in Finland. Germany had first indicated her changed feelings about the Finns through Ribbentrop's widely propagandized action of releasing Finnish arms shipments which Germany had confiscated in Norway during the invasion. Again on August 18, 1940, in connection with an agreement for an important arms purchase, Germany asked transit permission for Luftwaffe personnel via Finland to Norway. Finland acted favorably, since to have rejected it would have canceled delivery of the purchased arms. The Soviet Union offered no objections to Germany's transit request, the wording of which follows:

1. At the request of the Reich, the Finnish government permits transit of materiel and necessary personnel from northern Baltic ports, through Rovaniemi, along the Arctic road to Kirkenes in northern Norway.

2. The German government will inform the Finnish government, in sufficient time, as to which ports will be involved, the number of transports, their schedules of arrival and departure, as well as intended daily transit routes in northern Finland.

3. The German government will give the Finnish government notification at least twenty-four hours in advance of ship arrivals.

4. Materiel and men will be transported separately in different vehicles. The number of guards and officers who accompany the materiel transports will be fixed by a separate agreement.

The rift between Germany and Russia did not begin to show until in the spring of 1941, when Hitler's special envoy Schnurre proposed to President Ryti in Helsinki that Finland send one or several staff officers to Germany to discuss how military operations might be co-ordinated in case of a German-Russian clash. This was done, but the Finnish officers discussed only military problems.

The Finns stated clearly at the beginning of their discussions with Germany that Finland would not start an aggressive war. They added that they were not empowered to discuss or enter into any agreements to that end. The Germans at no time revealed any hint of the forthcoming Nazi attack on Russia. The lonely Finns, directly faced with the alternative of life or death for their country, were seeking desperately for a source of military supplies. The United States, England, France and the Scandinavian countries in turn had failed them—Germany remained their one last possible source.

The German Foreign Office officially informed Finland, on June 6th, that Russo-German relations would progress in a normal way. Although the political atmosphere was filled with contradictory rumors, no one could determine their source or the reasons for them. The Finnish government continued to believe that a new German-Soviet agreement would be signed. This is indicated by President Ryti's instructions, on May 30th, to try to see that the settlement would not be made at Finland's expense, as it had in 1939. He further wanted it made clear that Finland desired only to be guaranteed her independence, and that she hoped for the 1939 restoration of her boundaries.

These discussions proved to have been futile since it later became clear that Germany was not carrying on any negotiations of this nature with Russia. Mention of them here is of significance because they show that the Finnish government, in early June, 1941, continued to believe peace would be maintained.

The Finns were due for a rude awakening shock when in his proclamation on June 22nd, Hitler announced the German attack on Russia in which he stated:

Side by side with their Finnish comrades stand the victorious fighters of Narvik on the shores of the Arctic. German divisions, commanded by the conqueror of Norway, together with the heroes of Finnish independence, led by their Marshal, guard Finnish soil.

No pact, written, spoken or intimated in the Finnish-German

agreement, existed which justified Hitler's use of the "brother-hood in arms" phrase between Germany and Finland. He had no authority on which to base his statement. He was correct, however, to the extent of expectations and assumption that the Soviet government would attack Finland as a result of the Nazi attack on Russia. Only in this way would his "brotherhood in arms" automatically become a *fait accompli*, without any pact.

Hitler's phrase so troubled the Finns that their government informed the Western Powers, Germany included, that Finland did not consider herself at war with Russia, and furthermore that Finland's policy was one of strict neutrality and she would direct her concentrated effort toward keeping out of war.

Finland's definition of her position was of no avail. Hitler had made a ruthless but clever move.

The Soviet Union renewed its war on Finland immediately after the opening of Germany's attack on Russia. Soviet radios hurled imprecations against Finland and announced that two hundred million Russians could in their anger clear the "Finnish White Guard" from the face of the earth. On June 22nd, the same day Germany launched her attack on Russia, Russian planes began to bomb Finland and fire at Finnish border patrols. The Finns, however, withheld their fire. Finland was still striving to remain neutral. The day the Russo-German war started the Finnish Minister of Foreign Affairs notified all of its foreign legations that Finland would continue to remain neutral and continue diplomatic relations with Soviet Russia until and unless attacked. He also wired the Finnish Minister in Berlin that ". . . as far as Finland is concerned only defensive action is involved. It is clear that if Russia attacks we will defend ourselves. The presence of German forces in Finland is to be evaluated inde-pendently of the above and can at least at the moment be con-sidered as falling within the terms of the transit agreement."

Britain's Foreign Secretary Eden expressed satisfaction over Finland's position in a speech in Parliament on June 23rd. As late as June 24th, Germany did not include Finland in the list of countries that had joined Germany in the fight on Russia. Although Finland had no pact with Germany to join her in fighting Russia, implacable fate, which controls the destiny of men and nations, was leisurely at work creating new tests of endurance for the Finns.

Germany, with which Finland had such a slight tie, was now, however, at war with Russia. This placed Finland precariously at the edge of a great precipice between the devil and the raging sea in a strong offshore wind.

The Finns gave a demonstration of their courage by making a formal protest against the Soviet bombings. Moscow's action, then novel but now stereotyped, was to refuse to accept the protest. On the same day, however, Molotov stated in a speech that (a) no such bombings had occurred; (b) Finnish planes had flown over Russian territory.

Again more "bread baskets" to the poor of Helsinki; black is white; upside-down is right-side up; a lie is the truth, whether or no.

Russia severed all communications with Finland on June 23rd, and on June 25th,—again without a declaration of war—began that war with large-scale air attacks on all Finland, and Soviet artillery units began to fire upon Finnish army border units. After Parliament had given the government a unanimous vote of confidence the Finns began to defend themselves on June 28th.

As throughout their long history, the Finns were again involved in a war as the catspaw of great, ambitious and ruthless powers.

Lord Newton indicated in a July 22nd speech that the Western Powers understood the situation when he stated in the British House of Lords that there was a lot more to be said for the Finns than appeared at first glance and added that: "Finland is at this moment Europe's most sorely tried country. Finland's entry into the war happened because of her misfortune in having a certain arrangement with Germany. Finland did not design this, neither did she want to become a nation at war. The Russians are aware of their errors and are now negotiating with Yugoslavia, Czechoslovakia, and Poland. Is there any reason, therefore, why they should not approach Finland as well?"

The role thrust upon Finland was a difficult one, since her government and her people wanted only peace and independence. Accordingly, her resistance pleased neither Germany nor Russia. Germany's war was "a crusade against Bolshevism"; Finland's was one for defense, security and independence.

Finland's Social Democrat Cabinet Minister, Vaino Tanner, on October 28, 1941, declared in a radio address that Finland was fighting a defensive war for her own rights without having made political agreements with anyone, and added, "We are continuing that same defensive battle which we waged in hopeless circumstances during our winter war."

The Finnish Minister of Foreign Affairs in Berlin signed on behalf of his government the anticomintern pact, which was only of ideological significance, explaining his reasons for signing it by stating: "Through this Pact we can obtain information regarding the activity of the Communist International, discuss essential defensive measures, and carry them out in close cooperation."

A most important by-product of the pact, and of far greater consequence, was the Western Powers' use of it as a vehicle to turn public opinion against Finland. This was done by falsely charging that in signing the pact Finland demonstrated that she was ideologically inclined toward Hitlerism. America's participation in this propaganda against Finland is hard to explain, since American Ambassador to Moscow Joseph E. Davies, at that time, on August 2, 1939, after a careful study of Finland and her situation, had officially reported to the State Department:

The net impression which I get (and it is quite strong) from these various conversations is that the government of Finland is innately hostile to the Hitler concept and his governmental policies. Finland is instinctively not pro-German. . . . Finland's policy is based upon a realization of the exceedingly precarious geographical and military strategic position she occupies between two powerful enemy countries, and upon a determination realistically to avoid antagonizing either, if possible, and in any event to do her utmost to prevent herself from being converted into a battleground, whereby both her political independence and economic freedom and independent well-being might be destroyed.

President Ryti dealt with this situation in his speech at the opening of Parliament on February 3, 1942, when in discussing Finland's relations with Germany he said:

Friendly and confidential relations are natural in all circumstances. Such relations have not been prevented in the past by the fact that Germany's political and social system differs from our own, and that difference must not now either emerge as an obstacle. . . . Just as we consider it natural that no one from the outside will interfere in our internal affairs, and will not try to alter that system which we have developed for ourselves, and which we want to go on freely developing, so it is our responsibility to respect the systems other countries have adopted and found good and to leave every nation free to decide about such matters as their own affairs.

Earlier, when the German forces were advancing toward Leningrad, a German official stated to President Ryti that his government considered it desirable and advantageous for the Finns to annex Leningrad and the surrounding area. Ryti flatly refused to consider this proposal.

Later when Russia had to withdraw many of her military units from Finland to other fronts for the purpose of meeting the German onslaught, Finland's military forces acquired a more nearly equal basis with Communist forces, thus enabling the Finns to achieve their military objectives. When Finland had halted her attack, her Cabinet Minister Fagerholm explained Finland's limited war aims when he stated on August 2, 1943:

We are a democracy and do not believe in the permanence of dictatorships. Since December 5, 1941, Finnish military activities have been limited to guarding and patrolling, and Finland has in fact never fought for anything but her independence. We know that bolshevism means physical destruction, but we are not fighting an ideological battle or a war of conquest.

Finland began to reduce her field forces when she achieved her military objectives. Neither her stated limited war aims, nor her actions in making them effective were acceptable to the Western Powers.

The day Hitler began his attack on Russia, Winston Churchill declared that Britain would aid everyone who fought against Nazism and would consider everyone who co-operated with Germany an enemy.

Britain and Finland reached the severing of their ways in a friendly fashion. Soon thereafter, however, the Western Powers began to turn the heat on Finland. Whether they did this on their own initiative, or as a result of Soviet needling, cannot be known until the Russian war archives are available, if ever, for study.

Britain's memorandum concerning the severance of diplomatic relations with Finland in one part approached the point of being an ultimatum in that it stated that so long as Finland attacked Britain's ally's territory (Russia) it would be impossible to separate Finland's war from that of the general European war; therefore, if "the Finnish government continues the advance into purely Russian territory, a situation will arise which will force Great Britain to consider Finland as an open enemy, not only while the war lasts, but also when the peace is made."

Finland's reply, published October 8, 1941, stated in substance that ever since 1939 the Soviet Union had been the aggressor and Finland the defensive party; that some of Finland's territory which was not "purely" Russian, but primarily Finnish, was occupied by Russian forces; but that what was of more importance were the military considerations since "an effective defense, to which no one can deny Finland's right, is possible only by establishing the defense in those areas."

The old Britain of great days, when her word was law, on Russia's insistence spoke out in an ultimatum on November 8, 1941:

If Finland does not cease her military operations by the 5th of December, and, in addition, refrain from all active participation in hostilities, His Majesty's Government will have no alternative but to declare the existence of a state of war between the two countries.

Here was the voice of wrath of the aging great God Jove.

Finland replied gently to Britain's impotent ultimatum with the following official statement:

In the present situation there is reason to declare that Finland's armed forces are not far from achieving their strategic aims, that is, the liberation of the Finnish territories lost by the Moscow peace, and the neutralizing of those areas from which the enemy prepared to destroy Finland.

It is difficult for the Government of Finland to understand that its attitude should contain anything which could give the Government of Great Britain reason to declare a state of war between these two countries. Finland would deeply deplore it if that should happen.

Britain countered with a declaration of war against Finland on her Independence Day, December 6, 1941.

The United States followed Britain's action at a slower pace. On October 3, 1941, Secretary of State Hull stated in a press conference that:

The United States government is naturally interested in the question whether Finland will go on beyond her own boundaries—that is, her original boundaries, after having regained her lost territory —to take part in the general war. Because of the interest the United States government felt in this subject, it is also well understood why the British government was sufficiently concerned with this question to have sent a note to the Finnish government.

On the following October 27th, however, the United States

Minister in Helsinki handed the Finnish government a memorandum which said in part:

Insofar as the Finnish government is anxious to preserve the friendship of the United States now and in the future, the United States government must be given satisfactory assurances that the intention of the Finnish government is immediately to cease operations against Russian territory, and that Finnish forces will immediately be withdrawn (in principle) from the Russian territory to a line corresponding to the 1939 boundary between Finland and the Soviet Union.

In the event that attacks are made against shipments of military supplies from the United States en route to Russia via the Arctic Ocean, and such attack is presumably made or may be claimed to be made from Finnish-controlled territory, it must be assumed that in view of the public opinion now prevailing in the United States, such an incident must be assumed to lead to an immediate crisis in Finnish-American relations.

The United States Minister amplified this memorandum three days later with the following warning:

Without strengthening Finland's own future security, these military operations have in fact constituted a definite threat to the security of the United States. Therefore it must be made absolutely clear that unless her activity in this direction ceases immediately, Finland must lose the friendly support of the United States in those future difficulties which of necessity will result from such a decision.

Finland's case had now become a *cause célèbre* in world power politics. Innocent, protecting only her own land, striving to maintain her existence, fighting a powerful aggressor enemy, accepting aid from, but not fighting with, the only nation that had sent her the only help she had been able to buy or get from any source, Finland, with clear logic and unintimidated purpose, replied at length on November 11, 1941, to the State Department's memorandum. Her reply called attention to the nature of Finland's war; described it as purely a war of defense for existence; stated that Russia had made no peace proposals; exploded the State Department's argument that Finland's military activities threatened the security of the United States; and flatly refused to accept the United States' demand that Finnish forces be withdrawn to the 1939 Finnish boundary. And in conclusion:

It cannot be possible that the mighty United States demands that a small nation, who has been again attacked by a neighbor fifty times her size and who is fighting for her existence, should withdraw, while fighting is still continuing, to await a new attack behind boundaries whose defense, if the advantages hitherto gained are abandoned to the enemy, can, considering the differences in strength, easily become impossible.

These United States memoranda were prepared and sent Finland during a period when a Communist cell was actively operating in the higher echelons of the State Department.

Remember?

Since American good will toward Finland was an obstacle, some State Department officials tried to place Soviet Russia's interests ahead of those of the United States. The aim of these Soviet sympathizers was that of destroying American good will toward Finland by creating suspicions about her.

Top State Department officials, who were immersed in projects and situations of far greater consequence than Finland's plight, gave the State Department Communist cell its golden opportunity.

Another factor which worked to Finland's disadvantage was that truth in wartime is more difficult to find than the proverbial needle in a haystack. Propaganda, based on half truths mixed with emotion and prejudice, makes truth elusive. Coupled with this was Russia's ruthless singleness of purpose in gaining its own ends with complete disregard for what is right or just.

Finland's Situation Becomes Desperate

Finland's situation worsened after the German defeat at Stalingrad which ended Germany's drive to the eastward and also demonstrated that Russia would not collapse. Coupled with this was the fast-growing potential of Germany's enemies. The Western Powers now sought to weaken Germany further by launching an intensified propaganda campaign designed to win Germany's allies to their side. Finland became their chief target. Her moral position still was high, despite their previous propaganda efforts.

Since Finland had never fought as an ally of Germany and, moreover, had clearly demonstrated her unhappiness over the hard circumstances which had forced her to turn to Germany for aid as a last resort, her own people wanted to sever Finland's slender German relationship.

Finland's all-important question now became: How can we do this? She was wholly dependent on Germany except for some vitally needed food stuffs and raw materials which trickled in from Sweden. She was economically and militarily dependent upon German mercy. Germany controlled all of the Northland. She had built a great air base near Kemijarvi in the forests and hills, which today are slowly returning to their natural state as if in warning to man that his pigmy efforts are futile; had concentrated forces at all of Finland's communication centers as well as a vast supply of war matériel which included anti-aircraft installations. Finland knew that any move to break off relations would serve as the signal to start the German war machine against her. The Finns considered no surprise move, for to them that would have been dishonorable and, as they have demonstrated throughout their history, moral reasons come first with them and remain to the last. Russia was still at war with Finland, and despite the Soviet government's statements about its policy toward Finland—the sort of statements which the free world belatedly has learned to take not with a pinch of salt but with a tablespoon—Moscow had made no peace move, it had not made even a peace gesture, toward Finland.

The Finnish government repeatedly stated publicly that it was ready to make peace with Russia on the specific condition that the Western Powers give guarantees that the peace would last.

The next peace move came from the United States in the form of a memorandum which stated that it was proceeding on the assumption that Finland had confidence in the United States; therefore, America was tendering her good offices to help bring about peace between Finland and the Soviet Union. But America underlined the offer with the observation that *it likely would not be renewed*.

Finnish government officials reached the conclusion after long conferences that its acceptances would (a) *ipso facto* result in the termination of relations with Germany, and (b) place Finland at Russia's mercy while the United States stood by helplessly. The cautious Finns, not wanting to buy a pig-in-a-poke, accordingly asked the American Charge d'Affaires in Finland (a) what likely would be Russia's terms; (b) what about guarantees to Finland? Because they felt that it would be only right and proper for them to deal frankly with Germany, they sent their Foreign Minister to Berlin with directions to explain why Finland could not reject the offer without first learning what it envisaged. Ribbentrop expressed strong disapproval of the American offer. He said that if Finland made a separate peace, Germany would draw "extreme conclusions"; therefore Finland, to avoid such, must immediately inform the United States government that she would discontinue negotiations forthwith.

Finland's honorable procedure created a new difficulty for her in that Germany now began to press her for a political agreement which until then she had been able to avoid. Despite German pressure to force Finland to break off the negotiations, her officials waited to learn the answers to the questions they had submitted to the United States.

When the United States' answer came, it was to the effect that America knew nothing; it had merely wanted to help. Finland's reply memorandum expressed regret that, as she had neither received the desired information nor any indication of Russia's willingness to negotiate, she was unable to accept the offer of America's good offices.

Germany now not only renewed its demands on the political pact question, but Hitler, in October, 1943, wrote President Ryti at great length. Hitler first criticized Finland and then requested Finland to recognize Mussolini's new government. Finland replied without promises or commitments. Ribbentrop raised the political pact question again in December, 1943, and demanded an answer. Finland again said no. It should have been evident by now to the Germans that the Finns not only are stubborn but unyielding to any pressure or threat that tries to force their doing something they believe to be wrong.

After Italy collapsed in 1943, Finland was subjected to a more direct and effective propaganda campaign than at any previous time. Rumors filled the air waves and newspapers and were whispered in the chancelleries of Europe that Russia was ready to make peace with Finland. No authentic information, however, could be found to support them. Finland put out feelers to Russia, but none of them was acknowledged by Moscow.

A query reached Finland circuitously from the American government in August, 1943, which asked what position Finland would take if America were to land an expeditionary force in northern Norway: Would Finland oppose it? How would Finland free herself from the German forces? What supplies would she need?

Finland replied directly to the Secretary of State, Cordell Hull, on September 3rd, that (a) Finland would not fight American forces; (b) Americans should not permit Russians to enter Finnish territory; (c) negotiations would be begun with Germany for the withdrawal of German troops; (d) Finland in addition to her own harvests would need certain month liveries of food supplies.

Finland's reply fell into a State Department bottomless void. She learned nothing further about the query or her reply. The Allies' propaganda mills continued, meanwhile, to grind grist that was unfavorable to Finland. Illustration of American non-government comments was an article by Walter Lippman in 1943, in which he stated that it would be a problem to apply the principles of the Atlantic Charter to Finland, since Finland happened to be a neighbor of Russia—the inference being that small countries must fit their foreign policies to that of their neighbors. There also was the statement in an interview by former United States Ambassador Joseph E. Davies, who held it to be quite natural for Soviet Russia to want parts of Finland and that the neighbors of the Soviet Union must be allowed to join it "voluntarily," since the Soviet Union does not threaten American security.

What a different world it was in which these favorable statements to Soviet Russia and harmful statements to Finland were made!

Finland was now beset by criticisms from without as well as at home. The Finnish army had reached its strategic objectives in early 1942, after which it stood "at rest." The war continued to an extent, but its tempo was not sufficient to inspire or hold national unity. Casualties, privation, staggering costs, worsened the home front situation. The people began to grumble, as free men always do. Why shouldn't Finland get out of the war? the grumblers asked. They complained about the "black-out" of information, much of which was of such nature that even Finnish officials did not dare speak out.

One group of Finns on their own initiative formed the Finnish-American Society, in 1943, for the purpose of emphasizing the prevailing belief in Finland that the situation would become dangerously critical to Finland if the United States and Finland were to declare war on each other.

Some Finns criticized their government because it had not defined its war aims more clearly. The Social Democratic party, in a statement made November, 1943, did this by stating that: "The people of Finland have wanted to live in peace. . . . The prerequisite, however, is a peace that will guarantee our country's freedom and independence. We cannot bargain with these. . . ."

Peace Rumors Become Reality

A note from Moscow reached Finland by way of the Swedish Foreign Office in November, 1943, to the following effect:

1. If Finland is prepared to discuss peace, her representative would be welcomed in Moscow.
2. Before that, however, the Soviet Union must have a statement of Finland's observations and proposals. It would be important to keep the statement brief and general, and territories which had not belonged to Finland should not be demanded. The answer should be friendly and should in no event close the door to further conversations. If an understanding is reached, the peace itself can be worked out later.
3. Moscow has no intention of making Finland a province or of violating Finnish independence, unless forced to do so by future Finnish policy. Absolute secrecy regarding the negotiation is important.

When forwarding it the Swedish government expressed the belief that Sweden would be able to meet Finland's immediate food needs.

Finland pursued the Moscow offer in the hope that it would lead to official discussions. As a basis for discussions, the Finns asked that Finland's boundaries should be fixed as of 1939. They also expressed the hope that conversations would continue, but stated their country could not surrender cities and areas vital to its economy. The conversation appeared to have come to an abrupt end in that Moscow did not clarify Soviet peace terms.

Russia, having Finland on the fire, stepped up the propaganda heat and Russian airplanes bombed Helsinki on February 6th, eight days after the United States government entered the scene by playing the monkey's part in pulling Russia's chestnuts out of the fire. The United States "advised" Finland that the way to secure peace was to approach Russia (its saving grace, if any, was that it did not advise Finland to do so on *bended knee with hat in hand*) and hope for the best. In it Finland was told that "it is impossible to close one's eyes to the fact that the present conflict is a world war, in which no separate war can be acknowledged to exist." This note killed Finland's last hope from the United States. The British joined in the same hue and cry. The Finns now indeed stood alone in the world.

Left to her own resources Finland sent Mr. Paasikivi to Stockholm on February 12th to discuss the situation with the Russian Ambassador to Sweden, Madame Kollontay. She informed him that Moscow was prepared to accept a Finnish delegation immediately. Russian planes added a postscript to Madame Kollontay's suggestion by making one of their heaviest air raids on Helsinki. Inscrutable fate, as though determined to give the Finns the third degree, arranged for the German Minister to Finland to state officially that Germany would consider Finland guilty of downright treachery if she were to make a separate peace and that if she did, "Germany would draw her own conclusions"—whatever that might mean.

Russia, on February 19th, sent Finland her armistice terms, divided into two parts:

I. Terms to be accepted immediately:

1. The Soviet Union does not demand that Finland declare war on Germany, but naturally Finland must sever all relations with Germany. If Finland wants to remain neutral, she cannot allow the soldiers of a foreign power to remain within her borders. She must at least intern them. If this task is too difficult for Finland, the Soviet Union is ready to give the necessary support with airplanes and armed forces.

2. Restoration of the 1940 peace treaty. Withdrawal of Finnish forces to the 1940 boundary.

3. The immediate return of Russian prisoners and other Soviet citizens in internment camps and in labor service.

II. Questions which should be discussed:

4. Negotiations involving partial or total demobilization, to be conducted at Moscow.

5. Questions of reparations for damage caused by Finnish military operations and by the conquest of Soviet territory.

6. The question of Petsamo.

While it seemed impossible to the Finnish government to meet all of these harsh terms, the government presented the problem to a secret session of Parliament on February 29, 1944, after which a parliamentary majority of 105 to 80 voted to approve the governmental decision to estimate the situation. In the reply to Russia, the Finnish government expressed its serious desire to re-establish peace with Russia, stated that it had considered the armistice terms most carefully, and concluded by asking that Finland be given an opportunity to present her views regarding certain questions. Russia's reply of March 10th stated that the Finnish answer was totally unsatisfactory, since Russia's terms were "obvious minimum terms," and that when Finland had approved them it would be then in order to discuss ending hostilities.

The propaganda against Finland was again stepped up. The King of Sweden publicly expressed the hope that Finland would, as it were, seize time by the forelock; Cordell Hull voiced the hope that the negotiations would lead to the severance of Finland's military alliance with Germany; President Franklin D. Roosevelt publicly stated that it seemed strange to him and America that Finland had co-operated with Nazi Germany, and he felt that he was speaking on behalf of all Americans when he hoped that Finland would take advantage of the opportunity to free herself from that co-operation.

Historical perspective, with the facts stripped of the clouds which obscure them with war-engineered psychosis, serves to emphasize the hollowness and insincerity of many of these statements which were made in the stress and heat of battle.

It must be remembered that the Finns also were under the same stress and heat of battle. They stood alone in honor in a world where dishonor flourished like the green bay tree. They, however, kept their heads, and although they seemed to be standing alone, they did so with the conviction that the God of right, honor and justice stood with them. They had sacrificed supremely to maintain their freedom and independence. To date they had kept their heads, honor, freedom and independence. They continued to do so as the furies were loosed at them by the governments of the peoples they most trusted and admired.

They acted in character. Since Soviet Russia had refused Finland's request to start negotiations before accepting Russia's terms, they withheld approval of Russia's demands in the following statement:

The Finnish government regrets that the Soviet Union did not consider it possible to give Finland an opportunity to present her views on these various questions, and that negotiations have been declared possible only after the Finnish government has accepted the Russian terms. The Finnish government, which earnestly continues to seek to establish peaceful relations, and hopes that negotiations will be begun, cannot, however, accept in advance the terms in question, which deeply affect the existence of the nation without even knowing definitely their content and meaning.

Moscow countered on March 20th, through an intermediary, that the Finnish government "send one or two delegates to obtain from the Soviet Union an explanation of the armistice terms proposed by Russia."

The Finnish government complied with Moscow's request and, at the same time, released the following statement on the status of negotiations:

Since it has been claimed in certain quarters that Russia's original terms have been modified in some respects, and many sources have assured that a favorable modification of terms was possible, it is important that all this be clarified.

Finland's two delegates met in Moscow with Molotov and his aides on March 27th and 29th. Molotov told them that he considered the most important point of Russia's terms to be that of the Finns severing relations with the Germans and interning them. The Finns stated that they considered the adjustment of the 1940 boundaries to be the most important negotiation point, but Molotov was adamant. He did agree to scale downward a few minor demands, but when the Finnish delegates referred to the "terrifying" magnitude of the terms Molotov stated flatly that Soviet Russia terms were the minimum, and then significantly added that, in a sense, they were punishment for Finland's having been at war with Russia three different times during the previous twenty-five years. He neglected admitting that Russia had been the aggressor in each of the wars, and that Finland had only defended herself. Whereupon the Finnish delegates remonstrated over the magnitude and harshness of Moscow's terms, Molotov would dismiss them with the statement, "Russia has enough power to impose any terms she wishes."

At the conclusion of the conferences, Molotov gave the Finnish delegates Russia's armistice terms in the following form:

1. Severance of relations with Germany, and either internment or ousting of German forces and vessels in Finland by the end of April at the latest. In either case, Russia could lend Finland military aid.

2. Restoration of the Russo-Finnish treaty of 1940, and withdrawal of Finnish forces to the 1940 boundary, to be completed by several stages during April.

3. Immediate return of Allied and Russian prisoners-of-war as well as civilians, whether interned or employed by the Finns; if peace instead of armistice is concluded, the return of prisoners-of-war to be mutual.

4. A fifty-per-cent demobilization of the Finnish army, to be completed by the end of May, and reduction of the entire Finnish army to a peace-time footing during June and July. (To be included in the agreement, or to be made into a separate agreement to be signed simultaneously with the peace or armistice.)

5. For damages caused by Finnish military operations and occupation of Russian areas, reparations to the amount of 600,000,000 American dollars to be paid in five years in commodities (paper, cellulose, ships, various machinery and installations).

6. The return to Russia of Petsamo and the Petsamo region, which Russia voluntarily turned over to Finland in the peace treaties of 1920 and 1940.

7. Insofar as Finland approves the above six conditions, Russia will consider it possible to relinquish her lease of Hanko and the surrounding area without any compensation.

The government consulted some of Finland's leading economists who pointed out that Russian reparations demands would require fifty-five per cent of Finland's maximum possible production for five years and stated that to pay them the Finns would have to discover ways to live without eating. Parliament considered the Russian demands in secret session and gave the government a unanimous vote of confidence on April 18th. Following this, the Finnish government notified Russia that the proposed terms had been considered by the Finnish Parliament and government and that:

This consideration disclosed that the acceptance of these terms, which in part cannot be carried out for purely technical reasons, would actually weaken and destroy the possibilities for Finland to exist as an independent nation and, experts agree, would place a burden on the Finns which is far beyond her ability to bear.

The Finnish government, which earnestly desires the return of peaceful relations and lasting good relations with its eastern neighbor, regrets that the terms now proposed, which it has carefully considered, do not offer possibilities for the achieving of this goal.

Russia publicly announced on April 22nd, in a brief statement, that it had been informed that Finland had rejected the Soviet armistice terms as a basis for negotiations; therefore, negotiations had been ended. Clever and brainy and tricky as they are, Russian leaders frequently make significant mistakes. Vishinsky made one on the same day by stating in a government report the final phase of the negotiations which included Russia's demands.

No art of rhetoric was able to hide the bare bones of Russia's harsh and unjust demands. This was fortunate for Finland whose good reputation had been hurt by propaganda badgering, in that Moscow's cruel peace terms demonstrated clearly that Finland sought only to maintain her independence, while Soviet demands made Russia's intentions indisputably clear: Russia's purpose was to crush Finland either by armed force or economic demands. This served to decrease the efforts of even the Communist cell in the United States State Department to force Finland to accept Russia's terms.

Hitler deplored Finland's consideration of Russia's proposal. He wrote Field Marshal Mannerheim that he would not supply Finland with further weapons until Mannerheim gave her assurance that they would be effectively used against Russia. Hitler also stopped Germany's grain shipments to Finland, which had been provided in accordance with the German-Finnish trade treaty.

Delays, uncertainty, dwindling food supplies, unrest at home, Russia's unyielding attitude, German threats, two and a half years of *sitzkrieg* warfare, and prolonged privation and sacrifice now began to take their toll on Finland's spirit. Worse still, in the spring of 1944, every indication pointed toward Russia's resumption of armed hostilities against Finland in an effort to bring the Finns to their knees. Russia's successful repulse of the Germans at Stalingrad, and the invasion of France by the Western Powers had enabled Russia to shift more troops and war matériel to the Finnish front. The tired and poorly equipped Finnish army faced an overwhelmingly great Communist military force when Russia launched her attack on June 9th. These

new great Russian forces soon captured Finland's main line of
defense.

The Finnish government decided, in its efforts to avoid a
catastrophe, to form a new government. It did this as a result
of Moscow's repeated charge that its present government was
not representative. The Finns' hope was that a new government
might be able to bring about peace with Russia. Almost simultaneously with their reaching this decision, Russia sent word
that she was willing to conduct peace negotiations even with the
old government. Although the Finnish army defense had stiffened
and Germany offered to hurry planes and reinforcements, the
Finnish government preferred to negotiate with Russia. To this
end, the Finnish officials sent word to Russia through an intermediary that their country was prepared to end the war and
sever relations with Germany.

The plot now began to thicken. Russia agreed, on the condition that Finland first surrender. On the same day, June 23rd,
Ribbentrop arrived in Helsinki to demand a "clearly defined"
attitude about Finland's remaining to the end in war alongside of Germany; otherwise, he stated, Hitler would forthwith
cut off all supplies to Finland.

The two sharp horns of the dilemma which prodded the
Finns were whether to finally accept Germany as a war partner,
or continue to strive for peace with Soviet Russia. Field Marshal
Mannerheim urged the first alternative; President Ryti the second. Ryti finally yielded to Mannerheim, and, since it was
uncertain that Parliament would approve and also because parliamentary consent would have kept the pact in force under
another government, President Ryti demonstrated his greatness
and the completeness of his patriotism by concluding the pact
on his own responsibility and without countersignature, in the
form of a letter to the Reich Chancellor. In it he referred to
the conversations that had taken place and his belief that Germany would fulfill its promises of military assistance and other
future promised aid in assisting the Finns to defeat Russia's at-

tack on Finland. He added: "In this connection I beg to assure you that Finland has decided to wage war side by side with Germany until the danger which threatens Finland from Russia is removed." Ryti concluded with the following statement:

Taking into consideration the aid to a comrade-in-arms which Germany is giving to Finland in her present difficult situation, I declare as the President of Finland I shall not make peace with the Soviet Union except in agreement with the German Reich, and will not permit the Government of Finland, appointed by me, or any other persons, to take steps toward negotiations concerning peace, or any negotiations that might serve that end, except in agreement with the German Reich.

Ryti's action brought the heavens down on Finland. The United States severed diplomatic relations with her on June 30th. Germany at first sent important war materials but shortly thereafter sent only small supplies, a few troops and a few planes. She withdrew the latter about the middle of July. President Ryti resigned in an effort to ease the situation and General Mannerheim succeeded him.

The Final Act

The curtain now rises on the last act of the tragedy: Finland's valor and Russia's perfidy.

On September 4, 1944, Russia agreed to an armistice for the period of peace negotiations, with the stipulation that *the Finns were to stop firing on September 4th*, but that *the Russians were to continue to fire until September 5th*.

On September 18th, Molotov made numerous charges to the Finnish representatives without granting them an opportunity for rebuttal against the "bloody and criminal" government of Finland. He then demanded that they sign the preliminary peace agreement before noon of the following day. If they did not do so, he stated, Russia would occupy the whole of Finland. At

6 A.M. on the following morning an alerted secret session of the Finnish Parliament authorized their representatives to sign the Soviet-dictated peace terms.

The next chapter will analyze the implications as well as the cost burden Soviet Russia's peace terms placed on Finland.

A review of Finland's defensive actions against Russian aggression shows that Finland lost the war, was branded as a war criminal, and that Russia saddled her with the most staggering reparations load, when population and resources are considered, that any victor ever has placed on a defeated enemy.

Russia's charge that Finland was a "war criminal" cannot be supported by her foreign policy which never deviated from that of strict neutrality. Finland fought only to defend herself against an invader. Her primary military aim was that of trying to prevent her area from becoming a theater of war or of being occupied by Russia. Hard necessity forced her to follow the course she chose, and at each turn of events she tried to meet the most threatening danger. In the short view it is possible that her people were too stubbornly unyielding at times for their immediate best advantage. One of her major handicaps was that her people, devoutly cherishing freedom, were willing to die to retain it. Another of her handicaps was that justice lives in Finnish hearts. These are old-fashioned, out of place qualities in a world of ruthless power politics.

In September, 1943, a United States Department official summarized Finland's foreign policy by saying: "Tactically, Finland has played her cards badly and has not received the thanks of the West, of the Soviet Union or of Germany. An example of this was Finland's refusal to take part in the offensives demanded by Germany. Finland stayed put but failed to give the Western Powers any advance guarantees of her stand."

If appraised in a material way, loss of territory, lives lost, property destroyed and reparations costs, Finland's valiant fight against a ruthless invader seems to have been futile.

If appraised in a paraphrase of one of the most inspiring and challenging phrases ever conceived and created by man, the Finns can say with Job: "I have kept mine integrity."

When present-day nations have disappeared, seas dried up and the tallest mountains have been eroded into small hills, integrity will continue to come ahead of every other quality.

Chapter eighteen

Peace and Reparations

The setting of their tragedy revealed that the Finns had few alternatives from which to choose. They could continue to fight until Soviet Russia had killed their last soldier and destroyed their last home, or they could surrender and place themselves at the mercy of their conquerors and world opinion.

The setting showed also that Finland's surrender would be greatly to the advantage of Soviet Russia in that (a) it would release many Soviet divisions which were badly needed to occupy territories which Moscow intended to grab when Germany collapsed, and (b) it would give free exit to the Soviet's Baltic fleet from the Gulf of Finland and thereby give Moscow control of the Baltic.

Finland's new Prime Minister, A. Hackzell, in his radio address to the Finnish nation on September 2, 1944, which Parliament had approved, evaluated the situation and outlined the procedure for re-establishing peace between Finland and Russia.

He stated that Finland's situation required revaluation as unexpectedly unfavorable changes had taken place in the military situation since the preceding April. Earlier, he stated, the Finns had been able to halt the enemy's attacks, but the developments of World War II had left Finland almost more isolated than ever before. Germany, he said, was so hard pressed that she could send Finland neither war matériel nor vital food supplies. Germany's ally, Rumania, had surrendered on August 27th, and on

August 29th Bulgaria had announced her intention to withdraw from the war. France and all but northern Italy were lost to Germany, hence Finland could gain nothing by continuing her co-operation with Germany.

It was his government's belief, he added, that the political agreement which Finland had made with Germany under pressure, and which was born out of Finland's necessity to repel the Soviet's June offensive, was no longer valid, since ex-President Ryti had made it in his own name. Hackzell's speech cleared the way for formal peace negotiations with Russia.

These negotiations had been going on informally for some time. The Finnish government had queried the Soviet Ambassador in Stockholm on August 25th to learn if his government would be willing to receive a Finnish delegation to negotiate for an armistice or peace, or both. The reply, received on August 29th, set forth two preliminary conditions which Finland must fulfill before Russia would be prepared to accept a Finnish delegation. They were (a) Finland must publicly declare that she was severing relations with Germany, and (b) Finland must demand that the Germans withdraw their forces from Finnish territory within two weeks after the date the Finnish government had accepted the preliminary conditions, and in any case not later than September 15th. To make clear that these conditions were important, official and final, Moscow added that they were made in the name of Great Britain and had been approved by the United States.

When, on September 2nd, Prime Minister Hackzell presented his government's views to the Finnish Parliament and recommended that it accept the preliminary conditions, Parliament did so by a vote of 108 to 45. The forty-five Parliament members who voted in the negative did so on the grounds that Moscow had offered no guarantees which would assure Finland's independence.

Finland and Soviet Russia signed an armistice on September 4th. Aside from its historically unique and barbarically unchivalrous provisions, which required the Finns to discontinue all firing on September 4th but permitted the Red troops to continue to murder unarmed Finns until September 5th, it was more honorable and advantageous for Finland than had been the terms previously offered, because under it the Finns could begin negotiations without formal surrender, and Germany was given a brief, though insufficient period to withdraw her forces.

After having complied with Russia's preliminary demands, Finland sent her peace negotiators, headed by Premier Hackzell, to Moscow on September 6th, where they were forced to cool their heels until September 14th. The entry the late Senator Arthur H. Vandenberg made in his diary on May 1, 1946, while attending the meetings in Paris of the Council of Foreign Ministers, as advisor to Secretary of State James F. Byrnes, throws light on the problems which the Finnish peace delegation faced in Moscow:

There is no sense in carrying on this Punch-and-Judy business; it makes no contribution to better international relations, and it is beneath the dignity of the United States to be shoved around like a fourth-rate power by stubborn, contemptuous, irrational dictators from the Kremlin. . . . The tragedy of it all is that the rest of this sick world could agree on a total post-war program in twenty minutes. Only Moscow stands in the way.[1]

The Finnish delegation learned, on December 14th, that there was nothing to negotiate, as Russia had dictated the terms on the apparent assumption that *might* was *right*. The two governments signed a preliminary peace pact on September 19th, the terms of which were extremely close to the limit which would permit Finland's national existence.

The Finns' first duty under the pact was to free their soil of German military units. In compliance with Russia's conditions for holding negotiation meetings, the Government of Finland had, on September 2nd, formally requested the German

---

[1] *Private Papers of Senator Vandenberg*, ed. by A. H. Vandenberg, Jr. (Boston, Houghton Mifflin Co., 1952).

government to withdraw from Finland all of its military units stationed there. It took this action realizing that even with the best of good will and complete compliance with the request, the Germans could not meet the Moscow-made timetable. The Finns did believe, however, that Germany would co-operate and thereby not make Finland's precarious situation more difficult. Their belief could not have been more wrong in that the Germans showed that their fury, like that of the scorned woman's, was beyond anything known in hell.

Finland was now forced into another war with a great power, her third one within a five-year period. Fortunately for central and south Finland, but unfortunately for the Finns who lived in the Lapland province, the Germans had concentrated their forces in Lapland, nearly 200,000 well-equipped troops who were stationed in carefully fortified positions.

Nazi wrath became psychopathic when Finland requested the German government to withdraw its forces from Finnish soil and they hurried large forces of Storm Trooper demolition experts to Finland with orders to destroy everything.

What It Cost Finland to Remove German Troops

The cost of removing the Germans placed a new and unexpectedly heavy burden on Finland, which then was staggering under the already heavy load of the cost of defending herself from Russian aggression.

Finland suffered great losses during the 224 days of intense, fierce fighting which began on September 15, 1944, and ended with the last German soldier hurrying across the boundary to Norway on April 27, 1945. His departure cleared Finland of German troops and thereby fulfilled one of her preliminary armistice pledges.

Finland's effort to drive the Germans out cost the lives of 737 soldiers, 254 more missing and 27 frozen to death. Her wounded in this war totaled 2808.

In addition, the retiring fanatical, wrathful Germans, to carry out their orders to destroy everything, had either wantonly destroyed or confiscated property with a value of more than $600,000,000.

Some of the things the Germans destroyed could be considered as military objectives. These included more than seven hundred of the nine hundred more important highway bridges in Lapland and hundreds more culverts; every railroad bridge; railway tracks and rails twisted beyond use, and every other telephone or telegraph pole for hundreds of kilometers.

The things the Germans destroyed which could not in any sense be classified as military objectives were farm homes and buildings, even villages and towns, livestock and farm machinery. In addition, they planted many land mines, of which the Finns have found more than 7,000, but before clearing them out the mines had killed fifty civilians and seventy-five mine clearers.

In carrying out their scorched-earth program, the Germans destroyed 87 per cent of all homes and buildings in the capital of Lapland. One description of this attempted mortal blow at Rovaniemi, written in the summer of 1946, fourteen months after the Nazis had done their worst, states:

The time: After supper on a midsummer day in 1946. The sun is still high in the sky, for there is daylight around the clock at this season of the year.

The place: Rovaniemi, Finland, just under the Arctic Circle, the capital city of the Lapland province, nine out of ten of whose buildings had been war-destroyed two years earlier.

The setting: A one-story wooden barracks surrounded by gaunt chimneys and heaps and heaps of rubble which once had been homes. The stark chimneys warning mankind of the waste, horror and futility of war. Here and there homes and business buildings in different stages of construction are seen rising from the surrounding rubble.

The sound of hammer striking nail is heard as men and women, hard driven by the inevitable coming of the cold, hurry the hammer harder and faster. One-horse carts and charcoal-powdered trucks rumble along the streets carrying building materials and their large cans or barrels of water. The town has no water system, hence all water must be hauled from wells or the near-by river. Children's voices rise and fall on all sides as they play games in the piles of bricks and stones which once had been homes.

Six years later, in 1952, Finnish determination and industry has enabled Rovaniemi to rise phoenixlike from her ashes to become again the queen city of all the northern world. In Kittilä, which had a prewar population of 1500, the Nazis destroyed every building in it except the Lutheran church and a few small cattle sheds. They destroyed 90 per cent of the buildings in Enontekiö and partially destroyed many other towns and villages. Altogether they completely destroyed more than 25,000 homes and farm and business buildings, 130 communal or congregational buildings, killed 38,527 head of cattle, sheep and hogs, and broke more than 30,000 mowing and threshing machines, hayrakes, plows, harrows, scythes, spades, axes, saws and other farm equipment. To top this off, they confiscated 30,000 gross tons, plus 30 vessels of less than 500 tons of Finnish shipping.

During the period when the Nazis were unleashing hell's furies, Finland evacuated 47,000 Lapland residents to her central provinces. Approximately 40,000 other Lapland residents who were not in the direct line of Nazi destruction remained in their own homes or nearby forests until the terror had passed.

It is extremely doubtful if Finland, especially the Lapland province, could have survived without the help of Sweden, which in every form was given with magnificent generosity. The ramplike bridge which connects Tornio, Finland, and Haparanda, Sweden, became truly a bridge of life during the fall and winter of 1944. Over it, ahead of Nazi destruction, fled thousands of Finns. At one time more than two thousand per day poured across it into the peaceful, secure haven of friendly Sweden.

Few of them had adequate clothing; many babies were wrapped only in newspapers, and countless people walked barefooted, carrying their all on their backs or driving their cattle before them. But they came without red tape, hindrance or delay.

The Swedes fed and clothed these moneyless, hungry hordes, gave them shelter, and in as many as four or five special trains daily, hurried all 55,000 of them on to central and southern Sweden, there to place them in homes, hospitals and other institutions—and all of this without charge.

Soviet Russia's Stupendous Reparations Bill

The Russian-Finnish Paris peace treaty of 1947 is a cynical violation of the principles the Allies enumerated and agreed to, including Russia, in the Atlantic Charter which had stated that "signatories desire to see no territorial changes that do not accord with the freely expressed wish of the people concerned." In the treaty alliance between Great Britain and the Soviet Union they agreed "to act in accordance with the two principles of not seeking territorial aggrandizement for themselves and of non-interference in the internal affairs of other states."

How different are the ways which the Finns and the Communists follow. According to an old and still adhered to Finnish proverb, "A man's given word is as much a part of him as are the horns of an ox"; whereas the Communists ignore the provisions of the formal and solemn treaties to which they bind their government.

The Soviet government's reparations demands on Finland were far more severe than any that Satan himself had put in the minds of his other faithful minions. The Soviet Union's reparations bill was approved by nine United Nations governments, including the United Kingdom of Great Britain which officially, in the late fall of 1940, through Lord Halifax in a message to the Finnish people, had given assurances *that when*

*the Allies achieved victory, Finland would surely participate in
those advantages which a true and just peace would bring.*

Soviet Russia's demands were recorded and made final in the
peace treaty which Finland signed in Paris on February 10, 1947,
with Russia and nine of the allied nations. The United States
was not a party, because Uncle Sam had not declared war on
Finland. Some Finns today, exercising their hindsight, regret
that the United States did not declare war on Finland, since had
it done so it might have been able to force Soviet Russia to
modify its hard peace terms. These Finns add that even had the
United States declared war on Finland, the declaration would
not in any way have lessened Finland's admiration and abiding
friendship for America. As it was, Finland had no friend to
protect her at the Paris peace conference and thus stood alone
in her hour of trial.

Soviet Russia's attitude was that Finland had "shed Russian
blood" and therefore must pay heavily, even though she had
done it while defending herself. Although it was clearly evident
to the other participating nations as well as to Soviet Russia
that Russia was the aggressor and that Finland fought only in
defense of her independence, they gave no consideration to
Russia's wrongs and Finland's rights.

Finland's two defensive wars with Russia cost her in human
terms the lives of 84,200 men, 90 per cent of whom were between twenty and thirty-nine years old. It cost her the torn
bodies of 50,000 soldiers, left her with 50,000 war orphans and
24,000 war widows. Her losses in men killed represented 7 per
cent of the population capable of work and corresponds to the
surplus of births over deaths for the five year 1936–40 period.

Soviet Russia demanded, and nine United Nations supported
her demands, that Finland cede approximately 11 per cent of
her total area to Russia. About 420,000 Finns lived in this territory. An interesting historical footnote should be added here
because of its significance. Soviet Russia, in an effort to get this
group of nearly a half million Finns to live in the Communist

paradise, offered to permit them to remain in and own their old homes. The total number of Finns who accepted Russia's offer was *nineteen*.

The Finnish territory that Russia took comprised one of the few rich, fertile agricultural areas of Finland. With it went a large number of Finnish enterprises as well as homes and other property.

This Soviet demand increased the cost enormously to Finland for having fought to prevent herself from becoming a helpless unit in the so-called Union of Soviet Socialist "Republics." In addition to that was the task of providing homes for more than 425,000 homeless Finns.

Soviet Russia also demanded and secured from Finland a 50-year lease on the Peninsula of Porkkala territory, which is just outside Helsinki, for a naval base, as well as the right to use Finland's railways, waterways, roads and air routes to transport personnel and freight to the Porkkala naval base. This would be similar to a United States government lease to Soviet Russia of Staten Island and use of all transportation facilities. The Finns are allowed to send trains through their own former territory, but the passenger cars of these trains must be tightly locked and their windows covered with steel curtains, so that no one can see anything while Russian engineers take the trains through the territory.

One article of the Paris treaty bound Finland to apprehend and try persons accused (by Russia) of "having committed, ordered or abetted war crimes." Since those officials who were responsible for having decided on war or peace according to the constitution could not, under Finnish law as it then stood, be accused of crime against peace, Russia therefore demanded that Finland make a new, retroactive law—a procedure wholly incompatible with the established principles of penal law in all civilized countries. Finland had to yield and such a law was submitted to the Diet in August, 1945, and was passed the following

October. Soviet Russia wanted to vent her spleen against the high Finnish officials who had refused to do her bidding.

When Finland, under duress, had passed this law, which involved a deviation in many significant respects from the long and well-established principles of justice, the Soviet government presented General Mannerheim, the President of Finland, with a list of Finnish "war criminals" and an ultimatum that he sign it.

President Mannerheim, with a figurative if not an actual Soviet bayonet pressing against his back, studied the list carefully and saw that his name had not been included. He reached the highest point of the pinnacle of true greatness when he took his pen, wrote his own name at the top of the list and then placed his signature to the order.

The Communists, notwithstanding, did not include Mannerheim in the list of their Finnish "war criminals," because he was Finland's greatest war hero and they were still afraid, with all of their power and might, of the people of this small nation whom they had tied hand and foot and demilitarized. Their fear was well found. That it was well founded is pointed up by the passage of remarks by a Norwegian and a Finnish representative at a Scandinavian countries conference just after the war, at which the Norwegian expressed some doubt about the propriety of Finland being permitted to participate, since she had fought with Germany in World War II. The Finnish representative then asked him, "What did you do? At the start you didn't put up much fight against Germany!" The Norwegian lamely replied, "The Germans seized all of our war matériel and our soldiers. What could we do?"

"Yes, that is true," replied the Finn, bitingly, "but you still had your knives, didn't you?"

The Communists were still afraid of Finns' knives. They did not occupy the country. Soviet Russia forced Finland to "try" the list of her "war criminals" whom the Reds had selected, under the newly created retroactive law which could be likened to that of a demand by baseball fans for an umpire to change the rules in the middle of the game and thereby ensure the home team's victory. Under this law and by duress, Finland tried President Ryti and seven members of his cabinet and found them "guilty" of having opposed Russia's criminal aggression.

Included in the Paris peace treaty terms were provisions which required Finland to set free immediately all persons—meaning Communists—who had been imprisoned for their sabotaging efforts against their homeland during the war. Another Soviet Russian treaty stipulation was designed to protect their "pretty-boy" Boyd's possible treasonable activities by requiring Finland to "dissolve" all organizations of the "Fascist type." These included the Civic Guards, a voluntary Home Guard Organization which had been formed during the War of Independence, 1917–18; the Lotta Svärd, a voluntary women's auxiliary, likewise founded in 1918, which has served as a model for similar organizations in several countries; and the War Veterans' Union and other minor organizations of similar nature. The treaty also required Finland to legalize Communism.

The Paris peace treaty "closely restricted" Finland's armed forces to that of "meeting tasks of an internal character and the local defense of the frontiers." Soviet Russia, with a fifty to one ratio of military strength over Finland, was taking no chances and limited Finland's land army to a total personnel of 34,000, navy to 4500, and air force to 3000. In simple terms, Finland is a demilitarized state.

Soviet Russia also claimed and received all German assets in Finland by order of the Allied Control Council for Germany, although it was the Finns who, after great property losses, drove the Germans out.

The foregoing and other provisions seem harsh and unjust, but they apparently served only to whet the Communists' appetites for the main course which followed in the form of economic penalties for Finland's having dared to defend herself.

Soviet Russia demanded reparation damages—with no more true justice to recompense than a thief would have who stumbled and hurt himself while committing robbery—and secured helpless Finland's agreement to pay $300,000,000 in gold value of commodities (specified as to kind and quality) within six years at the rate of $50,000,000 per year. Huge as was Russia's bill, its size was doubled by the treaty specification that the value of the commodities Finland delivered would be assessed at world market prices in United States dollars at the rate which prevailed in 1938. Thus Russia's reparations bill actually was $600,000,000.

The treaty made no allowance to Finland for the price increases which had taken place between 1938 and the time schedule fixed for her to deliver the commodities. The treaty also specified that Finland's deliveries should consist of 33.7 per cent machinery and apparatus; 20 per cent new tonnage; 8.3 per cent cable products; 4.7 per cent old tonnage; and 33⅓ per cent wood products. Thus 62 per cent of Finland's reparation goods consisted of ship building and metal products which Finnish industry was not equipped to produce. In 1939, for example, Finland's metal industry, which now was to carry 62 per cent of the Russian penalty load, produced only 4 per cent of Finland's exports. To fulfill this enforced obligation, Finland had to build many new plants at great expense and purchase costly machinery and high-cost materials abroad in a scarce market. Since Russia imposed a 5-per-cent monthly penalty for all goods she did not deliver on specified schedule dates, Finland shouldered additional hardships.

There are innumerable stories in Finland which reveal the ingenuity and initiative of Finnish workers and officials' efforts to make deliveries on time. The Russians accepted no delivery without first having a swarm of inspectors go over it with microscopes. One spic-and-span-new ship passed their inspection except for one item—there was no clock in the captain's quarters. While the Soviet inspectors shouted imprecations the Finns hurried to town, found a clock and installed it with only seconds left to meet delivery schedules.

Another time, the Russian inspectors discovered a tiny spring missing from a great machine that already had been loaded on a train headed for the Russian border with only enough time for it to reach Russia by a given hour. It if failed to do so, the Russians would place a 5-per-cent penalty on the Finnish factory that made the machine. The Finns sent the train and machine on their way, hurried to a factory and waited while a factory worker made the spring, and then delivered it by plane and put it in place at the Russian border on schedule. Russia penalized Finland $253,000 for late deliveries the first year, 1945; and $266,000 the second. The penalties have been far less since that time. Finland has made many deliveries ahead of schedule. They amounted to $3,100,000 in 1947, but Russia refuses to credit them against the late delivery penalty account.

The Finnish government's first impression, after learning the details of Russia's demands, was that their country could not possibly fulfill them, since to do so would require 45 per cent of the entire nation's maximum production for a six-year period. The annual reparation payments would call for 5,500 million (prewar value) Finnish marks, or 5,090 million marks more than the surplus of Finland's foreign balance in 1938.

A comparison of the reparations burden which the United Nations placed on Italy—whose moral position as an aggressor was indefensible, while that of attacked Finland was above challenge—helps to emphasize the injustice of Finland's reparations bill. Italy, with a population of 45,000,000 people had to pay a $360,000,000 reparations bill, of which Russia received $100,-000,000, while Finland with 4,000,000 people was presented with a $600,000,000 reparations bill which Russia alone received.

Italy, moreover, was given a two-year period before having to begin payments, and Soviet Russia was to supply Italy's necessary raw materials. Finland had to begin her deliveries instantly and supply all of the necessary raw materials.

Russia later did scale Finland's reparations bill downward and extended the time for deliveries so that the total the Finns eventually will pay equals about $500,000,000 in today's currency.

No one, not even the Finns, believed that they could do it, but as of February, 1952, they had paid 95.4 per cent of their reparations bill and cheerful word comes from Finland in April, 1952, that "by September 19, 1952, the scheduled date for Finland's last delivery, the last little screw will have crossed the border."

When that date comes and the final delivery is made, the Finns can say as did the drunken Irishman in Pittsburgh forty years ago, after he had stopped a fast-moving, heavily loaded trolley car by standing in the middle of the tracks, "Thank God, Ireland's free."

Finland indeed will be free of the reparations load on September 19, 1952, but she will not yet be free of inflation, or of the effects of privation on her people, of sacrifice, of debt and all of its attendant evils.

America and Sweden have given Finland substantial financial help. The greater part of United States funds advanced to Finland by private banks and government lending agencies was once described by a Finnish cabinet member to be "like the Marshall Plan, but with one big difference; the difference being one between accepting a gift from a friend or a loan from a bank." The Finns did receive two and a half million dollars worth of UNRRA help for the German-destroyed Lapland. They would have been happy to have received more UNRRA or any Marshall Plan aid, but they could not do so because of the "hard fact of geography."

Inflation in Finland

Every country which participated in World War II is still suffering from economic instability. Those countries, such as Finland, which both participated in and were ravaged by the war, have suffered doubly.

Finland seemed to have turned the corner away from increasing economic instability in 1951. She did this through the simple but effective expedient of her people working harder to produce more goods for export, and by the effective and courageous steps her government took to halt the inflationary spiral by reestablishing an equilibrium between supply and demand.

The government's actions mainly consisted of adopting a new and more flexible system of adjusting wages to living costs, price reductions, credit restrictions, investment curtailments, tax reductions and lowered interest rates. At the end of 1951, Finland had nearly completed all of her postwar reconstruction, her war reparations to Russia, and had made substantial payments on the purchase account of new industrial and plant equipment which had been required to meet her war reparations bill. She also had reduced her public debt from 135.7 to 130.9 billion Finmarks (over $2,100,000).

Finland's total foreign public debt, according to preliminary estimates at the end of 1951, was the equivalent of 289 million dollars. Slightly more than 40 million dollars of it consists of credits extended to Finland by the Argentine, Brazilian and Colombian governments. The International Bank for Reconstruction and Development advanced them 12.5 million dollars. In terms of 1951 export volume and price level, Finland's longterm foreign debt was equal to the approximate value of 4½ months of her exports. Finland reduced her short-term credits by 14 billion Finmarks in 1951. The country's improved financial situation was reflected in a substantial increase in bank deposits which in 1951 reached an all-time high of over 200 billion Finmarks, nearly $100,000,000.

Despite this improved situation, some segments of the Finnish population have suffered unduly because of the Communist influence in the first postwar government which turned inflation loose. Now that the government has ousted Communists from key posts, it is doing everything possible to overcome Communist-created inflation evils and to check currency inflation.

The older, frugal generation in Finland has especially suffered because inflation has largely wiped out their lifetime savings, and also because Finland seems to have overlooked the generation which gave her independence.

The depreciation of the Finmark has placed some other groups in a precarious situation. The labor and farm worker pressure groups have gained for themselves wage increases that often were higher than the productivity of their work properly permitted, whereas salaried workers, especially those with university training, have suffered so greatly that their young people are entering the trades rather than pursuing their studies. This situation has created a dangerous social trend in a country which so vitally needs increasing numbers of technically and scientifically educated men and women.

Now, however, the Finns are keeping their eyes fixed and their efforts concentrated on their all-important task of stepping up production, to "get the bread wider," as they say. That done, they hold, it will be easier to divide the bread so that every class of society will get what its efforts entitle it to have.

At the present time the goal of every Finnish father and mother is to have at least four children. This is the case since statisticians have calculated that with only two children per family the Finnish population will be cut in half within a few generations; that it will remain stationary with three children, whereas with four children per family Finland will grow and remain strong. The government encourages this trend. During the war it issued extra ration cards for mothers of four or more children.

How does a Finnish family, consisting of father, mother and four children, divide its budget?

It spends an average of 45 per cent of its income for food which nutritional studies show is a fairly well-balanced diet. Milk and milk products come first. The Finns consume as great a quantity of them as does any other people, and milk is cheap and plentiful throughout Finland except in Lapland (where the people put salt instead of cream in their coffee). Scientific studies show also that when Finns store their potatoes in cool earth cellars they retain their vitamin C content far into the spring. Potatoes are plentiful and comparatively inexpensive in Finland.

Clothing is the next largest item in the Finnish budget and calls for 14 per cent of its income. Long and wet autumns and springs require that the children shall be well shod, and in winter, with the temperature 20 or more degrees below zero, they must be clothed to their nose tips.

At the present time, due to government rent regulations, our Finnish family spends only about 4 per cent of its income for rent. Government subsidies have brought rent costs down, but this is not a true saving, since the income producers are taxed for this purpose.

When the Finnish mother goes shopping for food or clothing, she has only a limited variety of articles from which to select. By far the greater part of the bread Finns eat is made of rye, a half-pound loaf of which costs around five cents. Meat, so a Finnish housewife thinks, is expensive—good beef costs one dollar per pound. Good meat is scarce since Finnish farmers raise only hogs for meat. The Finns largely rely on fish to supply their meat needs. They eat a great deal of Baltic herring—*silakka*—a smelt-size fat fish which they consider a delicacy that can be prepared in "a hundred different ways." This and the other fish they eat apparently supply them with their proteins and fat-soluble needs.

Sugar is now considered one of Finland's luxuries and is rationed, six pounds per month for each person. The Finns love coffee—no tea for them. Coffee also was rationed in 1951, a half pound per month, or three pounds for our family of six. The Finns run a special "coffee ship line" to Brazil to bring them coffee in exchange for paper and pulp. Butter, which is unrationed, costs the Finnish housewife about one dollar per pound, which she considers high; therefore, she buys rationed margarine when it is available.

What troubles the Finnish housewife most is that there are

so few green vegetables available in the winter that she can chose only from beets, carrots and potatoes.

The sturdiness, stamina and strength of Finnish bodies indicates that they, like Finnish qualities of character, have learned to thrive on simple but good fare.

Chapter nineteen

Finland's Present Foreign Policy

Finland demonstrated to understanding men that in her efforts to remain a free nation she, like Ruggles of Red Gap, could be "pushed just so far."

She suffered, not from moral guilt but because she was a small factor in a gigantic conflict. Her people should feel no sense of shame that their country met dishonor with honor, injustice with justice and blackmail with honest dealing. The last two thousand years of Christian practices and principles are wrong and should be cast aside if Finland was wrong in what she did and how she did it.

Finland declined an invitation to attend the European Economic Conference in 1947 (Marshall Plan) because it had become a "serious cause of difference between the great powers," and her policy always has been that of remaining "outside international conflicts." At the time, her government stated that she "sincerely wants to contribute to economic co-operation between the nations."

In 1947, Finland applied for membership in the United Nations. Russia and puppet Poland prevented her election with their negative votes.

Every evidence demonstrates that communism has failed to win the sympathy of the Finnish public, despite its having been well financed by Russia. The actual Communist party in Finland has never gained a dominant place in the country's political life.

Except for her direct dominance of Finland's economic life through reparations payments, her indirect efforts through the Comintern to advance the Communist cause in Finland, and her frowning but unvoiced disapproval of Finland's friendly relations with other nations, Russia has not overplayed her hand in Finland's internal affairs.

Stalin did create a flurry of concern in Finland in February, 1948, when he proposed in a letter to President Paasikivi that Soviet Russia and Finland conclude a mutual assistance pact.

Against whom, the reader asks? Why Germany, of course.

This proposal sounded ominous to Finland because the little nations which had signed similar pacts with Russia had had experiences similar to that of Czechoslovakia, the most recent victim of a Communist coup. Russia's proposed pact with Finland led the peoples of other countries to fear that Finland's end as a free, independent nation was nearing.

The sharp reaction of fellow travelers in other countries against Moscow's engineered Czechoslovakia coup startled even Moscow which, indifferent to the opinion of clear-thinking, honest men, tries always to retain the support of its deluded, muddled thinkers in other countries.

When he realized his mistake, Stalin let the intended Finnish firecracker fizz out in his hand. He was only fooling, anyway, he seemed to say. Molotov took his cue from Stalin and handed the Finnish delegation a proposal the terms of which were limited to the military implications of a possible unknown enemy attack on the Soviet Union through Finnish territory. If Stalin's original purpose was that of weakening Finnish morale in the forthcoming elections, he failed completely.

The Finns prepared and took with them a proposed pact which they were willing to sign. After Molotov had read its eight clauses he accepted its last six; then, after the manner of the Communist Korean Armistice members, he began to haggle. He stated that clauses one and two troubled him. The Finns yielded on the first clause but were adamant about accepting

Molotov's proposed changes of the second one because the meaning of his substitute offer was vague. The wary Finns, who had learned from experience that tragedies are the inevitable lot of every nation which gets caught in the quicksands of Soviet vagueness, held out for their own version.

Their stubborn determination to remain an independent nation, combined with their understanding of Russian deviousness, enabled them to avoid entering into an alliance with Soviet Russia which, Molotov explained at the first meeting, would be modeled after the Rumanian, Hungarian and Czechoslovakian-Russo treaties.

Even after the Finnish government had approved the treaty the Finnish Parliament debated it for weeks, during which period it took all necessary steps to prevent any of the "people's uprising" movements which had been such a successful Communist technique in other countries. Furthermore, since the Finns had never permitted Communist infiltration into their army and knew exactly who were undependable in the police forces, they remained calm about what had happened in Czechoslovakia.

The result of this and other Soviet Russian moves to gain control of Finland by hook or by crook is that the Finns have hardened in their resistance to communism.

Although Russia and Finland exist cheek-by-jowl, they are an entire civilization and an age apart in manners, customs, sense of honor and principles.

Finland, in religion, principles, political and economic procedures, respect for the individual's dignity and rights, culture, ways of living and outlook, is a part of western civilization. Her cross is that geographically she is partially surrounded by and thereby tied to the eastern civilization as it is expressed by Russia.

That which stands the Finns in good stead in their efforts to remain a free people and to hold the independence of their nation inviolate is that they think practically and realistically. Their ability to do so enables them to realize that regardless of the Soviet Union's record of shameful and shameless treatment of their country the Russians are their neighbors, and if they would permit, the Finns would make friends of them.

To that end the Finns have leaned over backward to be honest and scrupulous in fulfilling all of their treaty obligations with the Soviet Union.

The then Prime Minister, now President of Finland, Paasikivi, stated his belief, in the Independence Day address he delivered on December 6, 1944, that Finland's only means of building a peaceful and happier future was, then and henceforward, to conduct her foreign policy in such a manner as not to oppose the interests of the Soviet Union.

The principal objective of Finland's postwar policy has been that of doing everything, short of compromising her uncompromisable honor, to create and maintain good-neighbor relations with the Soviet Union.

Finland's purpose and intention to realize this objective was expressed by Foreign Minister R. Svento to a peace-festival gathering in Helsinki the day the Paris peace treaty was signed. Members of the Allied Control Commission and the Finnish government were present.

"We, on our part," Mr. Svento declared, speaking for the Finnish government and its people, "promise to you with whom we have been at war that we will never abandon the road of friendship and close co-operation which we have adopted towards the Soviet Union, and that we will continue to maintain friendly relations with Great Britain.

"We will not tolerate any attempts on Finnish territory to conspire against the cause of peace.

"We will not oppose the imperative norms of the new international law as agreed upon jointly by the Allied Nations."

This pledge denotes the disposition of the Finns to seek ways by which they can strengthen the foundations of their national independence with adoption of a good-neighbor policy.

Soviet Russia matched Finland's peace promises with a pledge not to interfere with Finland's internal affairs. These pledges prompted the Finns to reject the popular notion that the world is divided into two hostile parts. They determinedly refuse to classify themselves either behind or outside the iron curtain. This decision has helped them to keep on formally polite terms with Russia while at the same time they renewed their old friendships with the west.

Substantial evidence exists to support the belief that Russia's reparations demands have been in two ways tremendously helpful in defeating the spread of communism in Finland. First, since communism thrives only on human misery, Finland, without the full employment necessary to fill the Soviet Union's imperative reparations demands, would have had large numbers of unemployed workers at the war's end. Her industries were closed down. World markets had not yet revived, she was short of food supplies and other articles, and she was suffering from a vicious inflation cycle.[1] Russia's reparations requirements forced her to act on the double quick and revive her entire industrial plant, which in turn created full employment.

The second reason was that when the honest Finnish workmen saw how they were exploited for the Russian commissars, who often left the reparations shipment lying round for months after it arrived in Russia, their hearts were purified of the last confidence in the Soviet system.

The high-water mark of Communist influence in Finland came in 1945. Since that time Finnish Communists have lost key posts in government and labor unions. The Finns do not like communism, nor do they pretend that they do.

When, previous to the 1948 elections, Soviet Russia reduced her war reparations bill from $300,000,000 to $226,000,000, Finnish Communists shouted that the Finns should show their gratitude by voting Communist. The Finnish voters responded by

[1] The official exchange rate in Finland in 1944 was 49.35 Finmarks to 1 dollar, today it is 231 Finmarks, but the actual purchase power of the dollar is between 300 and 400 Finmarks. Since the value of the dollar also is depreciated in value, Finland has suffered doubly from inflation.

defeating a greater number of Communist candidates in that election than they had done in any previous election.

The Finns constantly face the same problems with Communists that other peoples face in their labor unions, in their local and national governments, and in their newspapers. But they watch more carefully and move more decisively when they are forced to deal with Communist trickery than do most other peoples. Some of the possible reasons for this are that although the Finns hate evil, they are capable of hating the evil of things they see in communism without also hating Communists, and also, because they know the Russian mind and its way of working (which so many peoples of the western world do not), they have developed a sixth sense of caution.

The voters of Finland, for example, ratified the alliance with Russia at the polls, while at the same time they repudiated communism. Soviet Russia had tried for months to induce the Finns to enter into its proposed alliance, but the Finns had said no and *no* and *no again*. Their continued refusals made a prophet of the English historian Francis Skirne, who wrote in 1903, "To dragoon the Finns into obedience is impossible—"

Regardless of the nature of Russian minor improprieties, the Finns tolerate them with true Christian forbearance and typical Finnish realism. They count all this as of little consequence when compared with their abiding purpose in life: living in harmony with other peoples, maintaining peace and protecting their independence.

Despite the Finns' neighborly attitude, the Russians fail to reciprocate in any way. For example, when, as sometimes happens during the summer, Finnish fishermen seek shelter from sudden storms in the Porkkala Islands (which are in the middle of the Finnish coast line), their relatives hear nothing from them for a month or two, nor are Finnish officials permitted to learn whether or not they are still alive. Usually after some anxious weeks they suddenly reappear. Where have they been? They reply that they have been confined incommunicado to their boats under arrest in some remote Russian harbor. Three young Finns disappeared in a storm near Kotka in 1951, but it was not until months later that an official note informed their parents that after the storm had driven their boat on to the Russian coast, the Reds had sentenced the youths "in due process of law" to spend three years in a Russian labor camp. Home owners everywhere who have to bear the cross of vicious neighbors are able to understand how great a trial the Russians are to the Finns, since their entire population is forced to live next door to such a neighbor.

They appear to be guided by a principle related closely to the one the late George B. Cortelyou followed. Mr. Cortelyou had served as private secretary to both Presidents Cleveland and McKinley, and later—under President Theodore Roosevelt—had successively filled three different cabinet positions with great distinction.

A friend once asked him, staunch Republican that he was, "What do you now think of your President, Uncle George?"

"I spent twenty years in and around the White House, David," Mr. Cortelyou replied, "and during that time I gained so much respect for the Presidency that I never speak ill of any President." Then, after a brief pause, he added, with his black eyes snapping: "But I can't help thinking!"

Nor can the Finns. And while they think, they watch.

They are extremely careful at all times to avoid saying or doing anything that might be offensive to the Russians, but they are in no way obsequious.

In November, 1951, when an American visitor drove up to his hotel in Lahti, he saw a great Soviet hammer-and-sickle red flag flying from a pole above the hotel's entrance. It was there to honor a visiting delegation of Soviet schoolteachers. Alongside it was an equally large Stars and Stripes, flying there in honor of the American visitor. That afternoon, after the local newspapermen had finished a lengthy interview with the American visitor, one of Lahti's leading citizens who was present suggested that it would be gracious for the newspapermen to report in the same issue that carried the American interview some mention of the visiting Russian schoolteachers.

Finnish newspapers are free from government censorship except in regard to what the press writes on foreign politics, which really means what the Finnish press writes about Soviet Russia. The Finnish government tries to keep the press from printing insulting or abusive comments about a foreign power.

This provision, however, allows editors considerable latitude, as is illustrated by an editorial in one Finnish newspaper in the fall of 1951. The editor commented on the large number of migrating Finns who had gone to settle in other lands, and mentioned the strange fact that records of migrants did not contain the name of even one lone Finn who had migrated to the "paradise" on the east—Russia.

In the 1901–1910 decade Finnish emigration totaled 158,000; in 1911–1920, it dropped to 67,000 persons. The greater number of migrating Finns went to the United States. Emigration today in Finland is not the serious problem it was thirty years ago.

The present, or would-be, destinations of Finnish emigrants are significant in that in 1949, 1,075 persons, their full quota, emigrated from Finland to the United States. This number would be much greater except for the United States immigration quota. The Finns always fill it and the waiting list is filled for several years to come.

The largest number of Finns in 1949 went to Sweden—2369 of them. Canada, in recent years, has taken Sweden's place.

How many Finns emigrated to Russia? One would expect the Finnish Communists to fall over themselves in emigrating to their ideal state. The fact is that not a single Finnish Communist emigrated to Russia in 1949, and only two did so in 1948. These figures indicate that not even Communists themselves choose to live in the U.S.S.R., which, according to Winston Churchill, is a terrible and terrorized police state ruled with complete cynicism by "a gang of ruthless and bloody-minded professors."

For their part the Finns, as the peoples of the other free nations, would be glad to get rid of them.

What will be Finland's ultimate fate?

Except for those who are able to read the Russian mind, if there are any such men, no one can answer that question.

Even a man capable of reading the Russian mind, and with full opportunity to do so, would be likely to fail to learn the answer since Russian Communists themselves seem uncertain of the future—except that they will continue to use force and trickery to gain their ends.

Finland is outmatched populationwise by Russia by a fifty to one ratio. The extent and variety of Russia's resources and wealth outmatch those of Finland by a similar or even greater ratio. But when it comes to moral strength, Finland is the greater of the two by an even greater ratio. The Finns' moral strength, with which they have met and stayed the brute strength of the Russians, is fortified by their attachment to their homeland. The roots of the Finns' attachment to their country run deep into the soil of freedom. Finland is a free man's country that keeps its doors of opportunity open for every one so that he may grow in grace. It does not deny political or other rights to anyone who is willing to accept the "code of morality of a common man's republic founded on the rule of law and the concept that the rights of the citizen take precedence over the claims of the state."

One of Finland's distinguished sons has written that the Finns love their country "because of its beauty."

To them it is a lovely land—a land of white and blue and deep green, of spruce and pine in winter, and in summer a land of silvery lakes, sparkling sea and verdant fields, ringed by forests in the softer greens of the days when the sun stands high in the heavens and hardly sets for weeks on end. Not a land of grandeur but of quiet, clean beauty that touches the heart and elevates the mind.[2]

[2] John H. Wuorinen, *Finland in World War II* (New York, The Ronald Press, 1948).

To the Finns it is a land worthy of the best that is in them, worth working and fighting—even dying—for.

The late Lord Lothian expressed to a London audience in 1924 his belief that there were three great domains of human action. The first, he said, was the *positive law* which prescribes the binding rules; the second, the domain of *free choice* in which men enjoy complete freedom. But in between these two domains, he added, there was a large and vitally important one in which neither positive law nor absolute freedom ruled: the domain of *obedience to the unenforceable* in which man is the enforcer of the law upon himself.

A thousand-year record of Finnish history demonstrates their adherence to and practice of the principles of all three of these domains, but shows that they give particular attention to the last one. They do so because it helps them to make the golden rule operative and thereby to strengthen and advance men's effort to create the good society.

They have followed this course because they hold the conviction that the principles of the golden rule flourished best in those lands where the soul of man is free.

The people of Finland today face an ominous future. They clearly realize this hard fact. They stand alone and unprotected from force on the world's water shed between the old and the new worlds, at the apex of the contest between gigantic, restless, surging forces, each of which is fighting for existence.

In a larger and more important sense, big little Finland does not stand alone and unprotected. Standing with her are the shades of every great leader in human history, whose words and deeds have helped most to gain for man the opportunity of realizing his glory and fulfilling his promise.

The Finns are protected with the indestructible armor of imperishable moral standards and practices.

It would be unwise to sell Finland's future freedom short!

Epilogue

"The Last Christmas Tree"

W. L. White speaking to you on this Christmas night from
Finland, the country where our legend of Santa Claus and his
reindeer first began. Reindeer still pull sleighs in the north of
Finland tonight, carrying supplies to the little nation's army
which is fighting to press back the great army which would
come in. But if part of our Christmas story began in Finland,
this is also the country where Christmas ends, for beyond the
line of its armies lies that great land where there is no Christmas
any more, and where the memory of its stories is dimming fast.
And this is why, since I have come from a front line post-of-
command of this Finnish army, I can tell you tonight about the
last Christmas tree. And although you have many finer ones in
America tonight, tall trees gay with tinsel, proud with sparkling
colored balls, and rich with presents underneath wrapped in
pretty papers and tied with silver cords, I think you will like
these even better when you know about that brave and sad last
little Christmas tree at the very edge of the land where Christmas ends.

[1] W. L. White, "young Bill White," a distinguished author and the son of
America's great editor, William Allen White, made this broadcast from Finland to the world over the Columbia Broadcasting Company's network on
Christmas Day 1939 from Helsinki after he had returned from a visit to the
Finnish-Russian front during the Winter War with Russia. Robert Sherwood,
while listening to Mr. White's broadcast, was inspired to write a most successful play, *There Shall be No Night*.

Even without our guide we might have found the last Christmas tree by following the sound of big guns from far off.
Presently when they were close, we left our cars and followed a
trail in the deep snow which wound toward the guns through
a tall spruce forest, the snow on their branches glistening in the
moonlight. The trail led past the second-line dugouts on through
the woods toward the guns, and sometimes we stepped aside to let
pass a horse-drawn sleigh, fitted to carry warm boilers of steam-
ing hot soup up to the men ahead. We were told to walk quietly
now. Talking in whispers, we passed places where the white
snow had been gashed deep by shell craters, and at last we came
to the front line post-of-command. The officer here greeted us
in a tired voice, saying we should go no further, as this forest
had only yesterday been retaken from the Russians whose lines
were a few hundred yards ahead, and his men had not had time
to dig safe trenches. Beyond us was no real front line but only
machine-gun nests, dugouts and a few shallow trenches, a place
where it was not safe for any man to crawl who had not first
seen the country by clear light of day. But perhaps we would
like to go down into his front line command post dugout, talk
to his men and see their Christmas tree.

The dugout was deep beneath snow and earth, and warmed
from the zero weather by a tiny stove. Tired men were lying
on the straw-strewn floor, and when they rose to greet us we
could see by the light of the shaded lantern that their faces were
weary and unshaven. The officer explained for this, saying fighting had been very hard, the enemy had greatly outnumbered
them, so when there was no fighting there was time for little
but sleep.

We asked him what the men would have for Christmas dinner
and he told us their mess kits would be filled with thick warm
pea soup, rich with pieces of mutton and pork, with plenty of
bread spread thick with butter, and for dessert porridge with
sugar. And then, because it was Christmas, the army had sent up

four Christmas hams, which would be sliced and eaten with the bread.

He said we should remember that several sledges had come laden with Christmas presents for the men—warm sweaters and socks knitted by their wives, or Christmas cookies and tarts baked by them, and there would be something for each man.

We asked when the men up ahead in the last machine gun posts and dugouts would get their presents, and he said not until tomorrow, but they would not mind, because each man knew why he must be there, and what must be done, and not one would wish himself in any other place, and because the people of this country love Christmas so much, each one could carry it with him in his heart.

Then we asked if, at our own risk, we might not crawl up and give them some of the cigarettes and sweets and tobacco we had brought. He shook his head, saying that if we made a noise and attracted Russian artillery there might be losses among his men, and this was not good to happen on Christmas night.

But tomorrow those men would get their presents in this dugout, and also the Christmas tree would be saved for them to see. The tiny tree was standing near the stove. Little red and white wax candles had been tied by men's clumsy fingers to its branches. The officer said the candles could not be lit, because this might be seen by the bombers through the dugout's canvas roof. Also tied to the green spruce twigs were a few gumdrops— the kind you buy twisted in colored wax papers. At the top was tied not a sparkling glass star but a cheap cardboard image of Santa Claus, and this was all. No strips of tinsel, no shining balls, no winking electric lights— You can be very glad that the Christmas tree in your home tonight is so much finer.

We asked the officer who sent these ornaments and he smiled kindly and said that they came from a very small girl whose father was out on the last line tonight, and with them a note from her mother explaining that the child was very young and could not understand why he could not come back to them even on Christmas, and had cried bitterly until they let her send him these little things so that at least he could have his own Christmas tree. So the tree would be kept as it was in the dugout until he came back from his outpost tomorrow.

So when you take your last look at your own fine tree tonight before turning out its lights, I think you will like it even better since you know about the last sad little Christmas tree of all, which could not even have its poor candles lit because it faces the land where there is no Christmas. Returning you now to Columbia in New York. . . .

PART TWO

Biographical Sketches

1. Baron Carl Gustaf Emil Mannerheim (1867–1951)

Field Marshal Mannerheim is unique in two ways: he is Finland's single great hero who was a military man, and as a statesman he held Finland together in its greatest crisis with little more than the force of his own inner greatness.

Fortunately for the people of Finland, when the deep in him called unto the great in them they responded to his call. Fortunately for the people of Finland, when they called on his statesmanship in two of their supreme crises he responded to their call, first to the regency in 1918, and next to the presidency in 1944. During the periods when he occupied those offices his military genius was swiftly transformed into the genius of statesmanship.

Fate seems to have had a large part in preparing him for the roles that he was called upon to fill for his country. He was the descendant of many generations of civil servants. As a young man he chose a military career and entered the Imperial Russian Army when Finland had a detached but friendly union with Russia.

Able, tall, handsome and a natural leader, he gradually rose to the rank of a major general in the Czar's army. Despite his long years of absence from Finland, there was where his heart belonged and he hurried back in 1917 when his homeland needed his services. Although Russia was then in the throes of its revolution, he traveled through large numbers of rebellious Russian soldiers in the full uniform of a Russian general, and because of his commanding appearance, they never molested him.

His knowledge of Russian ways and his understanding of Russian character and mentality helped him and his country through many crises. One of his aides has told how he and the other members of Mannerheim's staff once waited outside while some Russian staff officers strutted cockily into the General's office. Shortly after the door had been closed they heard Mannerheim shouting and storming at the top of his voice. Their hearts sank to their boots and remained there until the Russian visitors filed out with their tails between their legs, as it were. When Mannerheim's staff members hurried to him and breathlessly asked what terrible thing had happened, he replied casually, "Nothing at all. That's the only way to deal with Russians. You have to make them know who is boss."

Mannerheim, the great Field Marshal of Finland, rests in his long sleep on a gentle hillside in a cemetery which overlooks a children's bathing beach. There among the rows upon rows of thousands of small simple granite markers where his soldiers rest the Marshal lies alone in the midst of them. The marker on his resting place is exactly like the marker of each of his soldiers, except that it carries his name, just as each of the other markers carries the name of its soldier, flyer or nurse.

There in the grandeur and greatness of simplicity lies the idol of every non-Communist Finn, a man whose courage, ability and force lives to inspire all present and future liberty-loving Finns.

2. Jean Sibelius (1865–)

The study of man reveals many interesting sidelights on how societies and nations grow and fade, stand out sharply and become dim. No sidelight of a society or a people is more interesting than that of the geniuses it produces who seem to personify it. America has Washington and Lincoln, and Finland has Mannerheim and Sibelius.

Sibelius is Finland's soul expressed in music. All Finland realizes that he is. The Finns make this evident in many ways, one of which is that of fixing a period of each year as *The Week of Finnish Music*. The week begins on December 2nd, the birthday of Finland's great orchestra leader, Robert Kajanus, and ends on December 8th, Jean Sibelius' birthday.

During their festival music week the Finns, as only they can, present Sibelius' music throughout the country: his seven symphonies; symphonic poems, such as "Finlandia" and "Satu"; his dramatic music, chamber music and solo; choir songs and his one violin concerto.

A great Finnish poet, V. A. Koskenniemi, has written words for the hymn part of "Finlandia," and in recent years it has become one of the most popular songs in Finnish schools and public meetings. Sibelius' religious hymns are regularly sung in the churches of Finland. Some of his popular music, such as "Valse Triste," is played over and over again all over the world, and Hollywood once used it as a film theme. Honors and recognition have been showered on Sibelius from all over the world. Yale University in 1914 conferred on him the degree of Ph.D.L.C. Britain's famous conductor, Sir Thomas Beecham, and other great musical conductors, have added to their own distinction by becoming interpreters of Sibelius' music.

Now in the sunset of his life Sibelius lives quietly in his home in the country near Helsinki with his distinguished wife, who was the daughter of a family of culture. One of Mrs. Sibelius' brothers was a famous painter, another an author, and still another was the conductor of the Royal Orchestra of Stockholm. The Sibelius' five daughters include a great actress. The others are leading ladies in Finnish musical and social circles.

Following World War I, due to the fact that a German firm was Sibelius' publisher, he was for a period unable to get American royalties on his music until special legislation remedied the technicality.

When I went to Finland in the fall of 1951, my friend Miss Mary C. Smith, a great admirer of Jean Sibelius, asked me to carry to him her present. It was a box of fine cigars, which he loves. Within a few weeks she received a gracious note of thanks from him which is now one of her most prized possessions.

Fortunately for the sake of Jean Sibelius' taste for good cigars there are countless Americans who try in the same way to express their appreciation to him for his having given them an interpretation of the music of the spheres.

3. Juho Kusti Passikivi (1870-)

Finland's present president, Mr. Passikivi, was the son of a merchant in Tampere, Finland.

President Passikivi carries an aura of a block of granite, strong, unyielding, tough fibered and permanent. He has a strong face. From his penetrating look at one through strong-lensed glasses one gains the impression that he is a warmhearted, kindly, well-poised man who, when necessary, could be unyieldingly firm.

He reveals many sides during a visit. One is his wide range of interests and his great fund of general information. Once he talked at length and with detailed accurate knowledge of the American Constitution and our President's duties, then asked: "Why don't you amend your Constitution and relieve your President of his great mass of routine duties so that he may be free to devote his time and effort to the affairs of state?"

Once when he returned to Helsinki from Stockholm, where he had gone to initiate peace negotiations with the Russian ambassador during the Russo-Finnish crisis, he was anxiously queried by newspaper reporters about what had happened in Stockholm. After he had told them all he believed proper, he then began to describe with enthusiasm the large number of new books he had discovered in Stockholm which he had bought and would read as soon as he could. He speaks and reads English, Russian, German and Swedish.

President Passikivi is a born leader in that he possesses an excellent mind, which he has trained and disciplined, has high principles and a fixed purpose in life.

He majored in law and philosophy while a student at the University of Helsinki and began his career as a teacher of Finnish at the People's College in Lahti. When he discovered that no other faculty member was able to teach singing, he taught that too. Soon he initiated steps for advancing the spread of interest in cultural subjects to ever-wider population centers.

In 1901 he was made a doctor of jurisprudence, and from 1899 to 1902 he was a member of the faculty of the University of Helsinki. In the latter year he entered public service as General Director of the Treasury, which office he held until 1914. Banking next claimed his talents; in 1914 he became and until 1934 remained head of one of Finland's largest banks, Kansallis-Osake-Paulilis, except for a period during the dawn of Finland's independence when he served as Premier of Finland in 1918.

His real love was public service to which he returned in 1936 to become Finland's envoy to Stockholm. He continued in this position until 1940, when he spearheaded Finland's efforts to maintain her independence and at the same time maintain amicable relations with Russia. He was an admirable choice for this difficult task in every way, and not the least of his qualifications were his deliberate way of thinking, his bland, almost childlike face which masks his feelings, and his standing hair which, because of its natural upright position, prevented the Russians with their most frightful demands from detecting any sign of surprise in him.

When he had completed his difficult Russian mission in 1944, he again became premier and in 1946 Finland elected him president for a six-year term.

After we parted I turned at the door for a last look at him as he walked back to his office and felt then as keenly as I had during the visit that I was in the presence of greatness.

4. Risto Heikki Ryti (1889–)

One citizen of Finland is now emerging from the shadows of war's passions and prejudices into the clear light of sober judgment to be seen and appraised as a great man and true patriot. He is Risto Ryti, President of Finland during her trial by fire between 1940 and 1944.

He proved his greatness during Finland's most trying moment. This came in 1944 when the Allies were hurling imprecations at Finland for having permitted the German government to station troops on Finnish soil, an objection to which none of them had given expression when Finland granted the permission. Hitler was demanding his pound of flesh by calling on Finland to sign a political pact with Germany in return for the food, troops and war matériel he was sending Finland when Soviet Russia was trying to crush her with military might. The Finns were helpless but they refused to become Nazi allies. Defeat was certain without Germany's proffered help, and with defeat Finland would become an undistinguishable part of the Union of Soviet Socialist Republics.

Ryti opposed accepting German help on Hitler's terms. Mannerheim, who was responsible for the conduct of the war, insisted that without it Finland could not hold out. Ryti bowed to Mannerheim, but did so as President in a letter to Hitler. He purposely did not ask his government's consent, because that would have bound the Government of Finland irrevocably to Germany, whereas his agreement as an individual would have force only as long as he remained President.

It was because he did this that Soviet Russia forced Finland at the war's end to pass a retroactive law, try Ryti for treason and sentence him to a five-year prison term. Ryti is now a free man, as far as prison bars are concerned. His enforced confinement, however, has left him with visible scars, one of which is rheumatic trouble from which he hopes to get relief from the cortisone which friends in America have sent him.

Risto Ryti has other claims to fame, one of which is that Britain made him a Knight Commander of Victoria order; thus he really is *Sir* Risto Ryti. Another of his claims to fame is that he left his law profession in 1921 to become Minister of Finance of the Finnish government, then two years later to become Governor General of the Bank of Finland. Because of his unusual knowledge of financial affairs, he served on many international financial commissions both in and outside the League of Nations.

One of the greatest services he rendered his country was in insisting that Finland continue her post-World War I payments for food to the United States at the time other nations had established the precedent of ignoring them. Mr. Ryti told his friends in the Finnish Cabinet that neither they nor Finland ever would feel any remorse about having made these payments as gentlemen and men of honor should.

When we withdrew from the group at a dinner party in Helsinki to sit and visit together on a sofa, he told me that he had never anticipated the eventual happy result of those continued payments in the form of the scholarship fund. He had thought only of Finland's duty.

Slender, gentle, with fair coloring, delicate features and a warming smile that hovers easily on his lips, he seemed to be a man who was at peace with himself—"A varray parfit gentil knyght."

5. Alvar Aalto (1898–)

Wherever in the world the word *architecture* is known, the name *Aalto* is associated with it. This is as it should be because Aalto is the architects' architect of the world.

In addition to his being an architect, Aalto is a social philosopher. When he designs an industrial unit, he keeps two things foremost in his mind: its practicability, usefulness and convenience, and its arrangements that will enable the workers to know each other and to live in pleasant surroundings. The electrical appliance factory in Vassa he designed is an excellent illustration of his social philosophy. The workers work and eat in smallish buildings in a great fine woods and live in pleasant nearby homes. Time may demonstrate that a happy solution of today's industrial strife lies in the hands of architects.

Along with his remarkable abilities as an architect and social philosopher, Aalto has such unusual talents as a public speaker that he is able to enchant an audience. When he discerns evidence of special interest in some aspect of his prepared talk, he discards his written text and makes an entire speech by enlarging upon the part of the talk which aroused interest. Sometimes, when he illustrates his talks with chalk and blackboard, he appears to forget all about his audience; even so, it is able to follow easily his brilliant, logical and practical ideas.

Aalto, like Sibelius, lives in a place of which most other mortals catch only occasional glimpses.

6. Yrjo Ilvessalo (1892–)

One indication that inscrutable fate looks with favor on the Finnish people is her habit of providing them with leaders in a variety of fields of human activity.

When Finland had vital need for a military leader and statesman, destiny provided Mannerheim. In her supreme crisis in 1944, Finland required a president who was great enough to put country above self, and there was Ryti; when her people required homes, factories and institutional buildings, lo, there was Aalto; to guide her along the intricate dangerous postwar international path there was a Passikivi; to interpret her soul's aspirations to the world she had an incomparable Sibelius; to feed people she could turn to Virtanen for help.

Seemingly, fate had been more than generous with leadership for the doughty, intrepid Finns. But, as though she acted in the belief that some people might grumble (there are always such, as witness Lucifer's having been forced out of Heaven because of his grumbling about its imperfections), fate decided to fill Finland's cup to the brim by giving her a forester extraordinary.

His name is Yrjo Ilvessalo. He is a Finn of Finns, which means that he knows and loves trees. He knows all about the trees of Finland, and a great deal about the trees of twenty other countries in which he has made forestry studies.

Mr. Ilvessalo's greatest service to Finland has been that of making an exact study of his country's forest wealth. He and his staff have taken a careful census of Finland's forests, studied earth and vegetation and soil conditions, measured tree growth at definite intervals, and with almost superhuman accuracy gained for the Finns both a clear picture of their forest wealth and the information they need to conserve and increase it.

Mr. Ilvessalo is a member of Finland's twelve-member Academy which includes all fields in the arts, literature and the sciences. He has brought to his chosen work the abilities of a mathematician and a naturalist, a happy combination of exceptional talents for a nation which lives largely on its forests.

7. Frans Emil Sillanpää (1888–)

Frans Sillanpää, who received the Nobel prize in literature in 1939, now in his sixty-fourth year, has earned a distinguished place for himself in the literary world by having seen his books translated and published in sixteen different languages.

Mr. Sillanpää felt the urge to write when he was the schoolboy son of a tenant farmer. While a student at the University of Helsinki

he drifted from his interest in writing when the natural sciences
gripped him.

Following the end of Finland's "War of Freedom" in 1918, Mr.
Sillanpää, who had never lost his interest in farm life, began to concentrate on rural area social problems. This interest took him back
to his first love, nature. This was natural, since he was born in
Hameenkyto, which is a beautiful community ringed with small
farms, forests, rivers and lakes. (*Sillanpää* means "Bridges End" in
Finnish.)

The titles of some of Sillanpää's novels give an indication of the
subjects which most interest him: *The Life and the Sun; The Saintly
Misery; Fallen Asleep While Young; The Road of Man; People in
the Summer Night; The Month of August;* and *The Joys and the
Misery of Human Life.*

Mr. Sillanpää has not made many public appearances during recent years. He prefers to live in peace and quiet on his farm where,
like the good Finn that he is, he and his wife reared their eight
children. But when he does venture forth into the outer world everyone is able to recognize him by his great, flowing, Santa Claus-like
beard.

8. Miina Sillanpää (1866–)

Like so many other Finns and Americans who have made distinguished careers for themselves, Miina Sillanpää was, figuratively
speaking, born on the wrong side of the railroad tracks which she
crossed to become Finland's first cabinet minister.

The daughter of a tenant farmer, she became a factory worker
in a cotton mill when she was twelve years old and eight years later
she became a domestic servant. During these and the following
years, as she advanced to housekeeper, she studied continuously. Her
great native talents, excellent mind and a burning ambition to improve the lot of working women combined to make her a member
of the Finnish Diet in 1907. She continued to be a member, except
for some time out for other public service, until 1947.

One of Finland's large co-operative societies, Elanto, engaged her
as the inspector of its workers' cafeterias.

As far back as 1905, Miss Sillanpää began the publication of a

magazine for servants and soon expanded it to include all working
women. She made their problems her problems. She also became
interested in the plight of unmarried mothers. One outcome of her
interest in the latter group is that many towns in Finland have now
established new, large "First Homes" for unmarried mothers and
their babies.

It is safe to state beyond successful challenge that Miss Sillanpää
has done more than any other person to elevate the position women
hold in her country. Her distinguished service as a member of the
Diet has encouraged Finnish voters to elect other women to it. At
the present time, twenty-nine of the Diet's two hundred members
are women.

9. Dr. Sigfried Selim Sirrenius (1877–)

Nature, which has given Finland such a small variety of growing
things and so few natural resources, has been lavish with the variety
and richness of the leaders she has raised up for the Finns.

Dr. Sigfried Sirrenius, who is one of the world's finest spiritual
leaders, is an excellent illustration of this point. With his frame of
a giant and face of a saint, Dr. Sirrenius, now in his seventy-fifth
year, is a young man in his outlook, enthusiasms and vision. Although he is a pastor of the Evangelical Lutheran Church, the son of
a pastor and the husband of a pastor's daughter, his life's work has
been in a branch rather than in the main body of the church itself.

When he was twenty-eight years old, Dr. Sirrenius began his
service as a seaman's priest in Finland. He transferred his work to
London to a similar project which he continued for four years,
until 1912. During the next six years he worked in the Finnish
foreign mission field, but in 1918, at the age of forty-one, he found
himself and knew what he was born to do.

"Sippi," as Dr. Sirrenius is known to a host of friends in Finland,
England and America, made his great discovery during the white
heat of Finland's civil war when he began a service with industrial
workers. Soon thereafter he founded and continues to be head of
what is now called the League of Christian-Social Work Centers
which, after the manner of settlement houses in many American
cities, conducts work centers in many places in Finland.

Several of the directors of his work units have spent from a few months to a year or more in America's better-known settlement houses. One of Sippi's pupils, Heikki Waris, now Professor of Social Policy at the University of Helsinki, continues to live in a workers area just as he did when he was working with Sippi.

I first met Sippi at the barnlike Quaker relief workers' barracks in Rovaneimi in 1946. Someone had told me before he arrived that he, unlike every other Finn, preferred tea to coffee and that he liked it with lemon. This was a holdover habit that he had acquired while living in England. I had taken from Stockholm for the Quaker workers a suitcase filled with citrus and other fresh fruits. Upon learning of Sippi's preference, I had a dozen or so lemons ready for his coming. Whether it was the lemons, the pure goodness of the man that swept aside all barriers which man erects against man or what, the fact is that we immediately became "Sippi" and "David" to each other in all that such instantaneous response implies.

Sippi's rare qualities make him strong, firm, gentle, tender and kind, and all at the same time. He has dedicated his life to the cause of peace on earth and good will to all men. Out of that dedication has come the dream which he has made reality by establishing the International College at Hauho, described in the chapter on Education in Part One.

In America his name could have been Rufus M. Jones, or in India, Ghandi—great souls come from the same mold and are all akin.

10. Peter Evind Svinhufvd (1861–1944)

Finland's first regent, from May to December, 1918, Mr. Svin-hufvd later served as prime minister and still later, 1931–36, as President of the Republic. He had a long and interesting career as an opponent of Russia.

The son of a sea captain, he began his public career early in life. His first trouble with the Russians came in 1906, when the Russian Governor General dismissed him from the position he then held as an assessor of the Turku circuit court. His dismissal merely marked a change in his work, in that he soon became a judge in a rural community. In due course he was elected to membership in the Finnish Diet and was named Chairman (Speaker).

As a result of his having defended the laws of Finland against Russian pressure, the Czar's government banished him to Inner Russia in 1914 and kept him there until 1917. Following his return home, he brought Finland's declaration of independence to the Parliament in December, 1917.

When the Red forces captured Helsinki in 1918, Svinhufvd escaped on an ice breaker to Esthonia and went from there to Germany, from which place he returned to Vassa to join Finland's White Guard. Soon thereafter, he again became Chairman of the Government.

One of his major interests outside of law, government and politics was that of shooting and he became an expert marksman. He retained this skill well into his later years, continuing to win rifle championships in his class.

Svinhufvd's great contributions to his country were in the fields of leadership which opposed Russian domination, in establishing a republic and in his service as an interpreter and supporter of the law.

The Finns, who refer to Svinhufvd as *"Ukko Peppa,"* meaning "good old Peter," have erected a memorial stone in the community where he filled his last rural judgeship, to remind them that Finland's law comes first, ahead of everything else in the country.

11. Arthur Ilman Virtanen (1895–)

Throughout the world, what Sibelius is to music and Aalto is to architecture, Virtanen is to chemistry of livestock feed. Virtanen, in his fifty-seventh year, is a dynamo of activity who keeps one secretary busy answering the heavy correspondence he carries on in several different languages. As a scientist he thinks clearly; as a man of energy and wide range of knowledge he speaks with strong convictions, his sharp eyes peering out behind their glasses.

The Nobel Awards Committee acknowledged his genius by giving him the chemistry prize in 1945.

Virtanen, the son of a locomotive engineer, began his chemistry studies at the University of Helsinki and continued them first at Zurich and later at Stockholm.

When he returned home in 1919, he began work as chemist for Finland's large dairy co-operative society, Valio, in whose employ he is still engaged. Valio has built a six-story research institute where he and his assistants carry on their experiments. These he tries out on his own farm near the capital city.

America's inventive genius Charles Kettering believes that if man could discover what and how sunlight and other elements make vegetation green, he could solve many of his problems of existence. Virtanen has not yet discovered this secret, but he has pried from nature one way to keep fodder green in inexpensive earth silos and preserve all of its nutritional values and vitamins during the coldest of Finland's long winters. This process, carried out with simple acids, is known as A.I.V., after the initials of his name.

Another of his creations is that of a way to maintain the freshness of butter at such a high level that British buyers consider Finnish butter to be even fresher than Danish. Virtanen wrought this seeming miracle by developing a special butter salt, the secret of which was so well kept that the world did not learn its nature until after World War II when, as a symbol of gratitude to their generous northern country brothers, the Finns gave them the secret.

Because of Virtanen's genius, Finland's butter, cheese and milk are unsurpassed in the world. His genius ranges further afield in that he has discovered how to mix special bacteria cultures with pea seeds that enable the plants to absorb nitrates from the air.

Virtanen's life is more than milk, butter, cheese and cattle; he also is an ardent fisherman. No evidence exists to prove that he has learned how to make a fish strike when and where the fisherman wishes it to do so. But there is proof that he knows the chemistry of fish since he has demonstrated through his research and the application of his findings that a person who eats a few ounces of well-prepared fish each day will have no protein deficiency. His discovery of this fact helped the people of his war-famished country to emerge from the war in reasonably good physical condition.

A Declaration of Faith

*Three lectures on liberty
and freedom, delivered by
the author in Finland, 1951*

THE AMERICAN IDEAL *

Three missions brought me back to Finland.

I wanted to visit old and dear friends and gain from them the inspiration of their courage, integrity, industry and faith.

I felt a concern to bring your people a message of brotherly love and at the same time to give you an interpretation of those qualities and accomplishments which help to make America what it is in the hope that my interpretation would help to ease tensions in our troubled world.

Finns have earned the respect of the world because you personify those universal and timeless qualities which make a people great and a nation worthy of high destiny. You have achieved true greatness through uniting your national life with principles which are as durable as time and as universal as truth. All men who believe with you that the keystone of the good society is honesty and as the old Finnish proverb runs, "a man's given word is as much a part of him as are the horns of an ox," are inspired by your record. Without honesty there cannot be trust. Without trust there cannot be faith. Without faith man moves down from his place a little lower than the angels to a level with animals.

You have proof of my admiration and affection for you in my books, articles and talks about you and by my having induced and

* Delivered at the University of Helsinki, Finland, November 14, 1951.

258

secured passage of the Finnish educational bill by the American Congress which provides that Finland's future payments to the United States of its post-World War I debt, amounting to nearly $14,000,000, shall largely be used for the further education of your young people in American colleges and universities. Because it expresses the true heart of America, I am happy to have been the father and the nurse of that project.

You owe me nothing for what I did. Rather it is I who owe you much for demonstrating by what you do that there are people like you in the world. Your record inspired the idea and made my self-appointed task extremely easy. I had only to explain the plan to Congressional leaders and government officials. No urging was necessary. The Congress of the United States unanimously made a glowing, warm human idea into law both to help a hard-pressed people and to give recognition to great and fine qualities. By doing so it furnished proof that virtue does not always have to be its own reward.

My hope is that under the provisions of this law countless thousands of Finns and Americans will gain from their association with each other a deeper understanding of the brotherhood of man and glimpse in a new and fresh way that love is the greatest power for good in the world, and that out of this understanding there will come lasting friendships which may serve as bases for universal peace.

In this series of discussions I shall try to interpret to you some American ideals and something of American life in an effort to give you a glimpse of what I believe to be the heart and the enduring purpose of the people of my country.

At the same time I shall emphasize the place government has in the lives of men since no human activity takes precedence over government in that none enables civilization to advance so uniformly, none renders men more varied or greater services. The widespread bitter contentions which today sweep the world concerning the type and form of government that ultimately will prevail indicate that men everywhere consider government to be of paramount importance.

I shall emphasize my belief in the merits of the republican form of government. I admit its imperfections. They exist. Because men and women are not perfect, their governments therefore are not perfect. But Americans try to improve their government when abuses arise and become sufficiently disturbing. Because they realize that the processes of erosion have more completely changed the earth's surface than have all of the floods, earthquakes and tidal waves combined, and with far less disturbance to the life of mankind, they follow the evolutionary rather than the revolutionary process of change.

Entirely apart from their shortcomings as men and women, Americans are troubled by other things than governmental imperfections. In America as elsewhere erosive and destructive forces of change are at work. Also in America, as elsewhere, the pervasive, insinuating forces of science and engineering are pushing human frontiers ever outward and are thereby creating sweeping changes in the way men think and work and live.

Another unsettling factor which troubles highly mechanized America is that the people there are living in an ever advancing mechanical age. One of the difficulties which stems from the free life under which Americans live is that it tends to stimulate and activate the people's inquiring minds. The complications this situation creates are so great because Americans believe that everything man has done that is truly worth while has come from a free, inquiring spirit, they seek at all times to preserve that spirit. Its preservation is infinitely more important to them than is the preservation of any social, economic or political system.

Those Americans who in the long run by their character and ideals, by their principles and their deeds, are largely responsible for their country's true progress cannot be satisfied with any form of society or type of government which rests solely on economic theories or organizational proceedings. They want something more. That something is God. So they reach out and above themselves, toward the source of all life and light, seeking always for a better understanding of and a closer adherence to the eternal verities of truth, compassion, helpfulness, kindness and tolerance. All of these are implied in the ever-living truth of the Golden Rule—"Whatsoever ye would that others should do unto you, do you even so unto them." Millions of men have been killed in wars and millions more women and children have died of war-begot starvation and pestilence and millions more have lived in want and misery because men have ignored or trampled on that golden precept.

The quixotic idealism of Americans makes them believe that the Golden Rule expresses a universal and durable truth which if man obeyed would give him peace and prosperity.

I shall largely confine this talk to a discussion of the ideals of the American people despite Machiavelli's warning against "the perils of idealism." This is of primary importance because no one can state positively whether truth is *what should be* or *what is*. Is the ideal the truth? It should be, for it alone is real or vital in human life. The picture of the sunset, ocean or countryside is more beautiful, more understandable, than the real sunset, ocean or countryside. The picture, moreover, enables one to see the beauty of the real thing more clearly because, by omitting ugly details, it exalts the ideal, and thereby helps the observer to see things as they should be.

I warn you here that you will be listening to an optimist, even worse, to a vague, wistful idealist. I recognize "the simplicity of the materialistic view of life which contends dogmatically that things are bad and therefore will be worse." The conclusion is difficult to combat, "and yet"—in these two words lies the idealist's creed which carries the indefinable hope that his redeemer liveth, that life is worth while, that man's visions are God's reality.

The American pioneers, your relatives and my forebears, were imbued with a deeply religious purpose. In its more significant manifestations their religion was essentially one of optimism that was combined with an unshakable faith in the belief that kindness alone is able to pay dividends of lasting satisfaction in the human heart.

Our pioneers produced a race of undaunted optimists because the ethics of the Christian religion are basically hopeful. Because these ethics rest upon Christ's teachings, our pioneers believed that the good neighbor cannot achieve happiness by the possession of worldly goods alone. So they shared what they had with their neighbors and thereby created a pattern of life which has now become America's finest contribution to mankind—that of sharing what they had with strangers, friends or enemies.

The American people, who are charged by the credulous and

unthinking with being dollar worshipers, contributed more money to relieve the suffering and to improve the lot of mankind during the last three centuries than have all of the rest of the people of the world. Americans generously shared their lives and means with people they do not know and never will know because in their frail, fumbling, human way they try to make reality of the fundamental truth of the ethics Christ taught. This they find easy and natural to do because they have been schooled in neighborly, kindly acts.

I will have failed in my attempt to interpret to you something of America's effort and purpose unless I emphasize the generous spirit and practice of the American people, past and present. It is a spirit that has been nurtured in the warm and kind hearts of men and women who have come from every land. Going back and deeper into its origin we find it in Christ's injunction "Give all ye have to the poor." That injunction was what inspired the religiously inclined pioneers of America to bring it into full flower.

Large numbers of them had come to America with the universal dream of struggling parents in their hearts: that of creating a better and more secure life for their children than had been their lot. Because many of them had come from lands in which hard and durable custom had stratified class lines that kept generation after generation in the classification of society into which it had been born, they kept their society fluid in order that all of their citizens might be able to climb as high in the social structure as their talents, industry, integrity and consideration for others entitled them to do. Not "Who are you?" but "What are you?" and "What can you do?" became their test questions.

Perhaps I can best illustrate my point by giving you a picture of one typical American community in which I lived. I was born and grew up in a frontier, pioneer community. My childhood home was in what then was a part of the pioneer frontier of the United States, a farm in the semi-arid part of Kansas. We considered every one we knew as a neighbor, regardless of how distant his home might be. Hard pressed though we might be from crop failures all of us found ways to help neighbors who were even more hard pressed. Since there were few doctors, no hospitals and no nursing service, sickness and death became community problems. Children were born with the help of neighboring women and the sick were nursed by them. When the last call came everyone was prepared for his final rest by neighbors and hauled in wagons or buggies to a grave which neighbors had dug.

We were able to survive as a community because this co-operative spirit was combined with the sturdy self-reliance and hopefulness of the people. And I place their spirit of hopefulness high in the list. Regardless of how long droughts might last we were sure that tomorrow's clouds would bring rain to the dry ground and save wilting crops, next year there would be plenty, next year or the year after we would repair the house. In hard, severe winters we unfailingly believed that "times will be better in the spring." This kind of life kept our country hearts warm and kind, and because until my boyhood days the majority of Americans were country folk, their outlook became the outlook of all of the people.

I wish to underline their sturdy self-reliance by telling you that although they kept God fully informed of their troubles and hopes, they did not ask too much help from Him. One summer when the hot south winds were burning our crops to a crisp and the rivers were running dry, thus leaving the livestock without water, some neighbors asked a church leader to call a meeting and pray for rain. "What's the use," he replied, "the wind is from the southwest and southwest winds never bring rain."

At such times when hope seemed dead and God had forgotten us, we would be unexpectedly blessed with a year of bountiful crops, and because of our trials we would go our rounds a little more kindly toward and helpful to others. Good times or bad, however, we were always reaching out for something better in the belief that God helps those who help themselves. The wheat we were planting was unable to live healthfully through our severe winters, so we imported a new type of winter wheat from Russia. During dry seasons our native grasses produced little hay for winter feeding. To remedy this we brought alfalfa seed from Egypt, which produced miraculous hay crops in the driest seasons. Because our native corn produced small crops in dry years, we imported Kaffir corn seed from Africa, which, regardless of poor seasonal conditions, always produced a bountiful fodder crop. We truly were

> The heirs of all the ages
> In the foremost files of time.

So it went in our lives, always reaching out, always capitalizing on the world's knowledge and experience, its best products and its finest qualities of character and ideals. All of us—Baptist, Methodist, Presbyterian, Quaker and those who were members of other denominations—worshiped together in the Quaker valley schoolhouse. Government barely touched us except for tax collection and mail service. Unsanitary areas were made sanitary by volunteers, and highways were improved by them. All of us sought to make our community a good place in which any one could live because we believed that only thereby would it be a good place for everyone to live in. My parents, who were sixth-generation Americans, were one unit in the group of closely knit, American families. Our neighbors within a two-mile radius consisted of nine third-generation Americans and three Negro, four German and two Welsh families, one Danish, one English, one Russian and one Swedish family, all first-generation Americans. Because it exemplifies the quality which helped to make America what it is, I mention that when one of our Negro neighbors died without heirs he left all he had, his farm, home, goods and money, to an organization which was to maintain it as a recreation center for all needy boys, black or white.

Working together we helped to create a tiny segment of American life with co-operation, industry and self-reliance. These same qualities were at work in all other communities through the land before and since my childhood. They have helped to make America what it is today.

The spirit and purpose which permeated our community has been responsible for nearly every major move and most minor moves which Americans have made in their efforts to create better conditions for everyone. They have all been initiated, organized, developed, financed and first operated not by government but by the people themselves. Our government has trailed the people. It does not lead them.

The deep urge to be helpful to others which manifested itself in the community where I was born has not been confined to American borders. The peoples of the world outside of America have had evidence after evidence of American generosity. The billions of dollars and vast supplies of food and clothing and other goods that they have given to relieve suffering as well as the countless services that thousands of Americans have rendered in their efforts to reduce human need are convincing evidence of its reality. This flowering in philanthropy is one of the finest fruits of America's free enterprise system and free way of life.

Our public school system was originally created not by government but by the graduates of such universities as Harvard, Yale, Princeton and Columbia, all of which were created by and have been supported with voluntary gifts from their origin to the present day. The graduates of these and other privately established and financed colleges and universities gave America the beginnings of a public health program, and our first hospitals. My people, the Quakers, founded the first hospital for the insane at Frankford, Pennsylvania, over two hundred years ago and still support and direct its operation. When the Quakers founded it governments everywhere treated the mentally ill as criminals.

Unlike the procedure in older nations in which governments support art and natural history museums, opera and symphony associations and other cultural efforts, the American people originally contributed the money to create and since then they have continued to give the money which supports them. Americans seek to keep the heavy hand of government and the clumsy directions of bureaucrats at arm's length. This they could not do if taxpayers' money were so used. All such efforts are an expression of the purpose of Americans to be helpful to each other in their common effort to approach the goal of the good society. This manifestation of a dominant national characteristic, that of voluntarily sharing what they have with others, is a natural outgrowth of a people who practiced neighborly kindness and helpfulness.

Education has been a favored form of philanthropy in America from colonial days to the present time. Although only comparatively few of our early settlers were educated men and women, all of them were aspiring men and women. Because they were they realized the need of some education to help climb the ladder of success. Their duties as citizens in a self-governing country also served to stimulate their need and desire to learn, at least, something about the three R's—Reading, 'Riting, and 'Rithmetic.

The people as a whole, however, were slow to accept education as a function of government. Until a little more than a century ago, nearly all schools and higher institutions of learning were financed and conducted either by religious organizations or specially incorporated bodies such as those which continue to direct the operations of Harvard, Yale, and a few thousand other colleges, universities and private schools.

The battle for free elementary schools in America was won in the 1840's. Today public education, usually through high school, is provided throughout the nation. Still jealous of their rights and fearful of distant bureaucrats, community and state taxes provide most of the funds which they disburse. In the 1947–48 school year, these public schools, with an enrollment of twenty-four million pupils, cost the governments $4,300,000,000. Fifty-three per cent of this sum was supplied by local community taxes, five per cent by county, thirty-nine per cent by state and three per cent by federal taxes.

There also are 242 junior colleges in the United States which are tax-supported by municipalities. The junior college is something new in the American educational scheme which offers two years of instruction beyond the high school. Additional educational institutions have been created by each of the forty-eight states, which use tax funds to support one or more institutions such as general universities, agricultural, teachers, and technical colleges.

Apart from tax-supported schools are 13,000 private elementary and secondary schools which in 1947–48 had an enrollment of three million pupils. Most of these schools operate under religious auspices and are supported by student fees and philanthropy.

In 1948 there were 1788 institutions of higher learning in America, of which 630 were supported by tax funds and student fees, and 1158 by philanthropy and student fees. Two million, one hundred and sixteen thousand students were enrolled in these institutions that year. The cost of operating them was $1,884,000,000. Their total plant investment and endowment and other funds was $6,494,-000,000.

America also has a large number of emergency or special educational institutions. One group consists of the federal government's veterans educational work on which it spent $364,700,000 in 1948. A substantial portion of this sum went to newly and specially created trade training centers.

In addition to those mentioned there also are a large number of adult educational training courses, schools for the deaf and blind as well as for the physically handicapped. The majority of these institutions are supported by philanthropy. There are also 7,500 public, and 4,000 school and special libraries in America. In 1948, the American Library Association estimated that American libraries needed $500,000,000 for plant expansion alone.

Another popular form of education in America is the museum, of which there are approximately 3,000, about one half historical, and one third science and the rest are art museums. Nearly all of these are supported in part or wholly by philanthropy.

An important segment of American education, that of the private institution of higher learning, faces a crisis. The crisis has arisen because its facility has grown faster than has the support for it. Thus its success threatens it with disaster. At the same time ever higher tax levels, which limit giving, have slowed down endowment fund growth and reduced gifts for current operations and plant upkeep and expansion.

There has been a great deal of discussion about grants of federal funds to aid these institutions, but as yet the proposal remains in the discussion stage, because educators fear such grants would entail some kind of federal control. This they look upon with fear and trembling.

Another difficult factor in the federal grant-in-aid proposal is that a large number of our private colleges are operated under religious auspices, and such grants might involve the serious problem of proper separation of church and state—an American fetish. The most favored proposal of federal government grants-in-aid is that they provide scholarships.

Both advantages and disadvantages flow from the endowments of American private educational institutions. For example, forty-seven years ago this fall I left a Kansas farm with only enough money, and a pitifully small sum it was, to enter a well-endowed Quaker boarding school near Philadelphia. The cost for everything, board, room, tuition, books and medical care, was $180.00 per school year. It was so small because generous Quakers, who never knew that I would be born, had contributed to the school's endowment funds. Other Quakers, long since dead, had established scholarship funds. A scholarship of $80.00 per year was granted me. After the first year I earned an additional $100.00 per year by sweeping and putting in order the manual training shop twice each week. This I did on the morning after "shop" days by getting up at 5:30 and finishing the task before breakfast. The $100.00 I earned toward school costs, plus the $80.00 scholarship enabled me to start on the endless quest of gaining an education.

Except for changes in cost figures and scholarship grants, my four years' college course was quite similar to my school experience.

One of the advantages of the system which benefited me is that it enabled me to escape from an earth-bound farm existence and lead an always interesting and a somewhat useful life. Certainly had I remained on a Kansas farm I could not have fathered and nursed the Finnish-American educational fund. That is one advantage to the credit of the American educational system. Without mentioning others, one of its disadvantages is that, out of politeness, you feel compelled to sit here and listen to me tonight.

Mine is a typical American experience but it is not exceptional. Take Herbert Hoover, that great man who is Finland's true friend. He too was the beneficiary of the same spirit of generosity that has repaid society a million-fold. Between the two extreme examples of Mr. Hoover and myself there have been many millions of men and women who could not have achieved better, fuller and more useful lives without the help of funds which the American free enterprise system and the American spirit of generosity has provided. The sum total of their lives is expressed in the quality and character of the American people.

The vast numbers and great variety of American educational institutions and activities should, if education is a true aid in acquiring grace, make Americans a favored people—actually the best of the American people are no better than the best people in the rest of the world, nor are their worst people any worse than the worst ones elsewhere. How could they be otherwise? They are all of you of every country, one or more generations removed.

That which serves to make Americans different from the peoples of other countries is the alchemy of freedom. Freedom enabled Americans to dare big, to do big, and to brag big.

Your relatives and my forebears who went to America sought liberty above everything else, that which no man can have unless he is willing to give it to others: he does not strive to get it unless he has faith in his fellow men. Because your relatives and my forebears who found a new life in the new world had an abiding faith in others, they fixed their course by this faith and built their institution upon it.

The freedom they sought and gained is the real source of America's wealth. This inexhaustible treasure flows from the inherited and established right of a high degree of personal freedom for every American citizen to exercise his initiative, effort, movement, expression and worship. It is inevitable, therefore, that the laws of the land and the desires of the people should seek to provide justice and opportunity for every man. The laws fail sometimes and the people's desire occasionally becomes dulled, but, by and large, the American way of life through liberty does provide more complete justice, greater security, opportunity and comfort for more people than does any other government in the world.

Some years ago our government produced a motion picture that presented scenes in which raindrops pattered on fallen leaves of a western Pennsylvania mountainside, water rushed through the gashed gullies of Tennessee farms, then another in far-off northern Minnesota where a stream trickled along so small that it was hardly visible, next a hurrying brook in distant Montana, and another scene where the rain fell in torrents on Middle Western prairie grass. Other scenes showed the gathering of these tiny drops, rushing water, trickling streams, hurrying brooks and torrential downpours as they sped through woods and fields, past villages, cities, homes and industrial plants, to join other waters in small rivers, then in greater rivers and finally in the majestic Mississippi, fruit of all these myriad journeys.

Each raindrop, rivulet, brook, stream and river carried something of the soil it first knew—leaf-mold, silt, lime from the rocks it washed

—and these infinitesimal particles determined its character—crystal clear, clay or gumbo colored, brackish, soft, pure or impure. These colors and qualities, less the impurities cleansed away in flow, eventually blended themselves into a whole, which symbolizes the rich variety, vast resources and sweeping grandeur of United America.

How like the making of the Mississippi river has been the making of America! For three centuries the courageously aspiring of the world have been flowing there in endless streams to join its varied, vast, inspiring stream of life. Individuals one by one, then families shortly followed by groups, then shiploads, have come to American hills and valleys, mines and industries, villages and cities. Their roots reach back to every nation in the world. Each individual of each nationality brought from his homeland something of its spiritual chemistry, color, quality and character. The total of these individual contributions is impressive. During the one hundred seventeen years from 1820 to 1937, and disregarding prior emigration, more than thirty-eight million persons left their old homes to build new ones in America.

Allegiance to their adopted land could not prevent the newcomers from loving and even longing for the scenes where they were born. This love is the individual's anchor to windward throughout life. It both colors and enriches his life. It is, moreover, only as a man is capable of feeling this loyalty keenly and deeply that he becomes able to adapt himself to the home of his adoption, dedicate himself to its institutions and accept its ideals. America would not have been possible if man did not hold such loves close and warm in his heart and mind. And America is as great and determined, as tolerant and kind, as imperfect human beings can be, largely because for more than a century its strength has been constantly renewed with the fresh ambition and warm memories of stout-hearted men and sensitive women from all the world.

In America, as creeds and breeds rubbed elbows, ideas have been generated which touch the universal heart of mankind. Here the Protestant, Jew, Catholic and the free-thinker have done far more than wear American clothes, eat American food, use American slang. They discovered and claimed a new spiritual inheritance; found, clung to and established a new concept which places only the Creator ahead of man, which believes that self-respect and individual human dignity outrank the State. They have proved over and over again that the most precious heritages of mankind are above creed, color and boundaries; that while the finest fruits of human nature grow in every clime and ripen in every nation, they flourish most abundantly where the soul of man is free.

That is the story of America. As long as men are able to control the hate and envy in their hearts—there are no angels on earth—it will continue to be the story of America. Ours is the long pull, for which, as Carlyle said, social and political reformers need the time-sense of a geologist.

Unfortunately for their own and the nation's good, too many of our earlier newcomers were forced to live in badly or hastily constructed tenements and often were ruthlessly exploited. The wonder is not that they have been difficult to assimilate, but rather that the process of assimilation has met with such striking success. One finds their names represented in science, business, scholarship, letters, music, drama—in all the fine and applied arts. Larger numbers of them who were less fortunate and articulate, respected the laws of the land, kept their word, paid their debts, gave honest, competent service and lived neighborly lives.

America's greatest blessings are spiritual in nature, the only enduring realities in a material world. They partake of the warm heart of the Irish, the uncompromising integrity of the Scotch, the lyric quality of the Welsh, the bulldog determination of the English, the sturdiness of the Dutch and Danes, the courage of the Belgians, the fairness of the Swedes and Norwegians, the integrity and courage of the Finns, the thoroughness of the Germans, the quick intelligence of the Swiss, the alertness of the French, the artistry of the Italians, the unshakable faith in a life beyond of Central Europeans, the charitable services and idealism of the Jews, the yearning of the Russians, the beautiful, satisfying spirituals of the patient Negro, and the Indian's sixth sense of caution. These precious qualities, things of the spirit all, create the American type in which our pride may well be placed.

The mighty stream of American life, one hundred and fifty million tiny individual drops, immigrants or children of immigrants, Americans all, flows on, purifying itself, leaving bench-marks for

the historian as it merges all its precious freight of diverse characteristics.

The enduring purpose of Americans is to create the good society
of tolerant, fair, kindly, helpful individuals. And given time, unless
Satan outwits God, this purpose will be realized. In this long view
a thousand years are but a day. A single generation, like a watch in
the night, can catch only a glimpse of the majestic march of mankind. The full revelation of America requires time, tolerance and
faith!

A BRIEF LOOK BACKWARD—AND FORWARD *

In the first discussion I tried to interpret the ideals and the spiritual
purpose of the people of America as well as to present the hard core
of why Americans are the kind of people that they are.

My conclusions were: their religion gives them a faith in others,
prompts them to be kind, helpful and generous. Their struggle to
create a nation out of wilderness and desert taught them to be
neighborly, co-operative and generous. Their belief in the dignity
and importance of the individual man, whatever his creed, color or
nationality, inspired them to cling to their democratic ideal.

Even more important than these combined reasons, that which
makes Americans the kind of people they are is that they have kept
their vision fixed above men, by directing it above all men toward
God. This action has enabled them to rise above themselves and
above any man of woman born. The people of China furnish a
striking historical illustration of man's need to keep his vision high
through their failure to achieve true grandeur due to their practice
of worshiping their ancestors instead of God. They left the divine
out of their lives and formed their great concepts around the ances-
tor hero and thereby have failed to rise above the human level. The
ancient tablets tell us that God, not man, is the Lord of the earth.
It is a truism that unless man reaches up and out beyond himself he
cannot grow in spirit or strength.

Unfortunately the American God-in-every-man concept, which

* Delivered at the Finnish-American Society, Lahti, Finland, November 16,
1951.

rests on the proper consideration of the rights of others, is not always visible to the other peoples. One reason for this is that Americans believe in and practice freedom of expression. This procedure permits full comment about every ugly incident of their lives. Because crime makes sensational news stories, newspapers and radio broadcasts tend to report all crime and racketeering incidents. This practice of headlining criminal activities serves to give a false impression of American life since only a comparatively few Americans violate the law. Other governments which exercise news censorship undertake to blue-pencil news stories of wrongdoing within their borders. They, too, permit the world to get a false impression of what actually happens within their borders.

Contrasted with the sensational American news stories of criminal wrong-doing, are the peaceful ways and the virtuous, kindly, honest, helpful lives that the vast majority of American people live day in and day out, year in and year out. Since all such are without news value they are not heralded to the world.

I will not further discuss this phase of American life, because it stands on its own feet. I wish now to examine with you the virtues of our republican form of government, a type which permits political equality, which gives the people sovereignty; a government which is operated by representatives all of the people select by secret ballot under a constitution and laws they have created.

This discussion is timely because men throughout the world, pressed as they are by distress and confused as they are by dark doubts, seek a change in government. They are not sure of what they want because hungry men think only of their hunger and distress. They seek a magic formula by which they may be able to make their governments strong, swift and efficient.

Other than in periods of distress the goal of western civilization for more than one hundred generations has been to create and perfect a type of government that would give the individual citizen a high degree of personal freedom for the exercise of his initiative, effort, movement, and expression. Its success has rested upon his developing a sense of lawful independence and upon his accepting and exercising his civic responsibility.

Its fundamental purpose is to provide justice and opportunity for the common man. Wherever tried it has done this in a remarkable way. The greatest spiritual advances have resulted directly from the struggles and sacrifices of men to gain and hold it. Its by-products, in the form of material blessings, have provided more security and comfort and greater opportunity for more people for a longer period than have all other types of government combined.

My thesis is that civilized progress, according to the western world's interpretation, is attainable only by free men. I shall attempt to establish this by sketching briefly the beginnings and the development of western civilization and the parallel origin and development of the republican form of government.

Collaterally I shall try also to present a basis for sound and sure faith in mankind's upward progress by recalling to your thinking the most inspiring documents man has expressed in his noblest moments—expressions which reveal his deepest purpose and unceasing longing.

History reveals that the spiritual growth which marked the beginnings of western civilization began to manifest itself at about the same time and in the same place as the republican form of government. The time was about thirty-five centuries ago; the place, Judea. Until then but little consideration had been given to the common man's position in society or to his spiritual growth or to protect him from the ambition, greed, or caprice of rulers and fellow men.

Moses profoundly changed the status of the common man about 1650 B.C. by giving him an active share in government. He created the first republican government. Historians and writers on political science formerly assumed that civil liberty was the Greeks' gift to civilization. The late Oscar S. Straus corrected this misconception in his "Origin of Republican Form of Government." In two of the chapters of this book, Mr. Straus dealt with "The Hebrew Commonwealth, the First Federal Republic" and "The Hebrew Commonwealth and the Government of the United States."

He said, "The Hebrew Commonwealth originated and organized a civil polity which matured experience of after-ages selected as the most perfect form of government." The commonwealth of which he speaks embraced that period of Jewish history from the time of the Exodus from Egypt, about 1650 B.C., to the selection of Saul as King about 1099 B.C.

Moses, who was reared and educated in the house of Pharaoh,

was qualified to lead in the effort to establish the national independence and civil freedom of three million people. After he had
delivered his people from Egypt and brought them to Mt. Sinai, he
at first attempted to rule them singlehanded. His father-in-law,
Jethro, advised him to delegate authority. When Moses accepted
Jethro's advice he built the foundation on which the great nations
of our western civilization now rest. In following it Moses directed
his people to "take you or select for yourselves" and added, "Such
as you select I will make them rulers." These rulers, selected by the
people themselves on the basis of civil equality, came "out of all the
people," belonged to no particular tribe, family, or class.

Commenting on the world's first republic, Jonathan Mayhew, a
famous colonial preacher, in a sermon delivered in May, 1766, said:

"God gave Israel a king in his anger, because they had not sense and
virtue enough to like a free commonwealth and to have Himself for
their king—where the spirit of the Lord is, there is liberty."

Some students are of the opinion that, since Palestine lay between
Mesopotamia and Egypt, the Hebrews believed that a military dictatorship would give them protection. If this was the reason, the
citizens of present-day nations will find a striking moral lesson. Other
students hold that the Jews changed from a commonwealth to a
dictatorship because they grew weary of being good—as people
always do. They longed for a bit of panoply and pomp and for
ceremony, as men still do. They wanted some permanent ruler for
a hero. Even today most men must have their causes personified.

Before the change was made, however, the citizens of the first
republic gave western civilization its moral law, that definition of
individual conduct which is as vividly alive in its essential truth and
as fresh in its individual application as it was the moment Moses
returned with it from the mountain where he had received it from
the hands of God. Succeeding generations discover it with something
of the feeling Kant experienced when he said that two things filled
him with awe—the starry heavens and the moral law.

It is difficult to believe that the Ten Commandments' definitions
of individual conduct could come from the hearts and aspirations
of, and be accepted by, enslaved peoples. The word of the ruler is
law to all enslaved peoples. It must be obeyed. The individual fol-

lows his orders. The laws of Moses, on the contrary, rest upon the individual and his decisions. Only free men are deeply concerned to carry them out. They are a part of the everlasting to everlasting and they fix the great human pattern. They continue after thirty-six centuries to inspire man's progress and growth even though some men ignore them and some rulers strive to repeal them. But they can be neither ignored nor repealed. They continue to stand lofty, supreme, unquenchable, the first of the four great beacons of perpetual light which compellingly chart the course of mankind.

When, in 1099 B.C., the Hebrew people shifted their physical and spiritual troubles to their new king, Saul, they gradually lost their old vigor and force. The loss was gradual because the grandeur of great deeds and the grandeur of sunsets continue long after those who performed them are alive to tell the story; long after the sun has set. Even when the afterglow has faded, some of it still lives in the record; some of it lives in the memory.

Whether or not mankind, like the runner, is spent after a period of striving is yet to be determined. Whatever the reasons, the Hebrew Commonwealth passed out of existence. Its passing permitted the torch of liberty to grow dim and burn low for nearly five centuries.

It next flamed dimly in Grecian cities in the form of quasi-democracy where the whole people directly ruled public affairs, but it was not bright enough to create a beacon. Here constitutional law came into being. Here again the people claimed and maintained individual rights. Here again the duties and responsibilities of citizenship were accepted and exercised in crude beginnings which represented the best that could be done at that time. Even so there grew in the hearts of many Athenians an unshakable strength in their respect for law and their love of justice. Out of this growth and attitude flowered a growth and an understanding that gave the world its basic philosophy, some of its greatest art, and many valuable contributions to scientific progress.

A little later the torch of liberty again burned dimly in Rome, where, as in Grecian cities, it guided men for a considerable period. Rome also was greatly unlike a modern republic. The primary Roman concern might be summarized thus: establish and maintain orderly procedures and create and support property rights. For a considerable period Rome encouraged the growth of the individual in affairs of the state and in his sense of social relationships. The Roman citizen through his participation in public affairs, through his freedom of movement, through the discipline he received in the army, and in other ways, helped to create a mighty nation. He helped, too, to bring a sense of law and order into society; a plan of military and civil organization which emphasized the importance of co-operation. These and other activities of his found some expression in the fine arts, mostly in literature.

It was not until Rome had reached the zenith of her greatness that the finest of these expressions came from a young man who was a native of a Roman colony. His home was in a little town, called Nazareth. One day in an address he delivered on a mountainside, this young man gave the western world a set of ethical standards that will continue to stand throughout time as models. They too rest upon the individual. They deal with man's relation to man. They tend to elevate and purify his morals and thereby better fit him for self-government and free existence. Their appeal is primarily to free men. They do not seek to create a state in which men are puppets. They seek on the contrary to create a class of individuals who by their acceptance and performance of responsibilities and relationships are fit to create and rule a state. They too stand, lofty, supreme, unquenchable, the second of the four great beacons of perpetual light which compellingly chart the course of mankind.

In time the Romans also grew weary of well doing. Seductive demagogic voices whispered to them, as they do to men of all generations, that their old rights weren't worth preserving. In time the Romans believed the demagogues but when the individual had lost his rights the grandeur that was Rome began to recede; the purpose that had won victory on a thousand battlefields, that had subjugated and colonized every people of the western world, weakened and disappeared into history's pages.

The torch of freedom nearly sputtered out during the centuries of brutish barbarity which followed the end of the Roman republic. In all those centuries no man saw it long. The feudal lords and the divine right kings, whose power was held to come from either God or the Pope, ruled the bodies, souls, and minds of men.

Nevertheless nothing could dam back the aspirations for liberty which grew in the hearts of men and women during those dark centuries. It was their sure belief that "liberty is an endowment from the Creator of every individual man and woman upon which no power, whether economic or political, can encroach; that not even the government can deny that man is the master of the state, not the servant; that the sole purpose of government is to nurture and assure these liberties." These believers kept the torch burning, though dimly, with their aspirations and their sacrifices throughout those terrible centuries. Here and there in some city of Europe it flamed brightly for a moment, only again to sputter low.

England had gripped and carried the torch before the Renaissance roused the continent from its long apathy. She asserted the rights and the freedom of citizens and maintained them against arbitrary power. The republican form of government, however, made slow headway in England until Alfred, an ardent advocate of liberty and justice for all, came to the throne in 871. He improved his people's lot in many ways, but weak successors worsened it until it became well-nigh intolerable. The people were desperate when King John came to the throne in 1199. He outraged them by selling justice! By selling to the highest bidder his consent for widows to marry; by selling the care of minors and their estates for the best price he could get; by laying oppressive and unjust taxes; by crushing men under copes of lead, and by banishing men so that he could raid their states.

In time the barons and the people united and presented the Magna Charta to John with the demand that he grant it. He replied, "I will never grant such liberties as make me a slave."

Some of the passages of the great Charter still ring with force and clarity:

No freeman shall be taken or imprisoned, or disseised or outlawed or banished or anyways destroyed nor will we pass upon him, nor will we send upon him, unless by lawful judgment of his peers or by the law of the land.

We will sell to no man, we will not deny any man either justice or right.

About nineteen miles west of London, between the towns of Staines and Windsor, lies a meadow called Runnymede. On June

15th, in 1215, the barons' army camped on that meadow while King John faced the barons upon an island in the Thames. There the barons, backed by the people, forced John to place his seal upon the great charter. There on that day man erected the third of the four great beacons of perpetual light. The first had given him his moral law and the beginnings of civil liberty; the second had given him his ethical standards; the third one established his civil rights. Like the others it was not something newly conceived, suddenly created. It too had been nurtured by sacrifices and had grown out of hard experience and high aspiration and it was gained only after long struggle.

The men and women of Renaissance Europe slowly but surely became convinced that if the common man could be called upon to protect and extend his government, he also must have a say in its practices. It followed inevitably that if he were to be consulted he must first be informed. One result of their conviction was that national spirit development paralleled development of the individual's place in government. Man gained rights but these rights carried responsibilities. The individual man's increased importance brought many changes in his relationships—one of the most marked of which was that he frequently turned against the Church which had kept him in a state of tutelage for so many centuries.

The fourteenth and fifteenth centuries mark the period of the beginning of modern art, sculpture, music, literature and science. This period marks also the discovery of new continents, the establishment of new commercial interests, the subjugation of vast areas and savage tribes. As man's past lengthened and horizons broadened, his power of observation grew. More than ever he wanted to know and to obey the truth. The conflict which had centered around freedom of worship spread to civil relations and nationalism. The barriers that had so long imposed upon the exercise of reason were slowly broken down. The lost culture was restored. The humanists, who held as their ideal, absolute liberty for the reason kindled a renewed diffusion of the liberal spirit. These stirrings began to manifest themselves about the middle of the twelfth century and they flowered in a most amazing way between the second half of the thirteenth and the end of the fifteenth centuries.

This period heralded by Bacon, Dante and Wycliffe is glorious with the never-to-be-forgotten names of men who were born between 1400 and 1509. In that group are Gutenberg, Columbus, Savonarola, da Vinci, Copernicus, Michelangelo, Luther and Calvin.

No account of the progress of liberty would be complete that did not mention the contributions of European cities which existed in natural trade areas or fertile territories. Among them was the Hansa Confederation in the Low Countries, which was comprised of over seventy towns. It drove piracy from the northern seas and maintained trade depots in many distant centers. The Hansa Confederation and the quasi-democratic Italian city republics and Switzerland were the European seed beds of the republican form of government.

We now turn to America and the creation of the fourth great beacon. Its origins rested in the type of God-fearing people who settled the colonies; in the limited number of newspapers; in difficult and dangerous conditions of travel and in the lack of general education. The result was that the pulpit frequently became the forum. Pastors dealt with both politics and religion in their sermons. From their studies of the Bible these pastors knew more about the history of the Jewish people than of any other as well as how the Hebrew Commonwealth had been created and how it worked. They therefore borrowed generously from the Bible in creating the American republic.

The conditions which dominated the purposes and the way of life in the new world created in man's mysterious heart an insistent desire for political equality. Our colonial forebears sought political equality for themselves and when they had achieved it they recorded it in a living document, the American Constitution. It is the fourth of man's great beacons of light which stands, lofty, supreme, unquenchable, and compellingly charts the course of mankind.

These four beacons which are as timeless and as indestructible as the firmament contain the strained essence of man's strivings and wisdom. Administrations, rulers, governments and ideologies come and go, but these beacons always will guide men. They will do so because men are more than animals who are born to eat, work, sleep and die. These beacons and man who made them are a part of the everlasting to everlasting. That which is infinite in man's heart inspired the creation of the beacons. Because man is only a little lower than the angels he feels compelled to follow the course they fix.

Under the American Constitution man became a sovereign citizen of a republic; he was the master; the state, that is, government, was his creature, a common undertaking which he and his fellow citizens created and operated to care for their common interests and needs. Under it Americans sought to protect themselves against the caprice or design of rulers, of fellow men, and of their own misguided passions.

Under the beneficent protection of their constitution the American people have created a social, economic and political system which, according to Theodore Roosevelt, had inspired the common people he met everywhere in Europe to have a wistfulness about America, to look upon it "as a place of relief from the things that oppress and dismay them . . . freedom to live their own lives and make the most of themselves . . . in very truth the door of golden hope to the oppressed and down-trodden of all the world."

In his recently published memoirs Herbert Hoover stated: "In all my twenty years of professional traveling to and fro I landed from ships onto American soil from abroad at least one hundred times. To me every homecoming was an inspiration. I found always a more spontaneous kindliness, a greater neighborliness, a greater sense of individuality, a far deeper sense of equality, a lesser poverty, a greater comfort and security, and above all, a wider spread of education, a wider confidence of every parent in the unlimited future of his children than in any other country in the world." [1]

The American Constitution guaranteed to all citizens freedom of religion, speech, writing, the press, and movement, and the right to petition and of assembly. It made the humblest home inviolate, gave the private citizen the right to appeal to impartial courts against the state, against public officials and other citizens. It provided, by lawful methods, the means of turning one administration out and selecting another. Under it suffrage became universal and the ballot secret. Under it parliamentary government was guaranteed, title to property made secure, and the certainty provided of enjoying the rewards of one's own industry.

[1] *The Memoirs of Herbert Hoover* (New York, The Macmillan Company, 1951).

The freedom and protection the American Constitution provides for the individual and the duties it places upon him have brought unparalleled results. The American record of achievement and the spiritual and material contributions her citizens have made to the world during the 162 years of its official existence demonstrate beyond all doubt that true progress is the child of free, individual effort.

Under the American Constitution, for the first time in all history, a great nation has been able to produce all that it needs without slave labor.

Under it the individual holds a working share of responsibility in maintaining and strengthening the foundations on which the four great beacons of perpetual light rest—the maintenance of the moral law, the acceptance and use of the ethical standards, the upholding of the principles of civil liberty, and the active participation in the advantages and blessings of political equality and economic freedom. Each of these was created for individual man, each carries many advantages and each one rests upon his measuring up to the acceptance of the responsibility. But for the individual man none would have been created. None can be sustained save through him. Its guarantees protect the only lasting truths the western world has discovered in more than one hundred centuries. They are the only treasures man has wrought out of a long, turbulent existence. Take everything else he has wrought away from him and he will lose nothing that cannot be quickly replaced in better form. Take these away from him, leave him everything else, and he will have nothing.

The American system of government is under attack today. It is unnecessary to catalogue our mistakes. They exist. They are recognized. A determined people is making an honest effort to rectify them.

The dislocations of the war and the tragedies of its consequent depressions have caused Americans to search their hearts with a new earnestness which enables them to discover new truths and gain new light on old ones. Americans today are redefining and advancing the social goal. In this one as in each of man's former experiences, progress is coming out of spiritual travail. But only one sure step can be taken at a time; only that portion of the truth now revealed will be set down. The ultimate social goal remains undetermined, but a fifth beacon which compellingly charts the course of mankind is in the making in America.

The swift tempo of our lives and the vast increase in government facilities should insure the early creation—one that might be called, *access to equality of economic opportunity*. Fifteen centuries separated man's creation of the first two; twelve centuries separated his creation of the second and third ones; and five and a half centuries elapsed between his creation of the third and fourth beacons. Will only two centuries pass between his creation of the fourth and fifth ones?

Will the fifth beacon, as have the first four, further protect and advance the common man, be built around him, for him, of him to develop his talents, free his efforts, create and protect his self-respect and give him a sense of lawful independence?

Or will the coming change in government glorify the state through the subjugation of the individual?

Whether or not the principles of liberty and freedom—the most persistent traits in the wildest animal ever born—will survive through this period of world travail cannot now be foretold.

It may be that we of this generation in America are unworthy to hold the sacred rights and privileges which the republican form of government guarantees. It may be that, as in the past, man must grovel under the feet of dictators every so often. It may be that the blood of martyrs alone can purify the stream of civilization.

Inadequate though Americans yet may prove to be in this crisis that threatens free government, they cannot destroy man's insatiable desire and sure instinct for it. Another day and another generation are as sure to follow and re-create it as the stars and sun are to keep on shining. Some time again it will provide the blessings of liberty for a stronger, better generation because the march of the race is forward. Except in its weak or weary moments the race seeks ever higher, finer social, economic and political goals; strives, as I have tried to indicate, to establish and perpetuate that type of government which alone nurtures the golden hopes of men.

WHAT OF THE FUTURE? *

In the two previous discussions I undertook to interpret the ideals and to describe some of the things the American people have accomplished. I dwelt at length upon our form of government. Because men are not perfect, the American form of government is not perfect. As the decades have run into generations Americans have been able to follow but never quite reach the democratic ideal and goal because our aim always recedes into millennial irridescence. What is important is that we always chase it.

It is easy to demonstrate with statistics of material things, which add to the comfort, convenience, pleasure and opportunity and at the same time make life easier, that America is a land of fulfilled promise. Although Americans represent about 6 per cent of the world's population and occupy less than 6 per cent of the world's land area they own 85 per cent of the world's automobiles, 30 per cent of its improved highways, 35 per cent of its railway mileage, 46 per cent of its electric power capacity, 48 per cent of its radio sets, 54 per cent of its telephones, 60 per cent of its life insurance policies and 92 per cent of its modern bathtubs—which, of course, are inferior to the Finnish *sauna* but they nevertheless are useful aids to cleanliness.

The American output per wage earner in all manufacturing industries in the 1899–1939 forty-year period was increased 113 per cent with 33 per cent fewer work hours for which the worker was paid far higher wages than were paid any workers elsewhere in the world.

Today more American youths attend school and higher institutions of learning than in all of the rest of the world.

America has developed more mechanical power than has any other nation. It also produces more food, clothes, iron, copper, lead and coal.

America has a greater percentage of people who own their homes and farms than has any other nation. In few nations of the world do 20 per cent of the people enjoy the standard of living that 80 per cent of the Americans enjoy.

You may think by presenting these figures that I have been in-

* Delivered at the International College, Hauho, Finland, November 17, 1951.

dulging in the favorite American pastime of bragging. Instead I have given these facts because the proof of the pudding is in the eating. The proof of the blessings of liberty is in how it enables men to improve their lot.

A point which I must emphasize is that the American miracle of working and living has not come out of overall bureaucratic plans. It has instead come from the spirit of liberty which permeates America. Since free men place a high value on their time they seek to preserve human life and to improve conditions of living and working.

The American people have used their freedom so that human energy and individual initiative could enable the people to escape from the straitjacket of poverty and distress, to release them so that they may help to improve the working and living conditions of all men and women. Back-breaking drudgery, which has been the lot of men and women from the beginning of civilization and is still the lot of far too many men and women throughout the world, is the rare exception rather than the rule in America. The free American spirit has done this by substituting the power of steam, electricity and gasoline for human bodies—machines for human hands, free, untrammeled ideas for age-old routines.

One of the world's most troublesome problems today stems from the inability or refusal of peoples of different nations to understand or use words or terms accurately. For example, the term *democracy*, through use has become a cloak for political iniquity in many nations. Instead of being understood or used for what it is in such nations, democracy is an instrument or way of life which provides equality of rights and privileges. Leaders of nations who appreciate the significance and popularity of the true meaning of the word abuse it by using the term to describe their governments which rest on fear and force.

Capitalism is another term which has suffered from misuse. It is an ugly term in many areas. And because demagogues have encouraged the unthinking in the world to accept it as an opprobrious term, they apply it to the United States. In doing this they are wholly mistaken. Actually the system which exists in the United States is not capitalism. Instead it is one of competitive-free-enterprise and it has been that for nearly three quarters of a century.

Americans took the first steps in the 1880's to end the capitalistic system when their government created the first of its regulatory bodies, the Interstate Commerce Commission. It soon followed this with the adoption of the Sherman Antitrust Act which was designed to preserve competition. Then was when the competitive-free-enterprise system was created in the United States. These two measures with others placed the regulation of finance, industry and business operations of the people directly under the control of the government.

Faced with this change from the former *laissez-faire* policy of the government the enterprisers in all fields in America, if they were to stay in business, were forced to find ways to make profits by improving their methods of finance, manufacture, transportation and selling. This was their only way out since they no longer were able to keep prices high through combinations and agreements.

Contrasted with their new procedure is that of the nationals of many European governments who have used cartels and trusts as oppressive monopolies and prime manipulations to keep the price of products so high that they were out of the reach of the vast majority of people. One inevitable result was that the concerns in all such countries lost the values of competitive improvement in their industrial processes—the one certain way to reduce costs of production. It followed that their industrial equipment became obsolete, which compared most unfavorably with the ever-improving American industrial equipment.

This point is graphically illustrated with the findings of an exhaustive but as yet unpublished study the British Government conducted a few years ago. This report brings out the startling fact that, due to obsolete equipment, it took 2.1 British workmen to produce the amount of goods one American produced with modern equipment.

Under the competitive-free-enterprise system as it is working in America, enterprisers must rely for profits solely on their ability to finance their activities in producing better goods and distributing them at ever lower costs to the consumer. To do this they alertly seek ways to improve and increase the per man output with greater use of power, new and better machinery and improved transportation methods. Their savings through this practice enable them to pay the highest workingmen's wages in the world.

In 1850, American productivity depended 15 per cent on man's labor, 79 per cent on animals and 6 per cent on machines with which we produced twenty-seven cents' worth of goods per hour. In 1951, we are approaching the goal where human muscle will provide 3 per cent, animals 1 per cent and machines 96 per cent of the productive power of everything we grow, make or transport. This combination will turn out not twenty-seven cents' worth of goods per hour, but instead, one dollar and sixty-one cents' worth—an increase of nearly 600 per cent in one hundred years.

In 1850, the average man in the United States worked 12 hours a day, six days a week, or 72 hours weekly. Today the average work week in America is 8 hours for five days—a 40-hour week.

Fifty years ago the records show that the 1901 worker, after providing for family necessities, had only 17 per cent of his income left for everything else. Today, with far larger income, he has more than 35 per cent of it left for these other things such as education, automobile, refrigerator, radio, vacations and countless other items that make for a more abundant life.

This practice is not something new in America. Nails, for example, were forged slowly by hand until, in 1795, a Yankee genius created a machine which could turn out 60,000 nails per week. His invention enabled more families to build homes at less cost. Until 1844 pins sold for as much as twenty cents each. Another Yankee changed all of this with a machine he invented that could produce 2,000,000 pins each week. John Deere's plow made the prong-stick plow obsolete in America and thereby made our country the world's bread basket. Whitney's cotton gin made better cloth at lower prices available for all peoples, and Singer's sewing machine helped to fashion that cloth into clothing with less effort.

So it has gone in America where free inquiring minds and free-moving men have sought ever to find ways to make life easier and more secure. They were not satisfied to live in hunger, filth and disease, to work ceaselessly to keep life in poor, tormented bodies. That is not the way their dynamic, omnipotent God lived. It was not the way they wanted to live. So they have striven in their freedom to harness the forces of nature in the effort to create an economy of plenty by producing more and better goods at ever lower expense of time and labor.

Their sure belief, which rests on countless thousands of experiences, is that the dynamic forces which sustain economic security and assure progress in human comfort are nourished by freedom alone. With all of its faults the American system serves as the most effective ferment of progress the world knows.

Americans also believe with sure faith that civilization has been able to make marked advances only in those periods and areas where the critical faculty of the people has been free, alert and clear. To me the most significant and most satisfying accomplishment is that free America has never had a famine; depressions, yes—but never a famine in 162 years.

I have dwelt at some length on the America of yesterday and today. What the America of tomorrow will be like no one can safely say because forces of change, deep moving, powerful forces, are at work in America as they are in every other nation. In America, as elsewhere in the world, the hearts of the people are uneasy and their minds are troubled. War-engendered hates and tensions have created in man universal distrust of his fellow man. War waste has created terrible human want and distress, and, for the time being at least, war's practices have vitiated the power of spiritual forces.

The wars through which today's generations have lived, furthermore, have torn men from their spiritual, religious and ethical moorings. In civilized nations murder is a major crime. But war requires men to kill each other. Civilized nations penalize theft and rape. War makes a virtue of theft by calling it pillage and accepts rape as inevitable. War teaches hatred. Christ taught love. Two world wars in one generation have taught and encouraged too many people to hate others. The inevitable result is that millions of people throughout the world have found it difficult to shift from one ethical standard to another and then shift back again.

An additional reason why the world is in its present sorry condition is that our recent gigantic, cataclysmic wars have shot away or destroyed all of mankind's savings and his sense of security and they also have placed a heavy burden of mortgage on the backs of coming generations.

All men whose minds are gripped by the immediate present, and

most influenced by today's distress, doubts and alarms are inclined
to look with helplessness and foreboding toward the future. They
see ahead only more strife and struggle and hate and destruction of
that which men have ever held above price, human life and spiritual
purpose.

The foundations of earth are indeed wavering. All that man has
sacrificed and won seems to be crumbling. In many areas truth wears
the mask of a lie. Phantom shapes and ugly forms arise to frighten
us. The scales of man's purpose teeter in the balance as the preachers
of hate support their doctrine with force.

What they say and do concerns every man, woman and child in
the world today because they advocate the destruction of morals,
religion, truth, justice and freedom—in a word, God. Their tools are
violence, injustice, hatred, falsehood slogans. But let not your hearts
be troubled, neither let them be afraid. The new day will again
blossom forth if men will water the plant of life with love.

> Columns, pillars can be broken
> But the free heart will remain.

The God who created the firmament cannot be destroyed by all
of the empty words, violence, injustice and hatred of puny man.

Other men who have seen "yesterday, lived today and are not
afraid of tomorrow" have a surer faith. They believe beyond all
doubt that each man possesses a divine spark and believing this
they are able to face the future unafraid.

In the judgment of thinking men today's supreme question is: Is
man a *thing* destined to fit in a place rulers designate in order that
he may have food, shelter and clothes, or is he a part of the Infinite?

If man is a part of the Infinite, it follows that his future is secure.
Accept this as the answer and another question arises immediately:
How can man make his own and his fellow man's future secure?

I shall sketch a partial answer in my limited time by first considering the physical phase of man's present life. This seems in order
because hunger and want trouble the bodies and disturb the minds
of men. These, with the wars' destruction of so many physical things
that are necessary to the proper functioning of society as well as the
burden of colossal war debts, have a tendency to bewilder and con-
fuse men's minds and to fill their hearts with hopelessness.

Despite these difficult times we can see, if we will glance back at history 303 years ago, at the end of the Thirty Years War, the people of northwestern Europe from Bohemia to the English channel, from Finland and Sweden to Italy, must have felt similarly bewildered, confused and hopeless. Armies had fought all over that area for thirty years. The casualties, civilian and military, were counted by the millions. Cities and towns were "stormed, sacked and burned amidst horrors," according to an historian. Magdeburg was burned to the ground. Commerce was at a standstill; few buildings were repaired or new ones constructed for nearly a century; attendance at universities was negligible. Science was somnolent. Historians have recorded that from one-third to one-half of the men, women and children of Europe died in the terrible famine which followed the end of the Thirty Years War. This holocaust occurred because no free America then existed to provide food, medicine, a generous spirit and a Herbert Hoover.

Perhaps at no other period in human history until today were so many people as bewildered, confused and hopeless as were the two generations of northwest Europeans who lived following the end of the Thirty Years War. Yet had these stricken, troubled people but realized it, the great age was ahead, not behind them. Their children and their children's children wrought new and better homes, a finer way of life, untold opportunities, vast sources of wealth and from their co-operative and industrious effort revived, in a fresh and vivid way, the old, old concept of the dignity and worth of the individual human being.

The forebears of all Americans, except only the native Indians, saved civilization with things about which they knew but to which they had previously given little consideration: the discovery of the new world by Columbus 126 years before their terrible war began; the route to India which Vasco da Gama had found 120 years earlier, and the Straits of Magellan passage to India which was charted by the great navigator 98 years before the war started.

These and other discoveries and developments in the New World provided a vast variety of new products, both food and raw materials, and brought enormous quantities of new wealth in the form of gold and silver to the needy in the old world. These discoveries and developments also created new outlets for individual human energy, initiative and industry. They, in turn, gave impetus to the efforts of northwestern Europe's citizens to work their way out of their difficulties.

Three centuries ago when communication was slow and transportation difficult, inadequate and slow, a considerable period of time necessarily elapsed before those bewildered, confused, and hopeless people in the old battle areas realized that the new world could provide them with a sure way out of their difficulties.

Communication today is almost instantaneous and transportation is adequate and swift. New ideas, new forces and new instruments flow forth to society in swift endless streams. If man would take time today to appraise them he would see that if, through its governments, society would free the minds and hands of scientists, inventors and engineers, these experts could discover and develop new and fabulously wealthy continents, and thereby enable man to provide necessities and conveniences for everyone everywhere. pay today's colossal war debt and in time "realize his glory and fulfill his promise."

Men could gain the answers to every problem that troubles them today if they only had sense enough to select and commission a group of one hundred or more of the world's leading scientists, economists, educators, religious, labor and business leaders, and say to them, "Find the answers to the world's present major problems for us as a guide in our efforts to create the good society."

Given such an opportunity such a group of experts could prepare a program of soil conservation and use, improved farming and better food preservation methods which could feed the world's men, women and children and thereby banish famine from the earth. They could tell us also how we can ease the ancient burdens that rest on the backs of men and thereby give them more leisure as well as how best to use it.

Almost anyone can give illustrations of how science, invention and engineering have transformed our way of working and living and thereby contributed to our comfort and provided greater security. The changes they bring are so constant that we must sight back a century or so to realize their tremendous importance. A few illustrations will help you to see what I mean.

Less than one and a half centuries ago an English laborer devoted fourteen days of fifteen hours each to earn the cost of two bushels of wheat. Today an American workman can earn the cost of two bushels of wheat in less than half a day.

A century and a half ago an English workman's only agricultural tools were primitive cultivating and seeding equipment and a sickle or cradle and flail for harvesting and threshing wheat. He was hard pressed to produce five acres of that grain, whereas his American cousin today, using tractor and gang plows and modern seeding machinery, can easily prepare the soil and seed three hundred acres of wheat and harvest it with tractor and combine.

While watching Faraday making an experiment with electricity in his laboratory, the British statesman Gladstone asked him what electricity would be good for. Faraday replied, "It is something that you will be able to tax someday, sir." Their encounter took place only about one hundred years ago. Little was then known about this mysterious force which can be turned on or off as easily as water can be turned on or off at a faucet. Although man still knows little about electricity other than how to generate and harness it, yet it has been in existence since the dawn of creation. What man has learned about it has enabled him to remake his way of living and working.

The discovery and development of the blast furnace for making steel illustrates the transforming genius of scientists, inventors and engineers just as does the discovery and development of a multitude of other instruments and methods which enable modern man to produce more and better goods at lower prices with far less effort than could his grandfather. The transformation of life which test tubes have brought about holds true in other fields. For instance, according to its authorities, medical science has made greater progress during the past fifty years than it had during the previous thousand years, and thereby brought relief from pain which troubles the bodies of all men.

There has emerged from the test tubes of scientists in recent years such an uncountable number of discoveries as to make the story of Aladdin and his wonderful lamp seem commonplace. The laboratory has become the hope of the world today and the seat of its creation. Invaluable to mankind as have been its contributions, we dare not overlook the tragic truth that while the laboratory has given man increasing control over nature it has done little to help him gain control over himself. One reason for this is that the laboratory touches and trains so few of us and these few concentrate their efforts upon elements apart from the humanities—dislikes, unpredictable tempers and prejudices.

A major mistake that men make is their assumption that government is the only agency able to produce increased comfort and security for people. This mistaken assumption causes them to ignore the fact that the children of the test tubes, laboratories and factories have made greater and more varied contributions from which flow comfort and security for all men than have all the governments of Christendom. They are the new worlds for man to explore and conquer if his purpose is to find comfort, greater ease, security, and plenty. They, rather than ideologies and governments, hold the key to material progress.

Clearly the physical scientist has made experimentation and change the medium of man's present existence, but it has not changed the ancient goal of his soul, nor of eternal values.

The problems which follow in the wage of a growing multitude of inventions help to keep the minds of men upset and to center them on problems of living instead of upon problems of life. Progress in the physical sciences also has served to encourage men to expect miracles in the fields of the social, economic and political sciences. This is most unfortunate because advances in those sciences can come only with individual acceptance of and adherence to the principles of the Golden Rule.

One of the major mistakes modern man is making is that he tries with economic regimentation to force social, political and economic adjustment of the changed way of life that the physical sciences are creating. This is bad enough, but alas, economic regimentation is based upon spiritual regimentation. When a man is hedged about with regulations, restrictions, limitations and directions for his daily work and wants he soon finds, even with decent consideration of the rights of others, that he cannot think as he pleases, nor talk as he pleases nor find justice under law.

Despite its evident failures in some particulars the way of life that America has known for 162 years continues to be a better way of life than any other way people have ever followed in this world.

This is true because, under reason, Americans govern themselves, however badly, and by doing so they have nurtured a civilization that has given them a nearer approximation of justice than any great population ever before has known. I do not claim that America provides absolute justice for all men in all instances, but it does provide a net overall balance of justice for everyone which equals, even surpasses, the record in any other great nation.

The materialist may reply to this statement with the question: So what? Rich as America is, why can't it do everything it does and do it far better? You can afford it. His questions are akin to Adolf Hitler's statement that only a rich nation like America could afford democratic government.

Both the materialist and Hitler missed the real point which is that only a spiritually, economically and politically free people who are sure that nothing short of their own limitations is able to create the wealth America possesses.

Those people who contend that America is blessed above other nations with vast forests and mineral deposits and immense areas of productive land should check their facts. A careful check will prove that many other nations and areas also possess bountiful storehouses of natural resources such as oil, coal, gold, silver, iron ore, forests and good farm lands. China has immense coal deposits, South Africa gold, Mexico silver, the Near East oil, and South America, iron ore. Asia and Europe possess vast forces and all of them have great productive areas. Liberty is the one resource they lack. It is America's priceless resource. Nearly two and one-half centuries ago, when the struggling people of the other colonies sought to learn why Pennsylvania colonists had achieved such great progress and security, William Penn replied: "We put the power in the hands of the people." That continues to be America's central purpose: to keep the power in the hands of the people. That concept has demonstrated beyond all doubt that all of the people are wiser than a few of the people, regardless of how high placed or powerful those few may be.

Going hand in hand with the principle of placing the power in the hands of the people is another one which holds that a man is entitled to the fruits of his labor. Under the American system the individual stands out as all important, the power of the government is restricted to safeguard his individual freedom to think what he likes, to say what he likes and to do what he likes and to go where he likes, within the limits of proper regard for the opinions and rights of others.

The American founding fathers also sought to protect the inalienable rights of life, liberty and pursuit of happiness of the individual. The concept of government—with freedom of the individual as its keystone—has served to throw wide open the gates of ambition, initiative, inventive genius and industrial effort. From it has grown an unmatched industrial, business, transportation and agricultural system. America's more than 60,000,000 employed men and women work shorter work weeks under better conditions for better pay than do the employed of any other nation on earth.

It is in this way that the unparalleled wealth of America comes far less from the natural resources which God provided and far more from His conception of the freedom of the individual which He placed on tablets of stone for Moses to give to the world as His Ten Commandments.

This freedom of the individual concept as it has operated in America for nearly two centuries has proven to be priceless in enabling men and women to grow both spiritually and intellectually; and at the same time, through achievements that are recognized by all the world, it has been demonstrated to be the most productive system ever devised by man.

The American freedom of the individual concept has placed America in the forefront of industrial and agricultural production, provided the world's highest standard of living for workers, and enabled all of the people to attain an enviable spiritual and cultural level.

One bad feature which grew from this release of individual initiative, effort and energy was that a comparatively few men accumulated more of this world's goods than was beneficial for the whole of society. When this fault was recognized the American people acted to level down the high peaks of wealth with income, inheritance and death taxes.

I have tried in a limited period to give you some thoughts and convictions of the situations and conditions which, when I view the past, consider the present and give thought to the future, seem of major importance to me. My basic conclusion is that nothing transcends man's need for a free society because it alone best enables every individual to grow in grace, in consideration of the rights of his fellow men, in sympathy for the needy and oppressed, in tolerance for the opinions of others, and to free his talents so that he can make the most of himself. None of these things of the spirit can grow strong and become useful unless freedom is exercised. This is as necessary as is exercising and feeding the human body to make it strong and healthy. By the same token, man must feed and exercise his soul if he wants it to be strong and healthy. Courage, enterprise, initiative and other qualities of character, which are acquired only by long, sustained effort, tend to disappear quickly when they are not exercised. Brain cells become atrophied if not used just as lack of sight becomes hereditary to fish which live at the ocean's depth. Although it takes a long time for a people to raise itself to a high level of civilization, the time required for its descent into decadence is short when its character deteriorates.

I have dwelt at considerable length upon the American way of life, ideals and purpose, because Americans hold a fixed, unchangeable belief in the dignity and importance of the individual man, in the innate goodness and decency of man, and in the need to protect every man's sense of self-respect.

The late great American historian, Professor Carl L. Becker, once interpreted the underlying, fixed purpose of the traditional democratic ideology as follows:

To have faith in the dignity and worth of the individual man as an end in himself, to believe that it is better to be governed by persuasion than coercion, to believe that fraternal good will is more worthy than a selfish and contentious spirit, to believe in the long run all values are inseparable from the love of truth and the disinterested search for it, to believe that knowledge and the power it confers should be used to promote the welfare and happiness of all men rather than to serve the interests of those individuals and classes whom fortune and intelligence endow with temporary advantages—these are the values which are affirmed by the traditional democratic ideology. But they are older and more universal than democracy and do not depend upon it. They have a life of their own apart from any particular social system or type of civilization. They are the values which, since the time of Buddha and

Confucius, Solomon and Zoroaster, Plato and Aristotle, Socrates and Jesus, men have commonly used to measure the advance or decline of civilization, the values they have celebrated in their saints and sages whom they have agreed to canonize. They are the values that readily lend themselves to rational justification, yet need no justification.

In conclusion I leave with you an idea that the late Lord Lothian gave a London audience in 1924, when he stated that there were three great domains of human action. The first one was the positive law which prescribed the binding rules, the second the domain of free choice in which men enjoyed complete freedom. But in between these two domains, he stated, there was a large and important one in which neither positive law nor absolute freedom rules. This is the domain of obedience of the unenforceable in which man is the enforcer of the law upon himself.

The true greatness of a nation is measured by its people's obedience to the unenforceable.

And that, dearly beloved, ends the final lesson with my central thesis, namely, that the good society can be created only by acceptance and practice of the principles of the Golden Rule, and collaterally with that, that the principles of the Golden Rule flourish best in those lands where the soul of man is free.

Bibliography

BOOKS

Bank of Finland *Year Book*, 1950. Government Printing Office.

Encyclopedia Americana, The, Volume II, pp. 223-225, 1952 printing.

Finland Illustrated, 1949. Kivi, Helsinki.

Government *Year Book*, 1947. Government Printing Office.

Hippaká, Thomas A., *Indomitable Finland*. The Daylight Co., Washington, D.C.

Hoover, Herbert, *The Memoirs of Herbert Hoover*. The Macmillan Company, New York, 1951.

Jackson, J. Hamden, *Finland*. George Allen and Unwin Ltd., 1938.

Shearman, Hugh, *Finland, The Adventures of a Small Power*. Stevens & Sons, Ltd., London, 1950.

Strode, Hudson, *Finland Forever*. Harcourt Brace & Co., 1952 (New Ed.).

Wuorinen, Ph.D., John H., editor, *Finland and World War II*, The Ronald Press, New York, 1948.

PAMPHLETS

Aalto, A. Aino, Homage to. Ecole National Des Beaux Arts, Paris, 1950.

Agricultural Co-operation in Finland. Pellervo-Sura, Helsinki, 1949.

Alenius, Sigyn, *Finland between the Armistice and the Peace*. Söderstrom & Co., Helsinki, 1947.

Applied Art in Finland. Finnish Section, New York World's Fair, 1939.

Church of Finland, The. Finnish Committee of Lutheran World Federation, 1949.

Disabled Ex-Service Men's Association of Finland, The. Kirjapaino Asosakeyhtiö, 1949.

Economic Survey of Finland. Minister of Finance, Helsinki, 1951.

Forests of Present Day Finland, The, by Yrjö Ilvessalo, Helsinki, 1949.

Form of Government Act, etc. of Finland. Ministry of Foreign Affairs, Helsinki, 1949.

Mercantile Shipping of Finland. Telgmanisen Kirjapaino, Helsinki, 1949.

School System of Finland, The, by Niilo Kallio, Helsinki, 1949.

Sibelius and the Finnish Landscape, by Wendy Hall, Reprint from The Geographical Magazine, London, England.

Social Legislation and Work in Finland. Ministry of Social Affairs, Helsinki, 1949.

Social Welfare Information Service. United Nations, Vol. 6, No. 6, January-December, 1950.

Report of Self Help Counseling Mission, by Dr. Arthur E. Morgan to American Friends Service Committee, 1947.

MAGAZINES

Bank of Finland Monthly Bulletin, issues 1950–51.

Finland Pictorial, issues, April 1950 to November 1951.

Hansallis-Osake-Pannkki, quarterly economic review, four issues, Helsinki, 1951.

Finnish Trade Review, quarterly, June 1950, December 1951, Helsinki.

Saturday Evening Post, *Finland Hasn't Surrendered to Russia,* by Demaree Bess, June 26, 1948.

Saturday Evening Post, *How Finland Balks Her Communists,* by Demaree Bess, February 25, 1950.

Unitas, quarterly economic review, November 1949, Helsinki.

MEMORANDA

Annual Economic Report. American Legation Finland, Feb. 27, 1952 (59 pps.).

Finland's Original War Reparation Obligations and Their Fulfillment. Government of Finland, August 1950.

Index

Aalto, Alvar, 126, 144-147, 156, 159, 251
Aaltonen, Wäinö, 143
Accident Insurance Act, 111
Adventurer, The, 138
Aegean Sea, 29
Agricola, Michael, 39, 134
Ahti, God of Water, 5
Aland Islands, 44-46
Alaska, 3, 118
Alexander I, 10
Alexander III, Pope, 5, 7
American Relief Administration, 24
Antioch, 29
Anttila, Eva, 144
Arabia Company, 78, 144, 154
Arameans, 29
Arctic Circle, 4, 15, 215
Arctic Ocean, 47, 173, 194
Arwidsson, Ivar, 135, 176
Atlantic Ocean, 4, 29

Baltic Sea, 5, 45, 93, 211
Bank of Finland, 126
Barcelona, World's Exhibition at, 78
Beecham, Sir Thomas, 247
Belgium, 59, 71, 80
Bobrikoff, General, 10
Bonaparte, Napoleon, 45
Boston, 146
Bothnia, Gulf of, 4

Bowring, Sir John, 136
Bremen, 40
Bulgaria, 212
Bull, William James, 134
Byrnes, James F., 213
Byzantium, 9

Canada, 3, 71, 73, 236
Carlsen, Captain, 31
Carlyle, Thomas, 178
Central School of Industrial Art, 82
Central Federation of Employers, 106
Central League of Finnish Trade Unions, 105
Charles River, 146
China, 28, 51
Christian-Social Settlement Federation of Finland, 129
Churchill, Winston, 58, 178, 192, 236
Clemenceau, Georges, 26
Cleveland, Grover, 235
Cope, J. A., 74
Cornell University, 74
Cortelyou, George B., 235
Cuba, 171
Cygnaeus, Uno, 118-120
Czechoslovakia, 190, 230

Daladier, 183
Damascus, 29
Davies, Joseph E., 190, 199

301

Declaration of Faith, 258-297
Denmark, 59, 60, 71, 118
Dorpat, Treaty of, 47, 165, 167

Edelfelt, Albert, 141, 143
Eden, Anthony, 188
Egyptian, The, 138
Emäjoki River, 15
England, see Great Britain
Enontekiö, 216
Eric IX, 5, 6
Eriksson-Lihr, Dr. (M.D.), 159
Eriksson, Magnus, 19
Erkko, Foreign Minister, 167, 168
Estonia, 60, 166

Fagerholm, Cabinet Minister, 191
Finland:
  Agriculture, 85-90, 92, 256, 257
  Aland Islands problem, 44-46
  Arts: 131-147
    Architecture, 144-147
    Decorative, 144
    Literature, 132-138
    Music, 131-133
    Painting, 141-143
    Sculpture, 143-144
  Commerce, 97-103
  And Communism, 35-37, 54-59, 229-234
  Cooperative movement, 99-103
  Culture, 16-18, 21
  Economy, 57-63, 68
  Education, 116-130
  Emigration, 236-237
  And Fascism, 53-54
  Fishing, 92-93
  Forests, 65-74, 252
  Geography, 13-15
  And Germany, 38, 39, 187-210
  Government, 18-20, 35-37, 41-44
  Horticulture, 90-92
  Hospitals, 157-161
  Independence, recognition of, 24-27

Independence, War of, 39-40
Industry, 65-84
Industrial organization, 104-106
Industrial relations, 106-114
Karelian problem, 44-47
Land ownership, 47-50
Lapuan Movement, 53-59, 229-234
Location, 3-4
Origin, 4-12
People's character, 23-24, 28-34
Postal service, 96
Press, 139-140
Prohibition, 47, 49, 58
Radio, 96-97
Religion, 5-7, 39, 117, 118, 131, 254-255
And Russia, 9-12, 211-239, 255
Russo-German War, 187-210
Social Welfare, 148-154
Sports, 154
And Sweden, 5-10, 44, 45
Transportation, 94-96
Winter War, 77, 114, 155, 162-185
Women's status, 114-115
Finland, Gulf of, 4, 45, 166, 168, 169, 211
Finland and World War II, 170
Finnish Trades Union Organization, 104
Flying Enterprise, 31
Ford, Henry, 95
France, 51, 71, 164, 167, 170, 180, 187, 207
Friederich Karl, Prince of Hesse, 39
Friends Service Committee, 74

Gallen-Kallela, Akseli, 141-143
Germany, 38-41, 45, 52, 59, 71, 118, 124, 148, 163, 165, 167, 177, 180, 181, 186-215
Giedion, Sigfried, 146
Gilead, 29
Goethe, 138
Gosse, Sir Edmund, 135

Great Britain, 26, 51, 57, 70, 71, 88, 99,
    167, 170, 179, 180, 183, 187, 192,
    193, 201, 212, 217, 232
Greece, 29, 80
Greenland, 3
Gunther, Swedish Foreign Minister,
    181

Hackzell, A., 211-213
Hakkila, Väinö, 114
Halifax, Lord, 183, 185, 217
Häme, Province of, 6
Hameenkyto, 253
Hämeenlinna, 118
Hanko, 168, 169, 205
Hannuka, Governor, 18
Haparanda, 216
Harvard University, 123
Hauho, 127, 128, 129
Heath, Major Ferry, 24, 26
Heinola, 159
Helsinki, 18, 21, 36, 37, 38, 55, 78, 96,
    97, 123, 124, 126, 145, 154, 155,
    156, 159, 160, 161, 167, 173, 184,
    186, 189, 201, 207, 219, 232, 257,
    248, 256
Helsinki, University of, 74, 123, 124,
    143, 248, 252, 256
Henry, Patrick, 175
Hiawatha, 136
Hitler, Adolf, 51, 59, 166, 179, 183,
    187, 188, 192, 198, 206, 207, 249,
    250
Holland, 59, 71
Holsti, Mr., 26
Homer, 15, 135
Hoover, Herbert, 24-27, 37
Hull, Cordell, 193, 198, 202
Hwang-Ho River, 28

Ilvessalo, Yrjo, 251-252
Independence, War of, 39-40
Ingam, Lauri, 54
Institute of Technology, 125, 126

International Bank for Reconstruction
    and Development, 225
International College, 127-130, 255
Italy, 51, 164, 179, 198, 223
Ives, Burl, 135

Jamestown, Virginia, 112
Japan, 51, 164
Järnefelt, Mr., 133
Jordan River, 29
Jung, Dora, 144

Kaipainen, Mr., 144
Kajanis, Robert, 246
Kalevala, 135-137, 142
Kalinin, Mikhail I., 170, 171
Kallela, Akseli Gallen, see Gallen-Kal-
    lela, Akseli
Kallio, Kalervo, 144
Kallio, Kyosti, 139, 167
Kannaksen Ammattikoulut, 151
Kare, Kaulo, 138
Karelia, 166, 173, 175
Karelian Isthmus, 179, 183
Karelian Provinces, 44-47, 85, 135, 149,
    151
Karttunen, Laila, 144
Katrina, 137
Kemijarvi, 196
Kerensky, Mr., 36
Kiev, 9
Kipling, Rudyard, 66
Kirkenes, 186
Kittilä, 216
Kivi, Alexis, 132, 137
Kollontay, Madame, 201
Koskenniemi, V. A., 247
Kotka, 235
Kullervo, 137
Kuula, Toivo, 133
Kuusinen, O. W., 174, 177

Labor Agreement Act, 107
Labor Protection Act, 111
Lagoda, Lake, 179

Lahti, 38, 97, 145, 235, 248
Lapland, 4-5, 15, 18, 89, 93, 214, 215, 224
Lappohja Bay, 168
Lapua Movement, 54-58, 139
Last Christmas Tree, The, 239-242
Latvia, 60, 166
League of Christian-Social Work Centers, 254
League of Nations, 46, 59, 164, 177, 250, see Herbert Hoover
Leino, Eino, 137, 138
Leningrad, 164, 166, 167, 173, 191
Lihr, Eriksson, see Eriksson-Lihr, Dr.
Lincoln, Abraham, 58
Lippmann, Walter, 199
Literary Study Circle, 142
Lithuania, 60, 166
Logan, Colonel, 26
London, 238
Long, Andrew, 136
Longfellow, Henry W., 136
Lonnrot, Elias, 135-137, 142, 143
Lothian, Lord, 238
Louis, Joe, 92
Luther, 39
Luxembourg, 59
Lvov, Prince, 35

Macaulay, Thomas B., 158
McKinley, William, 235
Mainila, 172
Mannerheim, C. Gustaf, 30, 38, 40, 133, 156, 176, 183, 206-208, 220, 245-246, 250
Mäntynen, Jussi, 143
Marshall Plan, 224, 229
Massachusetts Institute of Technology, 146
Merry Wives of Windsor, 115
Minnesota, 3-4
Molotov, V. M., 166-173, 182, 184, 189, 204, 208, 230, 231
Molotov-Ribbentrop nonaggression and arbitration pact, 165, 170, 177

Morgan, Dr. Arthur, 90, 91
Morgan, James P., 24
Moscow, 166, 168-171, 174, 181-183, 197, 198, 200, 202-204, 211, 213, 230
Mussolini, Benito, 51, 198

Nestor Chronicle, 9
Neva River, 165
Newcastle, 74
Newton, Lord, 189
Nicholas I, 10
Nicholas II, 11
Northern Studies, 135
Norway, 3, 59, 60, 180, 181, 183, 187, 198, 214
Novgorod, 9
Nurmes Committee, 27
Nurmi, Paavo, 156

Oittinen, Mauno, 144
Okkonen, Onni, 143
Oslo Group, 59, 164
Outokumpu copper mine, 77

Paasikivi, Juho Kusti, 166, 167, 201, 230, 232, 248-249
Paris, 24, 141, 218; World's Exhibition in, 78
Pellervo Society, 102
People's Colleges, 122, 123, 248
Petsamo, 47, 166, 173, 202, 205
Philippine Islands, 171
Plato, 29
Poland, 71, 165, 190, 229
Porkkala Islands, 234
Porkkala, Peninsula of, 219
Pravada, 172
Putnam's Sons, G. P., 138

Ribbentrop, von, 166, 197, 198, 207, see Molotov-Ribbentrop nonaggression and arbitration pact
Rockefeller Foundation, 161
Roosevelt, Franklin D., 171, 202

Roosevelt, Theodore, 235
Rovaniemi, 18, 186, 215, 216, 255
Rumania, 211
Runneberg, Johan Ludvig, 135, 137,
    142, 143
Rurik, Czar, 9
Russia, see Union of Soviet Socialist
    Republics
Russian Revolution, 35, 105
Russo-German War, 187-210
Ryti, Risto, 174, 182, 186, 187, 190,
    191, 198, 207, 208, 221, 249-251

Saarinen, Eliel, 144
St. Petersburg, 35, 118
St. Vladimir, see Vladimir I
SAK, see Central League of Finnish
    Trade Unions
Salminen, Sally, 137
Salonika, World's Exhibition in, 78
Sandomat, 140
Sarkio, Kaarlo, 138
The Scale of Fate, 138
Schilkin, Mr., 144
Schnurre, Special Envoy, 186
School Reform Committee, 1946, 121
Seppänen, Unto, 138
Seven Brothers, 137
Shredin Peninsula, 166
Sibelius, Jean, 131, 132, 145, 156, 246-
    247
Siberia, 3, 118
Sillanpää, Frans Emil, 138, 252-253
Sillanpää, Munä, 114, 253-254
Sirrenius, Dr. Sigfried Selim, 254-255
Skirne, Francis, 234
Smith, Captain John, 112
Smith, Mary C., 247
Snellman, Johan Vilhelm, 137
Social High School of Helsinki, 124
Stahlberg, President, 57
Stalin, Joseph, 166-169, 172, 230
Stalingrad, 196, 206
Stockholm, 45, 46, 167, 170, 171, 182,
    183, 201, 248

Stockmann's Department Store, 97
Sullivan, John L., 182
Svinhufvd, Peter Evind, 3, 9, 40, 55-
    58, 256
Sweden, 3, 6, 19, 33, 59, 60, 71, 109,
    110, 118, 156, 179-183, 191, 201,
    216, 224, 236
    And Aland Islands, 44-46
    Conquers Finland, 5-9
Sweden-Finland Church Law, 1686,
    117
Switzerland, 119
Syria, 29

Tacitus, 32, 36
Tampere, 38, 79, 143, 248
Tanner, Vaino, 167, 190
Tapio, God of Forests, 5
Tech Town, see Institute of Technol-
    ogy
Tornio, 216
Toynbee, Arnold J., 28-30
Tuominen, Arvo, 175
Turku, 123, 139, 151, 255
Turku Archipelago, 93

Ukko, God of Air, 5
United Nations, 223, 229
United States, 23, 24, 29, 31, 42, 49,
    61-63, 68, 71, 80, 86, 90, 96, 112,
    113, 120, 123, 129, 133, 135, 140,
    144, 148, 166, 181, 187, 193-195,
    197, 198, 201, 212, 218, 219, 224,
    236
    Recognition of Finland, 24-27
Union of Soviet Socialist Republics,
    3, 5, 8, 17, 21, 32, 33, 44, 45, 56,
    57, 71, 73, 74, 77, 87, 124, 135,
    140, 142, 148, 152, 156, 162
    Conquers Finland, 9-12
    And Finland, 35-36, 41, 51, 211-228,
        229-236
    Karelian problem, 44-47
    Russo-German War, 187-210

Winter War, 77, 114, 155, 162-185
Union of the Youth of Finland, 124
Unsimaa, 161

Vaasa, 38, 55
Vallegren, Ville, 143
Vandenberg, Arthur H., 213
Versailles, 11
Viipuri, 38
Virtanen, Artturi Ilman, 88, 102, 256-257
Vishinsky, Andrei, 206
Vladimir I, 9

Wallenius, General, 57
Waltari, Mika, 138
Wanderer, The, 138
Waris, Heikki, 255

White, William L., 179, 239
Winter War, with Russia, 77, 114, 155, 162-185
Wittenberg, 39
Workers Cultural Union, 124
Workmen's Institutes, 122-123
World War I, 41, 45-47, 70, 77, 87, 180
World War II, 97, 224
Wuorinen, John H., 20, 133, 134

Yale Forestry School, 74
Yangtse River, 28, 29
Yartsev, 165
Ylppo, Dr. Arvo, 160
Yugoslavia, 190

Zhdanov, A. A., 164

A
Ï